To William Roy Foster (1953–2017)

Legal Writing Skills

A Guide to Writing Essays and Answering Problem Questions

Pearson

At Pearson, we have a simple mission: to help people make more of their lives through learning.

We combine innovative learning technology with trusted content and educational expertise to provide engaging and effective learning experiences that serve people wherever and whenever they are learning.

From classroom to boardroom, our curriculum materials, digital learning tools and testing programmes help to educate millions of people worldwide – more than any other private enterprise.

Every day our work helps learning flourish, and wherever learning flourishes, so do people.

To learn more, please visit us at **www.pearson.com/uk**

Legal Writing Skills

A Guide to Writing Essays and Answering Problem Questions

Fifth Edition

Steve Foster

Principal Lecturer in Law
Coventry Law School
Coventry University

Pearson

Harlow, England • London • New York • Boston • San Francisco • Toronto • Sydney
Dubai • Singapore • Hong Kong • Tokyo • Seoul • Taipei • New Delhi
Cape Town • São Paulo • Mexico City • Madrid • Amsterdam • Munich • Paris • Milan

Pearson Education Limited

KAO Two
KAO Park
Harlow, CM17 9NA
United Kingdom
Tel: +44 (0)1279 623623
Web: www.pearson.com/uk

First published 2007 (print)
Second edition published 2009 (print)
Third edition published 2013 (print)
Fourth edition published 2016 (print and electronic)
Fifth edition published 2019 (print and electronic)

© Pearson Education Limited 2007, 2009, 2013 (print)
© Pearson Education Limited 2016, 2019 (print and electronic)

ISBN: 978-1-292-25109-7 (print)
         978-1-292-25110-3 (PDF)
         978-1-292-25111-0 (ePub)

British Library Cataloguing-in-Publication Data
A catalogue record for the print edition is available from the British Library

Library of Congress Cataloging-in-Publication Data
Names: Foster, Steve, 1955- author.
Title: Legal writing skills / Dr. Steve Foster, principal lecturer in law,
   Coventry Law School, Coventry University.
Other titles: How to write better law essays
Description: Fifth edition. | Harlow, England; New York : Pearson, 2019. |
   Includes bibliographical references and index.
Identifiers: LCCN 2018042710| ISBN 9781292251097 (print : alk. paper) |
   ISBN 9781292251103 (PDF : alk. paper) | ISBN 9781292251110 (ePub : alk. paper)
Subjects: LCSH: Legal composition. | Exposition (Rhetoric) | Law
   examinations—England—Study guides. | LCGFT: Study guides
Classification: LCC KD404 .F67 2018 | DDC 808.06/634—dc23
LC record available at https://urldefense.proofpoint.com/v2/url?u=https-3A__lccn.loc.gov_2018042710&
d=DwIFAg&c=0YLnzTkWOdJlub_y7qAx8Q&r=Q1huLr_hfN5hBmNklTyEbqNkqKPJUy4ujVI9zNDFI
LM&m=jbbAu2BADSI6-BeJ_6Os8av3clBz3AmpUIfxPzpyabw&s=GVsYVmujy7glJiCwQYVg6rTCOQRy
ynvXFgsJglt0fU0&e=

10 9 8 7 6 5 4 3 2 1
23 22 21 20 19

Cover type based on © iarti/iStock/Getty Images Plus

Print edition typeset in 10/13 pt Janson MT Pro by Pearson CSC

NOTE THAT ANY PAGE CROSS REFERENCES REFER TO THE PRINT EDITION

Contents

how to conduct effective research and employ legal reasoning and critical thinking; how to cite and use legal authorities; how to avoid plagiarism; how to explain and apply legal principles and materials; and how to compile proper and appropriate bibliographies. With respect to plagiarism, the book stresses the benefits of employing proper referencing, and the rewards that students can obtain from good practice in this area. The text now adopts the full and new OSCOLA style of referencing; a slight variant on the style adopted in the previous editions.

The text is aimed at all levels of students, primarily those on undergraduate courses, joint law courses (e.g., Law and Business, Law and Economics, Law and Politics), professional courses such as GLD and ILEX, but also those studying A level and GSCE law. In addition, postgraduate law students, particularly those whose first degree is not in law and who will need some assistance in preparing and writing law assessments, may also use the text.

Since the publication of the first edition of the text, I have had time to reflect on the content of the original in the light of both my teaching practice and the suggestions of students and staff at Coventry and other academics and students who have provided useful and constructive feedback and criticism. Accordingly some changes and additions have been made to both the second, third and fourth editions and the present fifth edition. As with the fourth edition, the book is now divided into four parts, consisting of nine manageable chapters so as to make the information more digestible and easy to follow; although the order of the chapters has changed slightly to accommodate a more logical pattern of learning skills'. Part 1 includes basic guidance on note-taking, the employment of proper grammar, and some brief guidance on critical writing and how to write first-class assignments, to be supplemented with detailed examination of these skills later in the text. As with the previous edition, the chapter on postgraduate assessments, which appeared in the first and second editions, has now been placed on line; although some of that chapter on enhanced research and writing skills is included in Chapter 9.

As with the fourth edition I have included some more specific advice on the planning and structure of law assessments, and more guidance on analytical and critical writing skills, legal reasoning and legal research. I would be very pleased to receive any feedback on the book, including suggestions of what else could be included in the text.

I would like to thank everyone at Pearson for their help during the writing of this book and their assistance on the layout of the text. Also, thanks go to a number of anonymous referees who provided useful suggestions on how to improve the previous edition of the text. Special thanks go Owen Knight, who has helped me through all four editions of the text to the present Pearson team, and to Angela, who allowed me to reproduce some of her postgraduate coursework. The book is dedicated to our three children – Tom, Ben and Ella – and to my late brother, Roy.

Steve Foster

Introduction:
How to use this book

This book is intended to assist with your law studies, particularly in relation to the research, planning and presentation of your assessments. Each part of the text covers separate, although often interlinking, skills and should be consulted at appropriate stages of your course. The book needs to be consulted regularly: do not just read it – or one of its chapters – once and then hope that the advice sticks. In particular, the rules about legal referencing and citation are many and complex and you will need to revisit Chapter 7 on numerous occasions.

Part 1 of the text on general essay technique and presentational skills will help you come to terms with the sort of skills you need to display when undertaking an undergraduate course and when writing assignments for such courses. This part, consisting of Chapters 1 and 2, should, therefore, be read as soon as possible into your course because the content will help you reflect on the expectations of a law course and of your teachers. It will also help you identify any particular weakness or concern that you might have at this early stage of your study. Note, some aspects – such as research, critical thinking and legal reasoning will be dealt with in detail in subsequent chapters

Part 2 of the text (Chapters 3, 4 and 5) provide, respectively, detailed advice on critical thinking and employing legal logic in assessments so as to obtain higher marks, good and bad technique in writing assessments, and the technique required for answering problem questions. In particular:

Chapter 3 highlights good practice in terms of employing appropriate sources and in using critical thinking and legal logic to get better marks.

Chapter 4 gives examples of good and bad essays and offers specific guidance on how – and how not – to answer questions, highlighting common mistakes made by students and providing examples of poor and inappropriate presentation.

Chapter 5 deals with the technique required for answering problem questions, which you may receive at an early stage via seminar questions in subjects such as contract law, and which are often given as coursework and examination questions. Consult this chapter immediately after digesting the more general information in Chapters 1–2 as problem-solving is an essential skill for law students..

These chapters should be fully digested before you submit your first essay or problem-based assignment and then should be revisited after you have received feedback from your marked script.

Part 3 of the text (Chapters 6 and 7) deals with the research and use of legal material in writing law assessments, and legal citation and referencing in your assessment. Chapter 6 includes detailed guidance on how to conduct your research and both these chapters can be consulted at an early stage of your study, but will be particularly useful when you receive your first coursework assignment, whether it is in the form of an essay or problem question.

Finally, **Part 4** (Chapters 8 and 9) gives guidance on preparing for and writing examinations in law and explores the skills required for more advanced assessments. Chapter 8 will be of most use during the run-up to and the period of the examinations; however, it should be consulted as soon as possible into your studies. This will give you an indication of the skills that you will need to complete law examinations and, most importantly, it will show that succeeding in examinations is tied to good practice in your law study and your other assessments. Chapter 9 relates to extended and advanced assessments, including work at levels two and three of your degree, case notes, and dissertations. The chapter on extended essays may be useful to first-year students who have been given an extended essay to submit; generally, though, the chapter will be of most use in the second and third years of your undergraduate course (especially if you are required to submit a dissertation). This chapter should be consulted at the appropriate stage of your studies, but it may be looked at earlier to give you an idea of the standard of skills expected later on in your course and to allow you to practise and display these advanced skills as soon as possible. The chapter should be read alongside the earlier chapters in the text on legal research and using critical analysis and legal reasoning for it is in these assessments that those skills are particularly useful. The chapter on Postgraduate Assessments has been taken out, but some of its content has been included to enhance the current Chapter 9.

The book should help you adjust to your undergraduate study of law, particularly at the early stages, but do not dispense with it after your first term or first year. You should use and enhance these skills throughout your programme and hopefully the book will assist in this respect. Never underestimate the rewards of employing good writing and legal skills in your assessments; this can often make the difference between an average mark (or degree classification) and a good, or very good one. Good luck!

1

Preparing and writing law assignments

This part of the text addresses basic essay writing skills, including how to prepare and present law assignments. It begins by addressing basic but important matters such as time management, engaging with the legal area, the module and the module leader, and ensuring that the work that you have been asked to submit reflects the skills expected of you and represents your best work. Specifically, Part 1 gives advice on and covers the following matters:

- What to do when you get the assessment.
- Using notes and other sources to assist assessment performance, including a brief explanation of research techniques.
- The presentation of assessments including guidance on writing style and avoiding grammatical, spelling and typographical errors.
- Avoiding plagiarism.
- How to address and show a true understanding of the question.
- How to write critically and achieve first-class marks.

All these areas are illustrated by examples of good and poor skills and common errors made by students in the presentation of their work and their study patterns.

NOTE

Good students who engage in good study practices produce good essays, and poor essays are generally the product of poor student practices such as poor time management, lack of preparation and planning and a general failure to engage with their studies.

1

- - - - - - - - - - - - - -

Writing law assessments on undergraduate courses

Many students find it difficult to make the transition between A level (and other sub-degree courses) and undergraduate study. In particular they find that different and more enhanced skills are needed for the preparation and writing of assessments.

TIPS FOR UNDERGRADUATE ASSESSMENTS

Here are some observations and tips for undergraduate assessments:

- You may be writing academic essays for the first time, or you may have not written essays of any substantial length (essays on undergraduate courses range from 1,250 words to 4,000 words, with 1,500 to 2,000 words being the norm).

- You may have little or no experience in answering problem questions and applying legal principles to hypothetical scenarios.

- You will need to employ sound essay writing skills including good grammar and spelling, and will be expected to follow strict rules on citation and referencing of sources and the avoidance of plagiarism. Take advantage of any guidance the university and law school provide to you with respect to writing style, referencing and presentation of work (such as house style guides).

- You will be expected to undertake individual research and to read beyond your lecture notes and basic textbooks; in particular, secondary sources will be more advanced than those you encountered at A level and will adopt a more academic and lengthy style.

- You will be required to use legal materials (such as cases) in an appropriate and convincing manner in order to support your answers.

- The questions will tend to be more analytical and less descriptive and often ask you to take a critical approach.

- Lecturers may give little guidance on how to answer the question – you will be expected to find out the answer yourself.

- Lecturers do not generally allow you to bring drafts of your essay for correction before submission; you have to get it right on submission.

NOTE

The above point comes as a shock to many students, who expect the lecturer to guide them to a good or perfect answer through a series of submitted and returned drafts. Although there will be plenty of help available, the undergraduate student is expected to work out the answer and their approach to it for themselves.

- Learn to be independent in acquiring knowledge and in your research. Ensure that you read as much legal material as you can, including books, articles, cases and legal newspaper reports.

- Take your legal skills/method courses very seriously. They are the key to your success on the law programme, and to better marks in your assessments in substantive law subjects – there is little point in knowing all the principles and cases in contract if you do not know how to use and present those sources effectively.

The above points reflect the nature and level of undergraduate study. These skills can be acquired, or refined, quite quickly, although they are mostly learned by practice and will not be perfectly honed until the final years of study. Although you are not totally on your own, you will be expected to show an element of independence that you might not have been asked to display previously.

NOTE

Many students complain that they got a lower mark than their fellow students, even though they included the same sources and raised the same issues. Simply including the same sources and raising the same issues as other students on a sub-degree course will probably ensure a pass or good pass, but not on your undergraduate law programme. You will need to show an understanding of the material and clearly explain the source and information in the context of the question.

SOME COMMON COMPLAINTS

The lecturers *that set and mark your work* have many common complaints regarding the standard and style of student work. It is important that you do not give the lecturer the opportunity to identify these shortcomings in your work because you will invariably lose marks or risk failure.

COMMON COMPLAINTS FROM LECTURERS

Here are some of those complaints (gathered from staff at the author's university and from staff at other law schools who reviewed this text):

- Students do not answer the set question; instead they answer the question they set themselves.
- Students do not plan their answers and do not think about what they are going to say next.
- Students do not structure their answers and fail to deal with the issues logically and in order.
- Students write in an inappropriate and casual style, not suitable for the submission of law answers: 'I think Frank might have a good chance of winning his case,' rather than 'Given the existing case law in this area, the possibility of Frank succeeding in his action appears strong.'

- Students do not check their work thoroughly for spelling and typographical errors and for poor grammar before submission. Some sentences do not make sense and need rephrasing before submission.
- Students make lists of relevant points rather than writing in prose.
- Students do not cite cases or other legal sources properly, referring, for example, to 'the Carlill case' or 'it's in the Theft Act that . . . '
- Students do not understand and explain cases properly, and do not, or cannot, highlight the significance of the case. Instead they cite cases for the sake of it, regardless of whether it is relevant to the point they are making or the facts they are applying it to.
- Students do not reference their work properly and are often guilty of plagiarism, whether they intended to cheat or not.
- Students do not include a bibliography, or cannot construct their bibliography in an appropriate manner.

This and subsequent chapters address these issues, giving advice on how, and how not, to present your work and how to avoid these criticisms, and thus how to get the best possible marks.

NOTE

Most of the following advice applies to writing assessments in coursework and in examinations. However, some of the skills expected in coursework, such as referencing and layout, are not expected in examinations. In addition, you will need to display further and different skills in examinations. This matter is referred to again throughout this and subsequent chapters (**specific guidance on examination questions is given in Chapter 8**).

SOME BASIC POINTS

Let us start by identifying some basic points with respect to writing and researching your law assessments. Some may seem obvious to you, particularly if you are studying at undergraduate level. Students often ignore these rules to their detriment; whatever level you are studying at, the lecturer and marker will expect you to display these basic skills. This chapter highlights the disadvantages of ignoring these rules: you *will* lose marks if you do not follow them.

Time management

You will have been have been warned throughout your school and college life not to leave the research and presentation of your assessment until the last minute. Such advice is still (and particularly) relevant to your undergraduate and postgraduate studies, as is advice on basic time management.

Time is very often the main reason why students fail to follow the basic rules of good practice and why they fail to produce good, or even acceptable work: 'I started the planning and research late; when I got to the library the books were gone; I couldn't get hold of my friend in time to get a copy of the coursework instructions; there was no time to revise the work and proof-read as the work needed to be in.'

It is also a major reason for **poor referencing** and **plagiarism**: the student has no time to research and analyse sources and resorts to cutting and pasting from websites.

Provided you have done the necessary research, planned your answer and written out an appropriate draft, it is acceptable to write it up shortly before you submit it – this not only reflects human nature, but also allows you to modify your answer in line with information acquired since you started your original research. This approach is subject to one important proviso – always leave yourself enough time to check over your work and to account for things such as computer failure; few courses accept this as a reason for handing in late. **Never hand in your first or second draft; always submit your final, completed work.**

Respect for the module: engaging with the module and producing your best possible work

Teaching staff expect you to be as engrossed in the subject area as they are. They may be deluded in this respect, but they do not take kindly to students who do not show a desire to submit work which reflects their best effort. This will be reflected in the marking, for they believe that sloppily presented essays with countless grammatical and legal errors are a product of indifference towards the subject and their module.

Your lecturers expect you to have learnt the information and skills that they have taken time teaching you – nothing is more infuriating to them than when a student ignores the advice and information that they have presented in lectures and seminars – for example, when a student omits a recent case or other development that the lecturer has drawn the their attention to.

The staff teaching you will normally set and mark your work. Show them that you have attended and listened to their classes and that you have appreciated, even enjoyed, what you have been taught and what you have managed to discover by your research. All these efforts will be rewarded by the lecturer, who will recognise that you have made an effort to engage with the subject, to conduct thorough research, and to take care with the presentation of your work.

Getting on the module leader's 'wavelength', and tuning in to the area of law being studied

The module leader will expect you to display the basic knowledge and skills that they have provided in class, and to approach the subject in much the same manner as they delivered it.

Module leaders have their own styles, their own way of presenting things and their own views regarding the law and its efficiency and possible reform. It is not necessary that you agree with the module leader in all respects, but it is advisable that you are at least aware of and appreciate his or her views and style.

Regular attendance makes the law easier to digest and understand – the purpose of lectures and seminars is to highlight the main issues of the law and its difficulties, and the module leader is trying to help you with these matters. Irregular attendance often leads to gaps in your knowledge and appreciation and thus makes the assessment task more difficult.

Do not make a mistake in an assessment that the module leader has warned you about, or miss something that they have given to you; that will give the impression that you have not attended or listened.

NOTE-TAKING AND USING NOTES WITH OTHER SOURCES

A good set of lecture notes can be invaluable in studying and learning a particular subject and can be used constructively in the preparation of your assessment. The lecture handouts, and the notes you are given in lectures, provide a good indication of how that subject has been approached and taught and can usefully complement your textbooks in giving you a clear overview of the subject. It is essential, therefore, that you make the most of this resource and realise its potential (and limits) in the learning and assessment process.

TIPS FOR LECTURES AND NOTE-TAKING

- Attend lectures regularly: you cannot hope to build up solid knowledge of the module and a coherent set of notes if you attend irregularly. Inevitably you will miss some lectures, but establish a regular pattern of attendance from the start and keep to it.

- Do not come to lectures late – you will disrupt (and annoy) the class, and miss out on valuable information and the overall sense of the topic that is being covered. This will lead to a fractured set of notes and thus confusion and gaps in your knowledge.

- Ensure that you collect any new handouts distributed in the lectures or online and that at the very least you have a full set of lecture handouts relevant to the assessment task and at the end of the teaching term before you start to revise. Do not just collect the handouts – *read them* and use them in your studies.

- Do not rely on other people's notes: often there is an organised system where students share out attendance and photocopying duties. This is unwise and unfruitful; each student gets different things from the session and their notes are personal to them. Other students' notes rarely make full sense, and in fact are often never read!

- Try to familiarise yourself with the relevant topic before you attend the lecture. By reading the relevant chapter from the textbook before the lecture you will be able to follow the content of the lecture more easily and will not be under so much pressure to get everything down.

- Do not try to take everything down. Most lecturers will talk too fast for you to get down everything they say – lecturers very rarely dictate these days. Instead, ensure you get down the fundamental points and the gist of cases etc. If the lecturer uses slides etc., take a note of their content (or download them from websites if they are made available), and supplement them by adding your own notes.

- Do not stop listening and note-taking when the lecturer is talking generally or analysing the law. Many students religiously write down the facts of cases, but then switch off the moment s/he says, 'Now let's think about that case for a moment . . . ' Remember, you can get the facts of cases etc. from the text; it is the lecturer's structure of and views of the law that are most important and which should be noted.

- Revise your notes and fill in any gaps shortly after the lecture has finished, and do this on a regular basis. You can do this generally by consulting your texts and cases and materials texts, but often you might need to go to the primary source (e.g. a law report) to complete your notes. Do not leave this until revision as you will struggle to remember what 'check this in the book' meant when it was noted months ago.

- Lecture notes are not an authority in themselves and must never be cited as such in your coursework or in your bibliography. They can, however, be a useful companion when researching other primary and secondary sources.

- If the topic has been taught in lectures then consult your notes to see what has been covered and what approach the lecturer has taken to the topic. Read the relevant part of the textbook and other sources in conjunction with your notes. They should complement each other; you can look for the relevant section in the book that your notes cover, and you can use the points made in lectures to clarify things in the text.

- Take note of any new cases or developments that have been mentioned in the lectures, but which may not be covered in the text. Do not use your notes as a substitute for texts and other sources, however full your notes are. In particular, do not use your notes as a source of cases or other primary sources; go to a fuller source to get the details of cases etc.

NOTE

Essay writing skills are related to other study skills – organising your studies, attending and making the most of lectures, effective note-taking, and seminar preparation. Assessments are really hard work if you do not take an interest in and keep up to date with the subject.

WHAT SHOULD I DO WHEN I GET AN ASSIGNMENT?

Many inadequate essays are written by students who were not in the class (or accessing the relevant information online) when it was given to the other students, and who do not obtain the assignment in time to conduct proper research and planning. Get the work the moment it is distributed; if you missed the class ensure that you find out whether work was given out and how you can get hold of it.

Early preparation and research

This is absolutely vital – identify the subject matter of the essay and be thinking of the plan for it **almost the moment you receive the work**. No one is going to fly off to the library and start researching, but ensure you understand what the question is getting at; if you do not, then you can start finding out immediately.

Although you may not write the essay until perhaps much later, you need to be aware of the deadline and the subject matter of the essay. This allows you to:

- conduct proper library and other research;
- discuss the subject area and the question with other students;
- identify whether the subject matter or the question is particularly difficult, or whether it requires special research;
- take in information given in lectures and seminars which is relevant to the subject area and the question – you cannot do that whilst attending subsequent lectures if you are unaware of the title and its scope.

If you leave your research to the last moment, you will miss out on the most relevant and appropriate sources. The better-organised student will have gone to the library and taken the most useful books, leaving the badly organised student with out-of-date or inappropriate texts and other sources: **many such students resort to accessing inappropriate internet sources and, often, cutting and pasting and plagiarism.** Conduct your research in the library and on the internet as soon as you can, and photocopy relevant sources in preparation for the time that you begin to plan your answer.

Get to know the area involved in the question

Good writing skills apart, good assessments are written by students who know the relevant law, and poor ones by students who are unknowledgeable. A sound knowledge of the legal principles and sources is a prerequisite of success.

If you are already confident in the relevant legal area before you begin researching and writing, it is much easier to tackle the question. This allows you to concentrate on the specific task in hand (whether that is analysing an essay question or solving a problem question), and this confidence will be reflected throughout your answer.

At least ensure that you *understand* the question; if you do not understand it and attempt to decipher it much later on, you will misunderstand the question and the legal principles and end up submitting unsatisfactory work.

If the area is one that is to be, or already has been, covered in lectures and seminars, ensure that you attend those sessions, or get notes and materials from any missed sessions. Those sessions may also provide you with reading lists and other references to relevant cases and other materials.

Where an assessment is set on a topic specifically covered in seminars, students can be given a 'rehearsal' for the actual assessment in the seminar itself, ensure you prepare for, attend and contribute to the session.

If the area is not one covered in class, ensure you research it well in advance of typing up the assessment. As you do not have the benefit of lectures and seminars in the area, you are responsible for finding the relevant information (the lecturer may have given you a reading list, in which case obtain the texts and read the relevant information as soon as possible). In any case, you need to ensure that you fully understand the area. Conducting research and discussing the area with fellow students will help you achieve this, but expect the research and learning process to be more demanding.

Listening carefully (lecturers often drop hints)

The assessment has been set by your lecturer, who has a good idea of the answer and who expects you to cover specific issues in your answer (although the question rarely admits of one specific answer). Although your lecturer is not likely to tell you how to answer the question, some lecturers give general guidance on what skills should be employed and what general points should be covered. Regular attendance and listening to the lecturer (see the section on note-taking, above) have the following advantages:

- Lecturers gives their views on things such as the importance of a case, why it was decided in that way, whether a case was correctly decided, or why an Act of Parliament was passed or amended.

- They give their views on the morality of the law – this also gives you a good indication of whether, and the extent to which, the lecturer is asking for a 'black letter' or critical/analytical approach to the question.

- The lecture on a particular topic may follow a pattern similar to the one required to answer the question, or at least cover the most essential cases and principles. In other words, the lecturer shows you how the subject 'fits together'.

- They can explain difficult concepts and legal issues that are required to answer the question. For example, if the question asks, 'To what extent is the British Constitution consistent with constitutionalism?' the lecturer may be able to explain what constitutionalism is and may give examples of the British Constitution, which can be used in answering the question.

- The lecturing staff want you to answer the question and to do well; they are not out to trick you or make you fail. Work with them to get the best marks.

RESEARCHING FOR ASSESSMENTS

Chapter 6 provides more detailed information and advice on how to research law assessments, including what books, articles and other legal materials to use, and the process of researching legal materials. For present purposes here is some basic advice on how to research your assessments, including the timing of your research.

TIPS FOR RESEARCHING YOUR ASSESSMENT

- Examine the title as soon as possible after distribution and find out whether it is on an area covered, or to be covered, on the course (see earlier under 'What should I do when I get an assignment?').

- Read the question *carefully* to identify its scope, and thus the scope of your research.

EXAMPLE

You are set the question: 'What is the difference between law, rules of law and the rule of law?'

That question requires some thought and before you begin your research you at least need to be familiar with those terms and concepts. If you leave that until later then it is likely that your research and your answer will become confused, as you will begin to panic that you do not understand the concepts and thus what the question is after. **(Note: we will re-visit this question in Chapter 2.)**

- If the area has been covered on the course, ensure that you have all the handouts and lecture or seminar notes on the area. If you haven't, chase them up immediately.

- If the area is to be covered in lectures and seminars, ensure that you attend and prepare for those sessions and listen carefully to the lecturer for any hints and guidance (see earlier). If the area is not to be covered on the course, or will not be covered before submission, get to know the area as quickly as possible, and ensure that you have a basic understanding of that area before conducting further, more detailed research.

- Consult any recommended reading given by the lecturer, and carefully read and digest any advice given by the lecturer on the coursework instructions. In most cases (apart from specialist areas not covered in general texts, or where the assessment is in the form of a case study), you should begin by locating the relevant chapters in your textbooks (and cases and materials texts). This provides a foundation on which to research further material

- Textbooks provide some additional reading in a specific area (either in footnotes or in reading lists and bibliographies), and this is a useful starting point for locating further secondary sources. Cases and materials texts provide you with an excellent range of secondary (and primary) sources in the legal area, although you still may have to locate and read the full text of some of those materials.

- You should undertake searches on law websites and library catalogues to locate further sources and any new sources since the publication of the texts **(see Chapter 6 for detailed advice on this)**. Use appropriate websites to locate any new cases or statutory developments, and check whether they conflict with your texts and initial research (**again, see Chapter 6 for detailed advice on this**).

- Textbooks normally refer you to the primary sources necessary to answer the question. Identify which ones are particularly relevant, and whether you will need to access the source itself. If so, print off or photocopy those materials.

- Keep on the lookout for any developments during the period of research and writing up – you will impress the lecturer if you can incorporate new cases, developments or debates into your answer.

- Ensure that all your research relates to the question and is relevant to answering that question – do not just collect everything on constitutional law/contract/tort. You will locate a large amount of sources, and you need to check them for relevance *before* printing them off or photocopying them. Websites often provide useful abstracts of articles and books to assist you in this respect. It helps if you are conversant with the legal area, which allows you to identify whether a book, article or case is relevant; **in other words, make sure that you know what you are looking for.**

You should now be ready to begin writing out your work and including all your research in it. Sometimes you will need to discard material (either because you discover it is irrelevant or because of lack of space), and on other occasions you will need to undertake further research.

If it is time to undertake an assessment, read the above advice and then read the detailed guidance on research in Chapter 6 of the text.

2

Presentation of law assessments

Good lawyers present their work in a professional and appropriate manner. Students on undergraduate law programmes are expected to display similarly competent writing and presentational skills; your marks will suffer if you do not follow the basic rules outlined here. Students often complain that they are being marked on their grammatical ability instead of their legal knowledge, but both skills go hand in hand, especially in law where clarity is essential: **if you are on a law degree, you are on an English degree as well!**

- As potential legal advisers and graduate employees, you are expected to take pride in the presentation of your work and advice and to display competent skills in grammar and spelling.

- Poor grammar and structure make any advice you give difficult to follow.

- The complexity of the law calls for a clear writing style and a structured approach to addressing questions and problems.

- Undergraduate students are expected to display sound research skills and an ability to cite and utilise relevant legal and other materials.

- In general, students who gain good honours degrees in law can write competently and display sound essay-writing and problem-solving techniques. These students will, ultimately, be rewarded for these skills.

This chapter gives advice on how to present your work, but remember you must also work on and develop your own style of writing – one that will serve you on your degree and in your career.

WORD-PROCESSED WORK

You will be expected to word-process all your coursework assessments. Untidy and careless work does not create a good impression and is penalised, particularly when submitting undergraduate and postgraduate projects (**see Chapter 9**).

Concentrate on content, not 'fancy' presentation

Some students think it is vital to provide elaborate pictures of judges or scales of justice on the front of their work, and spend an inordinate amount of time on this aspect. Such embellishments are not to be discouraged, but ensure that the presentation is not better than the content.

Concentrate on a clear and structured layout, eliminating mistakes and untidy presentation. **Ensure that pages are in order, and that the bibliography is included.**

ADOPTING GOOD PRACTICE IN GRAMMAR, PUNCTUATION AND SPELLING

Although this section of the book will not provide detailed guidance, it will highlight some of the basic rules of grammar, punctuation and sentence construction. A common complaint of many module leaders on undergraduate programmes relates to the quality of the students' grammar, punctuation and spelling. Undergraduate assessments will test your proficiency in basic grammar and it is absolutely essential that you are able to adopt a sound, clear and appropriate writing style (see below).

Students who have not acquired the basic rules of grammar, punctuation and sentence construction before they come to university will find that their work will be heavily criticised and they will lose marks as a result.

Some allowance will be made if English is not your first language, but you need to practise and acquire a sound writing style early on in your course.

- Ensure that you know the components of a sentence (nouns, verbs, adverbs, adjectives, etc.), and that your sentences are thus complete and make sense.

EXAMPLE

'In R v *Smith* the judge clarified the requirements of the offence of murder.'

Not: 'In R v *Smith* the judge clarified.'

One of the objects of the sentence is missing from the second sentence, thus causing confusion.

- Ensure that your sentences flow and that your statements are related.

EXAMPLE

- 'The claimant could not show that s/he was induced by the misrepresentation. Which is why s/he failed in his/her action.'

  The second sentence does not survive on its own and should be connected to the first sentence: '... misrepresentation, which is why s/he failed in his/her action.' Alternatively, leave the first sentence and then start a new sentence: 'As a consequence the claimant failed in his/her action.'

- 'The judge held that the claimant had failed to establish all the elements of the tort of negligence. The judge held that the claimant had failed to establish that the defendant had broken a duty of care.'

  These two sentences look odd because they are related and need to be connected. Thus, you should write: 'The judge held that the claimant had failed to establish all the elements of negligence because s/he had failed to establish that the defendant had broken his/her duty of care.'

- 'The judge at first instance held that the advertisement was not an offer, in any case the customer had not accepted the terms of the advert, and there had not been any consideration shown by the customer.'

  Here there are three separate statements (clauses) which cannot be placed in one sentence simply by inserting a comma. Instead the author should create three separate sentences: 'The judge at

→

---

first instance held that the advertisement was not an offer. Further, s/he held that in any case the customer had not accepted the terms of the advert. Finally, s/he held that there had not been any consideration shown by the customer.'

Alternatively, the author could break the sentence up by using semi-colons: 'The judge at first instance held that the advertisement was not an offer; that in any case the customer had not accepted the terms of the advert; and finally that there had not been any consideration shown by the customer.'

- Always start a sentence with a capital letter.
- Do not forget to employ 'a' and 'the' (very common with students whose first language is not English).

EXAMPLE

The British constitution is largely un-codified; it is a feature of a constitution that . . . '

- Learn how to use commas, semi-colons and colons.

EXAMPLE

Use a comma to break up a sentence: 'The judge dismissed the action, finding that no contractual offer had been made to the claimant.'

Use a colon when you want to list a number of points: 'The judge listed the requirements of any valid interference with a human right: that the restriction is prescribed by law; that it pursues a legitimate aim; and that it is necessary and proportionate.'

Use a semi-colon to break up a list of points (as above) or to join two statements in a sentence: 'No contractual offer had been made; the advertisement was insufficiently clear in its terms.'

- Do not confuse tenses or plurals.

EXAMPLE

'In his judgment the judge notes that the advert was not an offer' (**use 'noted'** because you are referring to a judgment [note the spelling: 'judgment' not 'judgement'] that has already been given; you are not commentating on the judgment as it is being given).

'The matter was referred to the Court of Appeal and they decided in favour of the respondent' (use **'it'** not **'they'** as 'it' is one court, albeit with three judges).

'The judges has always shown respect to government ministers' (**'have'** as the sentence refers to more than one judge).

- Ensure that you learn the rules relating to the use of apostrophes. Misuse of apostrophes is common among students and causes irritation to markers.

EXAMPLE

An apostrophe can be used to denote that something belongs to something or somebody: **'the court's procedure'** (or **'the courts' procedure'** if referring to more than one court).

Or it can be used to abbreviate a number of words – **'they're'** (they are), **'don't'** (do not), **'it's'** (it is).

You do not normally contract full words, for example do not use **'can't'** for **'cannot'**.

Remember, if you use **'its'** to denote something belonging to it, you do not need an apostrophe as the word has already accommodated the apostrophe: **'The government is accountable to Parliament for its** [not **'it's'**] **unconstitutional behaviour.'**

- Avoid common spelling mistakes and misuse of words with different meanings.

EXAMPLE

Commonly misused by students are: 'their' (belonging to them) and 'there' (referring to a place); 'were' ('their Lordships were [not "where"] in agreement') and 'where' ('. . . where [not "were"] the parties made the agreement').

Never underestimate the benefits of employing good grammar

Students often feel that good grammar and style are very much secondary to knowledge of the law, and that lecturers will not penalise poor style, or reward good style. This is simply not true because lecturers do appreciate good grammar, spelling and style and are very often irritated by poor writing skills.

Further, a good writing style is imperative if you want your work to sound convincing; poor style not only sounds clumsy, it fails to convince the reader that the author knows what they are talking about.

Study and contrast the two examples below: extracts from an essay entitled 'Should celebrity privacy outweigh freedom of the press?'

EXAMPLE A

I think it's a bit of a nerve that celebrities like Niomi cambell and Max Moseley can bring privacy actions against the press. Because if they are well known then they should expect to have no privacy especially if they take drugs and have themselves filmed at sex orgies.

Freedom of the press is important in democracy states and should be upheld in every case no matter what. Obviously this does not mean that they can infringe peoples right to privacy but people like those I have mentioned above don't have a right to privacy so there shouldn't be any restriction on the press to report on their lives because that is what the pubic are interested in.

EXAMPLE B

Recent actions brought by celebrities against the British press to safe-guard their private and family lives raise the question whether such individuals have the right to privacy and whether press freedom can and should outweigh such a right? Although the law must attain a balance between these competing claims, it will be argued that in an effective and fair democracy press freedom should, at least in the majority of cases, outweigh celebrity privacy.

Cases involving the disclosure of private affairs of celebrities involves a conflict between the right to private life on the one hand and the protection of press freedom and the public right to know on the other. Both rights are protected under the Human Rights Act 1998 and the courts' role is to achieve a proportionate balance between these two rights, taking into account factors such as the status of the claimant, the nature of the information being disclosed (including any misbehaviour of the claimant) and the public interest in disclosure.

Student A will be very annoyed if they get a substantially lower mark in their essay than student B – A thinks that they have covered the same ground and made the same points as B. However, Student A not only commits errors in spelling and grammar, but also provides opinionated and unconvincing argument.

Student B's style is not only easy to follow, and more pleasurable to read for the marker, but provides evidence of an understanding of the issues and the arguments.

NOTE

You need to practise your writing skills. As a starting point, read sources that provide good practice in this respect (see the tips below). Ultimately you must adopt your own, good, style so that you can write assessments with confidence.

Read, read, read . . . and then do some more reading!

Studying law involves a tremendous amount of reading and perhaps sets law degrees apart from other courses. In order to gain the requisite knowledge and understanding you will be asked to read textbooks, articles, newspapers, case reports, statutes and a host of other materials.

TIPS ON READING SOURCES

- Reading appropriate legal sources not only provides you with substantive knowledge; constant reading of legal materials also familiarises you with legal jargon and the way in which legal academics and lawyers express themselves.

- More generally, constant reading of well-written and articulated sources will provide you with examples of good writing practice and how to employ the basic and more detailed rules of grammar, punctuation, spelling and sentence construction. This can in fact be a more effective way of learning and practising good grammar than simply sitting down and learning the ground rules.

- Get into the habit of constantly reading legal and other materials and adopt that style in *your own* writing; you will find that the style and all the rules of grammar begin to rub off on you and using proper grammar and spelling becomes second nature.

- Read quality newspapers every day; they provide you with a clear and informed style as well as useful legal and political articles.

- Read quality undergraduate textbooks and journals to learn how good legal writers express themselves: you will not get on with all of them, so look for a style which is both impressive and readable.

- Read novels and other books as regularly as you can. These can be of any style you prefer and do not have to be particularly 'highbrow' as long as the author writes well and appropriately.

- When you are reading the above materials, take time to study the style of writing, the sentence construction and the use of punctuation.

- Take notice of the spelling of certain words that you have always found difficult, and look up words whose meaning you are unsure of.

- Avoid using the casual style adopted on many internet sites and magazines – this style may be an effective way in which to communicate quickly and informally, but it is an inappropriate one to use on your course. Constant reading of these sites and materials (as opposed to textbooks etc.) will become ingrained in you and as a result you will write in that casual style in your assessments.

Spelling and typographical errors

Many students submit work with countless spelling and typographical errors. This is unprofessional, creates a poor impression and irritates the marker – it should be avoided wherever possible. Some minor mistakes are inevitable, however much editing you do, but leave adequate time to check for these errors.

- Use the grammar and spell check on your word-processor.
- Do not submit the work until all errors have been identified and corrected.

These matters *are* relevant to the quality of your work and to the mark that will be awarded. In particular, for project work grammar and punctuation are an essential criterion for awarding marks and determining classification.

CLEAR AND COHERENT WRITING STYLE

Some students have their work returned with comments such as, '*You deal with most of the legal issues, but your writing style and structure is poor, and your answer unclear.*' This is very frustrating for students who feel that they should be marked on their legal knowledge and not their proficiency in English and their essay skills, but a good writing style is essential to clarity and to success in law assessments.

You need to become confident when writing assessments and in adopting your own writing style. You cannot rely solely on the words of authors.

Try practising these skills by setting yourself the task of explaining a legal concept or case in your own words: for example, read the relevant pages in your text on 'offers and invitations to treat' and then in no more than 100 words explain the difference.

Law is complicated enough without it being explained in a muddled and clumsy way. Ensure that you write in a clear and appropriate manner, and that the reader understands what you are saying, as shown in the following example.

EXAMPLE

'A legally binding contract requires agreement, consideration and an intention to create legal relations.'

Not: 'For a contract what you need is an agreement and as well as that consideration as well as intention.'

Learn and employ the basic rules of grammar and punctuation. Again, the best way to acquire these skills is to read law texts and articles and other good, simple prose. Do not adopt the informal style used when talking to friends and fellow students. Let us look at some examples.

Casual language

Many students use casual phrases and present their work in an informal manner. These lapses create a poor impression – that the student does not read legal materials and has not yet learned how to express him- or herself as a law student.

Formal law language may sound unusual (and a little pompous) at first, but it will soon become second nature.

EXAMPLE

Do not say: 'I don't think Billy has got a chance of winning this case as he was drunk.'

The style is unprofessional and not what is expected of someone who is aspiring to become a professional lawyer. Can you imagine paying a lawyer for advice and getting that reply? In addition, it is subjective and not based on any authority.

Instead say: 'Given that James was drunk and failed to see the sign placed by the hole, it is unlikely that he will prove that the council breached any duty of care owed towards him, as required by the relevant case law [give case name and reference].'

In the above example, the former style is too casual; the latter uses the style adopted by lawyers, textbooks and other legal literature. It *does* matter which style you adopt: assessments are presented in a formal setting and will be marked by someone who uses appropriate language.

EXAMPLE

Do not use phrases such as **'As I said before'** (use **'As mentioned above'**), or **'Everyone these days is unhappy about law and order'** (use **'Given the increasing number of serious public order offences committed in England and Wales** [provide figures and source], **there is increasing public concern with respect to law and order'**).

You will soon learn how to express yourself by reading the right materials, and expressing yourself in that way will become natural.

EXAMPLE

The layperson might say: 'He went to court and won his case by getting £10,000.'

As a law student you must not express yourself in that way. Instead, the lawyer and the law student would say: **'The claimant brought an action for breach of contract and the High Court awarded him compensation of £10,000, representing his loss of profit.'**

Uninformed and unsupported opinion

EXAMPLE

Do not say: **'Everybody knows that judges are snobby and out of touch.'**

The comment is too casual and is unsupported by any evidence. It is a throwaway remark likely to be made by an uninformed layperson. You will be expected to be more objective and to provide authority for your opinions.

$\rightarrow$

Instead say: 'The common public view is that judges are middle class and out of touch with the common person. This view is also held by Professor Foster [quote text or article] and indeed figures show that most senior judges received a public school education [provide source and relevant figures].'

Muddled and inadequate explanations of the law or cases

It is essential that you provide clear and simple explanations of the legal principles and any relevant cases. A muddled style confuses the reader and indicates that you are uncertain on the law.

EXAMPLE

Do not say: 'After the Human Rights Act the judges can now use the European Convention to assist the individual in securing his human rights. Before the Act the judges couldn't do that, but they could take the Convention into account sometimes.'

This statement is confused and vague and does not inform the reader of the position of the Convention in domestic law, both before and after the Act. It also does not give any authority for the proposition.

Instead say: 'Before the Human Rights Act 1998 came into force the courts could use the European Convention only in cases where there was an uncertainty in a statute or the common law [authority]. However, since the Act came into force, judges must take into account the case law of the Convention (s. 2) and must interpret statutes in line with the Convention wherever possible (s. 3). Consequently, the Convention can be used directly in the domestic courts when adjudicating on human rights disputes.'

The reader now understands what the student is saying, and it is apparent that the student understands the legal position and has consulted the relevant sources.

There is little value in mentioning a case or a legal principle if you cannot show that you appreciate its meaning or impact and can articulate that.

In particular, you need to learn how to explain a case in simple and clear terms, often using very few words. Examples of this are given in **Part 2 of the text.**

Appropriate writing skills: example essay – you be the marker

Below is an example of a short essay which might be given to students in the first week or so of their law studies, perhaps for presentation in induction week or in the first seminar. The purpose of such essays is to test the student's general writing skills and their powers of legal logic and reasoning. The titles appear quite simple, but without the necessary skills and confidence, such assignments are difficult.

Examine the title below and the instructions given to the students, who must attempt to answer the question in approximately 500 words.

'Should human rights thrive in times of terrorism?'

- You may read texts and articles on terrorism and human rights to get some general ideas, but you should use your own words to construct your arguments.

- For this piece you do not need to reference your work by citing other authors, because this piece should be written *in your own words* and should reflect your own opinions. (You may include a list of references at the end to show your research.)

- Write the piece in the style of a clear and well-informed newspaper article – for example, the leading articles in a newspaper such as *The Times*. Thus, write clearly and appropriately, employing good grammar and writing style.

- Write in an objective manner and base your views on a reasonably sound understanding of the general issues – the protection of human dignity and liberty, the need to protect national security and public safety (especially in times of emergency), the role of democracy and of the courts in upholding, and limiting, human rights.

- Try to include arguments for and against the granting of human rights in this context.

Now look at both the poor and sound answers below. Try to identify the errors made in the poor answer and the skills shown in the sound one.

A: A poor answer

Read this answer and identify what errors the author has made with respect to grammar, style and structure. Using the above criteria, assign a mark to the essay and give some constructive and critical feedback to assist the student in improving his performance for the next, related, piece of work.

Although a lot of liberal, lefty civil libertarians think that terrorists should have human rights, I think its ridiculus to say that terorists should have the same human rights as we have. After all, they have thretened the whole country with their terrorist activitiys and they cant expect to have there rights protected otherwise the society will be under constant threat from terrorism and the goverment wont be able to do there job properly.

Human Rights belong to law abiding citizens and if people break the law and threaten society with acts of terrorism then we should withdraw their rights altogether. The Human Rights Act should not be used as a charter for criminals and terrorists and people like that should give up there rights and leave the act to be applied to individuals who deserve protection.

Take the recent arguments over extending the period the police are allowed to question terrorists. Given that the country is in danger, surely it cant be unreasonable to detain these people a little bit longer than normal. As long as the country is made safe it should not be up to the courts and human rights lawyers to decide how long we can detain terrorists. Although it isnt right to torture or kill them, less serious rights such as liberty, freedom of speech and the right to a fair trial should not stand in the way of protecting society from the threat of terrorism. In fact I think there is room for arguing that the death penalty should be brought back for terrorists and that the police should be allowed to use whatever force they think is right if it results in information that will save lives and restore order to the country.

On the other hand, it can be argued that upholding human rights in the terrorist context is essential to maintaining the rule of law and a healthy democracy, as well as allowing the state to fulfil its obligations, both in domestic law and under international treaties such as the European Convention on Human Rights. This is all very well and good, but surely the rights of a few terrorists can not stand in the way of the interests of society as a whole. Human rights have no place at all when public safety and national security is in trouble and it is wrong for the judges to question the relevant law and the efforts and bravery of the police and armed forces who are trying their best to balance human rights with the public interest. What rights have the courts got anyway as they arent even elected to protect us. Not like Parliament and the government who have been elected to protect our homes and our lives and the lives of our children. Those who argue that human rights should not be lost in these times should ask themselves and important question: what if it was youre children who got killed in the bombings?

In conclusion, although there may be sound reasons for giving terrorists rights, I cant think of any them and would say, no, terrorists shouldn't have human rights.

B: A sound answer

Study this answer and identify its qualities with respect to what the question expected of the student. In particular, compare it with the poor answer, above. Using the above criteria, assign a mark to the essay and give some constructive and critical feedback to assist the student in improving his performance for the next piece of work.

Every healthy democratic state prides itself on its human rights record and its willingness to uphold principles of equality, human dignity, liberty and due process. These principles are invariably contained in domestic law and form part of the state's international obligations, and a breach of them gives rise to possible breaches of the law and national and international criticism. However, these rights cannot be enjoyed absolutely and in times of emergency they may need to be compromised for the sake of the state and the rights of its citizens.

Events such as 9/11 and the bombings in London in 2005 have resulted in the passing of a number of legislative provisions which were intended to restrict individual liberty and human rights in the name of public safety and national security. Recently, for example, legislation has been rejected extending the period of police questioning of those suspected of terrorist offences to 42 days. This begs the question whether the enjoyment of human rights can survive emergency situations such as the imminent threat of terrorism and whether those suspected or found guilty of acts of terrorism should be able to rely on human rights law.

International law provides some guidance in this respect, accepting that states may further restrict some human rights during times of war and other public emergency, and stating clearly that such measures cannot infringe on the most fundamental rights such as the right to life and freedom from torture. In other cases, however, the exceptional measures must be reasonable and proportionate; but who decides where the balance lies between protecting basic rights and safeguarding national security and public safety?

Although basic notions of civilised society should not be abused even in times of emergency, it should be accepted that for a true democracy to survive in the face of terrorist threats extra measures need to be taken which invariably impact on personal freedom and normally accepted ideas of justice. Thus, although it can never be acceptable to torture a suspected, or indeed convicted, terrorist, that individual's right to liberty of the person or a fair trial will need to be compromised when the special dangers posed by the terrorist threat require giving state authorities extra powers of questioning, or where the traditional rules of a fair trial (such as the gathering and disclosure of relevant evidence) would not be appropriate and would greatly injure the general public interest.

Equally, during such times it should be accepted that the balance must be achieved by democratically elected and accountable government, and not, ultimately, by judges applying abstract and inflexible principles of justice. Thus, human rights law accepts that basic rights must be compromised during these times and, subject to evidence of clear abuse of power, judges should leave the balancing exercise to the laws of Parliament and the judgment of accountable government officers.

In conclusion, basic human rights should survive in times of terrorism, but they should not *thrive* to the detriment of the greater public good in securing public safety, or obstruct government's bona fide efforts to protect its territory and its citizens.

Clear and structured paragraphs

You should write in paragraphs and not in unconnected sentences or lists or bullet points. Every paragraph should contain a number of related sentences, dealing with one or more specific legal issues in turn. Look at an example of how not to do it.

EXAMPLE

Assume that the student is answering the question, *'What are the essential features of the British Constitution?'* An unstructured answer might look something like this:

'The British Constitution is unwritten, but most other constitutions are written in a formal document.

Some constitutions are rigid and cannot be changed except without a special procedure. This is not true of the British constitution, which is flexible. The sources of the British Constitution are both legal and nonlegal and consist of statutes, case law and constitutional conventions. Parliament is regarded as sovereign and can pass whatever law it wants.

The British Constitution has no formal bill of rights, and Parliament can pass whatever law it chooses. A central feature of the British Constitution is democracy and the House of Commons is elected. Other features are the rule of law and the separation of powers.'

The student has made a number of relevant observations about the British Constitution, but the piece is not written in clear and structured paragraphs. The answer jumps from one point to the next and confuses the reader. A structured answer requires three or four separate and clear paragraphs identifying the central features of the British Constitution.

EXAMPLE

Paragraph 1 – The unwritten nature of the British Constitution. Contrast with other constitutions such as USA and explain why the constitution is unwritten and where the British Constitution can be found.

Paragraph 2 – The informality and flexibility of the British Constitution. Absence of any formal and rigid constitutional law, reliance on general sources of law, and lack of any higher or supreme law.

Paragraph 3 – Absence of a formal bill of rights. Explanation of common law system of protecting rights, parliamentary sovereignty and human rights, and the effect of the Human Rights Act 1998 on human rights protection.

Paragraph 4 – Importance of constitutionalism and the control of government power in the British Constitution: the place of the rule of law and the separation of powers in the British Constitution.

Use the style adopted in textbooks. Undergraduate texts adopt a sound prose style, presenting the work in structured paragraphs under clear headings and sub-headings. You should adopt this style.

- Do not use sub-degree texts that adopt a bullet-point style.
- Use headings and sub-headings sparingly and only when necessary to indicate that you are dealing with separate issues.
- Lists should be avoided unless it is appropriate to employ them. For example, during a judgment a judge may have made a list of relevant issues to be considered when deciding whether a claim should be successful.

The point, evidence and evaluation/analysis system

In respect of paragraph construction it is useful to follow the **point, evidence evaluation (PEE)**, or **point, evidence, analysis (PEA)** system. This involves:

- making a point that is relevant to answering the question ('An essential feature of the British Constitution is that it is based on parliamentary sovereignty')

- providing **evidence** (e.g. a case which supports and illustrates that point)
- **evaluating/analysing** that evidence in the context of the question.

Thus, a central feature of the British Constitution is that it is un-entrenched and that sovereignty rests in an organ of government, rather than the constitution itself: **this analysis shows that *you* understand the (relevant) point that you have made.**

Why don't students write in paragraphs?

- Many students do not plan their answers before they start writing and do not think about what they are going to set down.
- Some students simply copy out points from the book because they are reading them for the first time or they do not realise that certain points are, or are not, connected.
- Some students do not know how to write in paragraphs and have not written in this style before – accordingly they make lists or write in one-sentence paragraphs.

When you are planning your essay, think about what information is going to go into particular paragraphs: see the example paragraphs on the British Constitution above.

AVOIDING PLAGIARISM

Plagiarism has become a major issue in academic courses, leading to university disciplinary procedures being invoked, and, occasionally, students being expelled from the course. It is essential that students are aware of the ground rules in this area.

What is plagiarism?

Plagiarism involves the use of others' ideas or words and presenting them as your own. It is a form of cheating, no less serious than cheating in examinations.

If you are on an academic course you will have to display *your* knowledge and skills: you cannot expect to be rewarded for submitting others' work without credit and analysis.

Some examples of plagiarism are given in the poor answer to the contract law practice question in Chapter 5.

Copying from other students

Copying from other students is also plagiarism and is a form of cheating. It involves copying another student's work and passing it off as your own. Although you may be encouraged to discuss an assessment with another student and to share some research material, the written work must be your own.

Never show a fellow student your written work – either in draft or final form – before submission of the work. Remember, both parties can be penalised if one student knowingly allows another student to copy his or her own work.

You can also be guilty of **self-plagiarism** – where you use your previous work in your present assignment. University plagiarism checks often flag these similarities up, so please seek your own law school policy on this.

Why is plagiarism wrong and why should you avoid it?

Plagiarism is wrong because it represents academic dishonesty – the student has represented themselves as having knowledge and skills that they do not possess, and would be rewarded for that if not detected.

Plagiarism is a form of cheating, and you will be penalised: from the deduction of marks, through the award of a mark of zero for that piece (or the whole module), to expulsion from the course.

In addition, professional bodies such as the Law Society may be informed of such events, jeopardising your career.

NOTE

Marks can be deducted from assessments for **poor academic practice** falling short of plagiarism – for example, where a student copies (and then credits) large sections of an author's work: this is not plagiarism, but it is poor academic practice as there is a lack of individual analysis expected from the student.

Make sure you read the university's policy on plagiarism and abide by it. If you are in any doubt, consult your tutor, lecturer or course leader.

Why do students plagiarise?

Most students who plagiarise do not do so intentionally or with a view to gaining an unfair advantage. These students plagiarise because they do not know the rules on plagiarism and do not appreciate that they are plagiarising (neither of which is an excuse).

- Some students think it is acceptable to copy from texts without crediting the source. They assume that the lecturer will know that they are using a particular book or article and that it is not their own work.

- Some students do not bother to credit a source in the main body of the work because they have mentioned the source in their bibliography. You must credit the source even though the source is listed in your bibliography.

- Some students do intend to plagiarise to gain an advantage in the assessment. They hope that the lecturer will accept the view as the student's own and will be impressed by the student's research or grasp of the law.

- Many students plagiarise because they feel they need to. They have no real grasp of the legal principles or the question and use authors for this purpose. However, instead of plagiarising, the student can credit the author (getting credit for the research – we will look at this in more detail later).

- Because many students do not understand the basic principles, they find it difficult to know whether these views are relevant to the question and to providing an appropriate answer. Thus, much of the plagiariser's work is irrelevant to the task in hand, in addition to being plagiarism.

- Most plagiarism is immediately identifiable. Unless the student has a very good writing style and academic approach, the style of the answer shifts dramatically (**see the poor answer in Chapter 5**). The university mechanism for detecting plagiarism will usually detect the copied sources, and in any case the lecturer is usually able to identify the source from his or her previous research and knowledge.

How can I reference the source and avoid plagiarism?

You can avoid charges of plagiarism by clearly crediting your sources. (**Chapters 6 and 7 provide fuller information on how to cite and reference legal sources.**) If you have read and relied on a source, put it in your bibliography and supply the reference in the main body of the essay. Make it clear that the view you are putting forward is not your own, but someone else's.

EXAMPLE

'It has been suggested that the case law under the Human Rights Act 1998 has provided very few examples of a "hands-on" approach to the protection of human rights in England and Wales [create a foot-note and put "See Steve Foster, 'Human Rights and the 1998 Act' [2005] EHRLR 66, at page 71"].'

Here you will be rewarded by the lecturer because the footnote provides evidence that you have researched and read a relevant article, and that you are capable of including a relevant source at an appropriate stage of your work. You can gain extra marks by showing your appreciation of that view, perhaps by pointing to cases that back it up or contradict it, and by putting forward your views on this matter.

Good referencing not only avoids charges of plagiarism, it rewards the students for good research and referencing skills.

NOTE

Your university will provide you with its in-house rules about plagiarism: ensure that you read and understand them fully. If you are unsure, ask your lecturers and course tutors.

PROVIDING AUTHORITY

Providing legal authority in your answers is related to the avoidance of plagiarism – if you credit and cite your sources you can thereby avoid a charge of plagiarism – but they are not the same. To say that it is an offence to commit an act or theft, or that there is a case on whether adverts are offers, is not plagiarism – it is simply unsupported by legal authority.

If you learn the rules on avoiding plagiarism and the use of authority you will avoid any discipline as well as getting reward for using authority in your assessments.

As a law student you are expected to provide legal and other authority for your work, whether it is primary authority – the relevant Act of Parliament or case authority – or secondary authority – textbooks or journal articles. You cannot write law assessments without providing authority and you will fail unless you do so, even if your answer is well written and generally logical.

In addition, providing and citing authority avoids a charge of plagiarism (see earlier). There is nothing wrong with the following statement:

> 'The Human Rights Act has been described as of great constitutional significance and indeed it provides judges with enhanced powers with respect to the protection of human rights.'

However, a law student must provide authority. The Act's year should be added (1998), the author who described it as significant (and who has been alluded to) should be identified, and the provisions which give the judges enhanced powers should be cited.

The rules on providing authority are detailed in Chapters 6 and 7, but note the following points:

- Never simply make a statement without providing authority – 'an agreement is not a contract unless the parties have provided consideration and consideration must be sufficient' [Provide the case name and reference].

- You do not need to provide authority for obvious statements and accepted principles – for example, **'England and Wales have a common law, as opposed to a civil law, system.'** (Even then the student can refer the reader to a textbook for further information.)

- Always provide specific case or statutory authority, rather than saying **'this is covered by statute or a case'**.

- Do not *just* provide your opinion on the law – **'I think the law needs amending as it is unjust'**. Explain what the law says and why it could be unjust.

- If you are going to provide an opinion, make sure you are aware of academic views on the matter and base that opinion on an appreciation of those views and of the law in general, even if you subsequently wish to disagree with that view.

- If your view is the same as the author's, then make sure you credit it.

- If asked to give legal advice (**see problem questions in Chapter 5**), make sure your advice/opinion is based on a knowledge and appreciation of the legal principles.

Proper citation and referencing of sources

Proper citation and referencing of sources is discussed in detail in Chapters 6 and 7, but you will be expected to adopt the rules on citation and referencing used in undergraduate (as opposed to sub-degree) texts.

- **Citing** a case means labelling the case in the appropriate way, giving the case its proper title. **Referencing** the case means identifying its correct source – for example, the law report.

- Always *cite* the case or other legal source properly.

EXAMPLE

Do not say: **'This was decided in the case of Mrs Donogue.'**

Instead say: **'This was decided in *Donogue* v *Stevenson*** [reference via footnote, or year of case in an exam].'

Alternatively, if you have already mentioned the case, you can say **'this was decided in *Donogue*,'** and put either *Donogue* v *Stevenson* with the reference in a footnote or **'see above, note 1'** in a footnote.

- Always provide the correct reference for that source.

EXAMPLE

'The "neighbour" principle was established in *Donogue* v *Stevenson* [1932] AC 562' [Appeal Cases for the year 1932, starting at page 562].

This is (one of) the official law report(s) where the case can be located and should be used in coursework). Do not put **'page 33 of Smith, *Tort Law*,'** even if you did find the case there, the text is not the primary source. In an exam, it is sufficient to put (1932) after the name of the case.

Using footnotes

Consult the lecturer as to whether you should use footnotes, but generally footnotes are expected in coursework assessments in law. They give your coursework an air of professionalism and indicate that you are developing relevant legal and writing skills. Footnotes also allow you to provide legal authority for your answer and to credit relevant sources, avoiding any charge of plagiarism.

Footnotes can be created easily on your word processor (there may be variations to this simple process):

- Put the cursor at the place where you want to create the footnote mark. For example, **'This can be illustrated by the case of *Donoghue* v *Stevenson*'** (you want your footnote number to appear here and you are going to create a footnote at the bottom of the page).

- Go to 'Reference' at the top of your screen and click on footnotes (or reference, then footnotes).

- Click on footnote and you will have a choice of 'automatic' (in number order) or 'custom' (symbols such as *).

- Press automatic and then the footnote number will appear and you will be taken to the bottom of the page where you can fill in the appropriate text.

- Click back on the main screen to return to your essay.

What to put in footnotes

Footnotes can be used to give a relevant legal reference – a book, Act of Parliament or case.

EXAMPLE

'The leading case in this area is *Smith* v *Foster*[1] . . . This rule is now covered in the Public Order Act 1986[2] . . . It has been suggested that this case is wrongly decided as paying too little attention to procedural justice.[3]'

---

[1][1996] 2 All ER 333
[2]Section 13(1)
[3]Steve Foster. 'Procedural Fairness and the Human Rights Act 1998' (2005) 68 MLR 660, at 668

Footnotes also can be used to provide further, ancillary, information that may not deserve a mention in the main body of your essay. In particular, they can be used in extended essays and projects to refer to a variety of academic sources:

EXAMPLE

'In that case the House of Lords held that the position would be different had the contract been in writing.[4] This view has subsequently received constant criticism.[5]'

---

[4]Per Lord Bridge at page 77. His Lordship also opined that the normal rule would not apply if there was an independent witness to the agreement (at page 81). For a critical account of that obiter, see Steve Foster. 'A Bridge Too Far' (2005) 23 OJLS 33, at 45

[5]See Steve Foster 'Extending the law' [1997] PL 223; Steve Foster 'Extending the law again' [1998] EHRLR 246; and Steve Foster 'Time for revision" (2005) 68 MLR 330. For a general discussion on this area, see Steve Foster *Criminal Law and Human Rights* (2nd ed, OUP 2015)

Be careful when using extensive footnotes; they are common in legal journals and textbooks, but may be discouraged in student assessments. Check with the lecturer whether they count towards your word limit. Some lecturers may not read any text in footnotes.

With respect to **plagiarism** (see above), do not copy (or copy and paste) an author's footnotes: the information in footnotes is a product of the author's research and you cannot copy them into your assessments, even if you have credited the author's words and ideas in the main text. Your footnotes should contain sources that *you* have accessed and read.

Appropriate, true and properly cited bibliography

You should provide a list of sources that you have used for the research and preparation of the assessment at the end of the work, on a separate page. The rules on bibliographies – including how to cite and reference sources in them – are discussed in greater detail in Chapters 6 and 7, but note:

- It should contain an appropriate range of materials (depending on the level of your study and the nature of the task) from textbooks, journal articles and primary sources.

- Do not include inappropriate sources, such as sub-degree texts or Wikipedia.

- It should contain all the material that you researched and read for the work.

- It should not contain anything that you have not read (at least in part).

- It can contain material not specifically referred to in the main text of the work, but generally you should try to refer to as many references as possible during the work. If you don't, the lecturer may draw the conclusion that much of your bibliography is purely for show.

- Ensure that the bibliography is properly cited and referenced (**see Chapters 6 and 7 for details**).

- You may wish to separate primary and secondary sources. You also may wish to separate specific primary sources (Acts of Parliament, cases, treaties) and secondary sources (books, articles). Consult your lecturer on these details.

READING OVER YOUR ANSWER

In addition to revising your answer as you go along – to accommodate new sources and ideas – it is essential that you read over and proof-read your work before submission. This is ignored by many students, not because they don't care whether they submit clear and structured work, but because they leave insufficient time to check over their work before submission. Presenting sloppy work with countless errors and which ignores basic legal and English skills gives a poor impression and leads to marks being deducted; in extreme cases the student may fail. Well-written, structured and logical answers allow markers to concentrate on the legal content and gives the impression that the student knows what he or she is talking about.

- Spend almost as much time checking your original work as you do writing the assessment.

- Check work for basic spelling and typographical mistakes and for poor grammar, unclear structure and inadequate explanation.

- Do not submit your first draft – work on the piece until it is acceptable.

- Give yourself at least a whole day to check your final draft.

- If you get a friend to read the work, ensure you choose someone who is very competent in English (do not use a fellow law student on the course because of the possibility of plagiarism).

- Use the grammar and spell check functions on your computer, but be aware of legal phrases that the computer may not be aware of (e.g. Latin phrases). A common error is students describing a tortious action (an action in tort) as 'tortuous' (laborious) on the instruction of the computer.

Why don't students follow these rules?

Students don't follow these rules either because they do not care how the work is presented (this is uncommon, but some students feel that presentation is irrelevant), or because they do not have the time or inclination to check the work before submission. The problem starts earlier, with late preparation, poor research and hurried writing. The student is left with little or no time to check the work for even basic errors.

ANSWERING THE QUESTION

The key to success and higher marks is the ability to address and answer the set question – the student who appreciates what the question is getting at, and has the ability to answer the question, will end up with higher marks. Even if the content of the answer is sound, many students fail, or fail to get good marks, because they have not understood, or have deliberately ignored, the question.

- Lecturers set questions that they know the answer to (or at least have a sound idea of what should be included in the answer).
- Lecturers deliberately set testing questions and in the main avoid wholly descriptive questions, such as 'What are the essential requirements of a legally binding contract?'
- Lecturers tend to set questions which require students to use their legal skills (analysis, criticism) and to research beyond the basic text or which require analysis or (in the case of problem questions) application to the facts of a scenario.

Answer the question that is set

Many students fail, or fail to do well, because they simply refuse to answer, or are incapable of answering, the question. There is nothing more frustrating to a student than when they get the following type of comment:

> You show a good knowledge of the general legal area, but you simply have not answered the question, and as a result most of your content is irrelevant. **30%**

Do not select your own question

Many students *choose* to ignore the question set by the module leader and instead select their own question. For example, a student when asked the question 'What is a constitution?' or 'What is the purpose of a legal system?' may turn the question round and instead address the question 'What are the sources of the British Constitution?' or 'What are the features of the English legal system?' They do this because the answer to *their* question is provided in the textbook!

In doing so the student has ignored the question (carefully) selected by the module leader and has given an answer to another question. Even if the student touches on the specific question, the answer, logically, does not follow the pattern expected by the module leader, and in the worst-case scenario the answer is totally irrelevant.

Equally important, the answer does not address the specific nuances of the question. In the above example, the question asks the student to look at constitutions or legal systems in the abstract – it asks the student to identify the characteristics and content of a constitution/legal system – and the answer instead gives information about one particular constitution or legal system.

The student does not display the knowledge and understanding required from the question and has not answered the question. Instead they have copied out general descriptive information from a textbook without thinking 'am I actually answering the question by supplying this information?'

Although this may be tolerated to a great extent on sub-degree courses, it is not tolerated at undergraduate and postgraduate levels. The module leader expects you to identify the specific legal problems raised by the question, and to address those aspects in your answer. Otherwise the module leader would set questions such as '*Write all (or anything) you know about constitutions/legal systems*'.

Do not write in the general area – the 'scatter-gun' or 'dartboard' approach

Some students simply identify the general legal area and write in that general area (as covered in the text). Imagine if a client asked a solicitor about a personal contractual problem and was met with a mini lecture on the law relating to the formation of a contract. The client would feel cheated because the solicitor has merely told the client the general legal position and then, in effect, told the client to answer the specific question him- or herself. It is the same with student assessments: the module leader has not asked you to copy out the relevant pages of the text (although some of that information can be used in constructing your answer).

Analyse the question and its components and make a plan of your answer

Look at the question carefully and identify the relevant area of law and the main components of the question.

EXAMPLE QUESTION

'In terms of procedure and purpose, what is the distinction between civil and criminal law? Is this distinction always sustainable in practice?'

The question is about the difference between civil and criminal law, but cannot be answered simply by listing the basic distinctions. You can start with basic definitions and distinctions, but your answer must concentrate on the headings of *procedure and purpose.* You can then address the final part of the question by giving examples of both divisions, and, more importantly, giving examples where the distinction is blurred.

Your plan should look something like this:

- Define criminal and civil law and explain the *basic distinction.*
- Explain the difference in respect of legal *procedure* – how a case is brought, parties to an action.
- Explain the difference with respect to the *purpose* of both – regulating private relationships and activities, providing compensation (as opposed) to protecting society, punishing.
- Give examples where the distinction is uncertain or blurred, for example, where some conduct might attract criminal and civil liability, private criminal prosecutions, juries in civil cases, exemplary damages.

Thus, before you begin to type your answer and before you finalise your research, you must make a plan of your answer (to the question that has been set). You should know what you are going to say, and in what order, before you begin writing. You can refer to that plan in structuring your answer and check your work at the end to see whether you have followed that plan and answered the question.

EXAMPLE QUESTION

'The British Constitution is unwritten, informal and flexible. Indeed, it could be argued that there is no British Constitution. Discuss.'

- You could start with a brief definition of a constitution and what a constitution is and what it should contain.

- You can then discuss what is meant by the terms 'unwritten, informal and flexible' with respect to the British Constitution, comparing it with written, formal and rigid constitutions.

- You can answer the second part of the question by examining the relevance of those characteristics to the question of whether a constitution exists – is rigidity and formality necessary?

- You could provide evidence of the British Constitution to argue that it does exist – that there is an established system of government and principles of constitutional conduct, and recent constitutional reform.

- You could provide evidence to support the argument that it does not exist – lack of a fundamental, supreme law, sovereignty of Parliament as opposed to sovereignty of the constitution.

- You could then reach a conclusion as to the truth of the statement.

NOTE

Only the students who *truly* appreciate what a constitution is are going to answer the question properly: if you ask yourself the question 'what is a constitution?' and you cannot answer this without referring to a textbook definition, then you are unlikely to get good marks for your answer – it will appear that you are simply copying out of the book, hoping that you are answering the question, but failing to convince the marker that you truly understand.

Introductions, main text and conclusions

Coursework should be approached in three stages – the introduction, the main text and the conclusion. In other words, say what you are going to say, say it, and say what you have said.

The **introduction** is your opportunity to show that you understand the question and the legal issues – it should be brief and tell the reader what needs to be covered and how it is to be covered.

EXAMPLE

'This question ("*Is law the same as justice?*") asks whether the formal law is equivalent to the general notion of justice. To answer the question one needs to appreciate the various meanings of both law and

---

justice, and to identify the central characteristics and qualities of each. Thus, by examining various definitions and ideas of both, and by providing a number of examples, one should be able to conclude whether the two concepts are indeed the same.

With respect to law, we can note that law has been defined as . . . '

A good introduction also indicates to the marker that the author is familiar with the relevant legal rules and concepts, and the legal dilemma raised by the question. For example, below is a sound introduction to the question '*What is the difference between law, rules of law and the rule of law?*'

EXAMPLE

'Every developed state requires a system of law to regulate the behaviour and actions of its citizens and of the government itself. This law will be made and enforced formally, and will produce specific rules of law, governing particular areas of conduct, such as the law of contract, employment law and land law. In addition that society will agree to abide by the formal law and to resolve disputes in accordance with the law – known as the rule of law. This essay will explore these concepts in order to distinguish the nature and function of each.'

With problem questions, the introduction can identify all the relevant legal issues.

EXAMPLE

'This question relates to the formation of a contract and whether X and Y have entered into such a contract. In particular, it must be determined whether X made an offer, whether Y accepted that offer, and whether both parties have provided sufficient consideration for each other's promises.'

Alternatively, you may dispense with a general introduction and include a specific introduction as you deal with each point.

> **EXAMPLE**
>
> 'The first point to consider is whether X made a firm offer to Y, or whether his or her statement was a mere invitation to treat.'

The **main text** should deal with each point in turn, identified in your plan, addressing all aspects of the question and providing relevant legal authority for each point.

The **conclusion** should contain a summary of the issues dealt with in the main text, along with the student's own concluding remarks. Note: markers will examine the conclusion (often before the main text) to see whether the student has understood and answered the question.

> **EXAMPLE**
>
> 'In conclusion it is submitted that the notions of law and justice do not necessarily coincide, and that formal law can exist without it meeting the requirements of basic notions of justice. [You can expand by referring to some specific points in that respect and by referring to authority already referred to in the main text.] However, provided the substantive law contains those requirements and reflects such notions, it can be seen that law is, or perhaps should be, the same as justice.'

NOTE

Do not include new information or ideas in your conclusion. Many students do this because they remember a point that they have left out in the main text. This causes confusion to the reader and suggests that the student is either muddled or poorly organised.

Make sure the content of your answer is relevant

- Check continually whether what you are writing is relevant to the question. It should be easy to do this provided you have the necessary knowledge to identify the main points raised by the question and have made a clear plan of the answer.

- If it is a problem question, place yourself in the position of the person to be advised: would he or she need to know that information? Is the point relevant to his or her situation?

- In an essay question, check that you are addressing all the issues and that you are not including information simply because it is covered in the textbook and relates to the relevant legal area.

Address the problems in problem questions

Chapter 5 addresses the techniques necessary to answer problem questions. Remember, you are asked to give advice to the affected parties, not to write generally in the legal area. The scenario raises legal and factual problems.

- Was a contract concluded at that stage?
- Did the parties follow the legal formalities of a contract?
- Did their behaviour indicate agreement?

The parties want these problems addressed and answered, and you will not be able to avoid them by simply writing in the general legal area.

Why don't students answer the question?

There are many reasons why students do not answer the set question

REASONS WHY STUDENTS FAIL TO ANSWER THE QUESTION

- Students simply do not understand the question or what the question is getting at.

- In problem questions (**addressed in Chapter 5**), students cannot identify which aspects of (contract) law are raised in the scenario. In such a case students either guess at what areas are alluded to, or write everything about the law of contract just to be on the safe side.

- In addition, the wording of, or the words used in, the question can confuse students: *'The British Constitution is mythical and principally unconstitutional. Discuss.'* Here students do not appreciate the use of the words 'mythical' and 'unconstitutional', but having seen the words 'British Constitution' feel that it is safe simply to explain the sources and features of the British Constitution.

- They understand what the question is getting at, and what is required to answer it, but do not have the knowledge or research time to provide the answer. For example, in exams students identify what a problem question is getting at, but do not know anything about those areas (consideration/ misrepresentation). Instead of writing nothing, they talk about what they do know (offer and acceptance/intention to create legal relations).

- With coursework assessments, a question asking for personal or academic analysis (or for them to get to grips with a concept such as 'constitutional-ism') is ignored by students because that would require further research or asks students to articulate on a topic they have little or no view on.

- They know the answer to another, simpler question – generally one that can be answered by reading and copying out the general textbook.

- Students ignore the question and substitute another question which they do know the answer to, and which can be answered by looking at the general textbook. 'What is the purpose of law?' may become 'How is the law classified?' Students do this because the text provides lots of information on the classification of law, but little on what law is and its purpose.

In order to answer a question properly, you need to:

- Look at the question carefully.
- Identify the words that define the question.
- Be prepared to solve the question and undertake the necessary research.

Below are some examples of testing questions that are likely to be misread or misunderstood by students.

EXAMPLE QUESTION

'What is a legal system and what is its purpose?'

This question is *not* asking you to outline the nature and sources of the English legal system. Many students simply describe the English legal system because that is what they find in their textbooks. But the question is asking you to define *a* legal system and to explain its *purpose*.

You need to appreciate the nature and purpose of a legal system – what it does, what it consists of, how it interacts with the law and the constitution. You can then describe its purpose (which should become evident once you have defined a legal system) – that it

→

has and what purposes it achieves. A knowledge of the rules of contract may help you appreciate the reasons why people enter into them – they formalise the parties' agreement, provide evidence of their agreement, finalise the terms and the rights and duties of the parties, allow individuals and companies to arrange their business affairs and to provide redress if the agreement is breached. Simply stating the law does not address the question why people enter into them.

In all of the above examples, you have been asked a searching question that cannot be answered simply by looking at the textbook. It requires you to appreciate particular concepts and to think *why* the law (or a legal system or a constitution) exists. The lecturer is asking you to reflect on what you are studying and what you have been taught. In most cases the lecturer has addressed these issues in lectures and seminars, and if you have not attended lectures and engaged with the subject (or you are not prepared to research beyond the main text), you may struggle with the question.

How can I ensure that I answer the question?

The key to understanding the question is the *real* understanding of the legal issues – what a constitution *really* is, as opposed to copying out information about constitutions from a textbook without any reflection.

Misreading or misunderstanding the question can happen to anyone, particularly during the tension of an examination. However, you can avoid this problem by reflecting on certain rules.

TIPS FOR ANSWERING QUESTIONS

- Read the question carefully.
- Identify the specific context or angle of the question and topic, not the general words or areas.
- In the case of coursework assessments, read and follow any guidance given by the lecturer and discuss the title with (reliable and knowledgeable) fellow students.

- Ensure that you are conversant in that legal area before you begin writing the answer. Many students answer the wrong question because they have a limited knowledge of the area and are unable to identify the central issues.
- Attend all relevant classes where the question, or at least the subject area, will be discussed.
- If the question uses unfamiliar terms, find out what they mean and do the necessary research beyond the text to allow you to tackle the question.
- Expect the question to be demanding and for it to require you to think about the answer and to do further research.

A choice of questions

If you are given a choice of questions, choose one that suits your knowledge and your specific skills. If one area has been covered in lectures and seminars and the other needs individual research, you may be better advised to choose the former, unless you have good research skills and you are particularly interested in that legal area.

- Some students prefer to tackle problem questions rather than essays (**see Chapter 5**), but ensure you have a sound knowledge of the law and good problem-solving skills.
- Some students are more confident with analytical questions (*'Critically examine the central features of the British Constitution'*) rather than more descriptive questions (*'Using case law, explain how section 1 of the Theft Act 1968 has been interpreted by the courts.'*).
- Some students prefer interdisciplinary questions, requiring a (political) perspective (*'To what extent is the British Constitution consistent with basic notions of democracy?'*).

Different types of question

You should identify early on what type of question has been set. This dictates your research, your writing style and your overall approach to the question.

Questions on legal theory, concepts and institutions, or substantive law

Some questions relate to substantive legal topics (contract, tort, criminal law) and require the student to be conversant with specific legal principles.

EXAMPLE QUESTIONS

- *What is a contract? What are the essential requirements of a legally binding contract?*
- *The courts will only impose a duty of care on the defendant if they feel it is just to do so. Discuss.*
- *In what circumstances does and should the criminal law impose strict liability?*

These questions require a knowledge and discussion of the relevant substantive law. They can be answered adopting a critical approach, and some require an appreciation of specific concepts (such as justice), but essentially they require you to be conversant with the relevant legal principles and sources.

Other questions refer instead to legal concepts (e.g. the law, the rule of law, justice) or institutions (e.g. constitutions, legal systems, courts).

EXAMPLE QUESTIONS

- *What is law? Is law the same as justice?*
- *Explain what is meant by the rule of law. Why do we prefer to live by the rule of law rather than by the rule of men?*
- *What is a constitution and what purpose does it achieve?*
- *What is the function of a legal system?*

These questions cannot be answered by simply explaining specific legal rules. They are asking you to appreciate and explain certain concepts or ideas. You need to employ accepted definitions and views on, for example, what law is, and to discuss those concepts and views in the context of the question.

For example, you cannot answer the question '*What is law?*' by saying that 'the law of contract is an example of law and the rules of contract are as follows . . .' However, once you have identified what law is, you may be able to use specific laws in illustration:

'. . . law can govern and regulate private relationships and activities, such as family law, contract law or property law.'

When you have defined justice you can use a law to illustrate a specific aspect of justice:

'. . . a fundamental principle of justice is that every citizen should have access to the courts and, where necessary, access to free legal advice and representation. In this respect, the Access to Justice Act 1999 provides that . . . '

Essay and problem questions

The skills required to tackle problem-type questions are addressed in Chapter 5. For present purposes, essay questions test the following skills:

- your ability to research a specific legal topic;
- your legal knowledge of that legal area;
- your ability to offer a critical and analytical account of the law;
- your ability to address the question and to structure a logical and academically sound answer;
- your ability to use relevant legal sources in support of the answer and to employ relevant citation and referencing skills.

Problem questions require you to employ most of the above skills, but in particular you must concentrate on the following:

- identifying the relevant legal areas and the specific legal problems faced by the parties;
- applying relevant legal principles and cases to the facts of the scenario;
- providing the parties with clear, correct and constructive legal advice.

In problem questions, the style of the answer will be different in many respects – your account of the law will be less academic and critical and your advice will be more practical. However, you will still be expected to employ other academic and writing skills, such as sound grammar and spelling, clear use of case law and other authority, and proper citations and references.

Descriptive and analytical questions

Some questions require a reasonably descriptive account of the relevant legal principles and sources. They are principally testing your legal knowledge and your ability to give a clear and correct account of the law.

EXAMPLE QUESTION

'What is the difference between a contractual offer and an invitation to treat?'

This question can be answered by examining the legal principles as established in the relevant case law, and by giving examples of offers and invitations. It does not call for any critical account of the law or the cases, although a good answer would highlight and comment on any illogical or inconsistent case law and would include some academic opinion.

Other questions call for a much more critical and analytical approach of the law. Here you need to appreciate the law and its rationale and to be able to critically assess its effectiveness.

EXAMPLE QUESTION

'Existing case law with respect to the adequacy of consideration shows that the courts have failed to settle on any definite legal principles. Discuss.'

This question cannot be answered by simply outlining the principles and case law on consideration. It is asking you to address the quote, which implies that the law is in a state of confusion and lacks principle, relying instead perhaps on flexibility, which is causing confusion. You must identify the relevant legal areas (performance of existing duties, part performance of contractual obligations) and analyse those decisions to see whether the statement is indeed true. You should be conversant with academic opinion in this area and should use textbooks and journal articles to support your answer.

In addition, some questions ask for the student's own opinion or assessment of the law.

EXAMPLE QUESTION

'Critically examine the central provisions of the Human Rights Act 1998. In your opinion, do you believe that the Act is democratically and constitutionally sound?'

The first part of the question asks for a critical assessment. You need to highlight the controversial provisions of the Act – not simply list each and every provision – and highlight the legal and constitutional problems. You need to be aware of, and to use, academic opinion in this respect.

Then you are asked for your own opinion. This often throws students, who either feel that they can say anything at this point or are uncomfortable with offering their own view. For the former group, the question is not giving you carte blanche to comment on the Act. Your opinion must be based on an appreciation of the Act's provisions and of the arguments for and against the passing of the Act and of its provisions. For the latter, you are not expected to provide an entirely individual view on the matter and can base your views on *your appreciation* of accepted academic commentary.

It is perfectly acceptable to say:

'. . . although the Act appears to allow a shift of power between Parliament and the courts, it should be stressed that the courts' new powers have been granted by Parliament itself. This view is supported by Foster [provide citation and reference] who feels that the Act is neither undemocratically nor unconstitutionally unsound. Thus it is submitted that the Act is neither undemocratic nor unconstitutional simply because the courts are vested with greater powers.'

It is *not acceptable* to offer entirely subjective and unsupported opinion:

'In my view it is unacceptable for the judges to question the law and to decide whether the law is in breach of human rights. That is not the court's job – they are not elected like Parliament, and they should just declare what the law is.'

This opinion exposes a lack of understanding of the role of the courts in protecting human rights and is unsupported by established legal opinion.

What is the lecturer after? What does the lecturer expect from the student?

The lecturer's expectations depend on the nature of the question (see earlier).

Other questions are difficult for the following reasons:

- They require you to **cover a number of legal areas** (for example, a problem question which covers offer and acceptance, consideration, breach and damages). You need a broad knowledge of the course to tackle these questions (attending lectures and seminars on a regular basis helps enormously), and you need to devote an appropriate amount of time to each area.
- They require you to **display a thorough knowledge of a specific legal area,** or a case or number of cases. For these questions you need to research beyond your basic textbook and may need to access full law reports and case notes on relevant cases.
- They require you to **employ skills such as statutory or case interpretation.** The answers to these questions do not appear in any textbook and you need to look carefully at the wording of the statute or the decision of a previous case to allow you to answer the question. Never underestimate the acquisition of general and basic skills in tackling questions in substantive legal areas.
- They require you to have some **knowledge of recent events or political and social affairs.** A lot of students struggle with questions which require some knowledge of politics or recent affairs. If you are not naturally a 'political animal', acquire a textbook that adopts a more political approach to the subject and try to get to terms with at least the basic political or other arguments. As a law student you should read a good broadsheet newspaper, particularly if you are studying subjects such as Public Law or Law in Society.

What sort of skills do I have to employ?

You should examine the question closely at an early stage and consider the sort of skills you are going to need to tackle that question. This allows you to acquire the skills before you write the assessment. In general, to tackle law assessments you need to employ the following skills:

- Careful and selective research.
- An ability to grasp concepts and legal principles.
- A sound knowledge of the relevant legal area.
- An understanding of cases and other legal sources and their relevance to the question.

- An ability to explain concepts and legal sources in a simple and clear fashion.
- Clear writing and English skills.

In addition, the question might expect you to show other skills, such as critical analysis or contextual awareness. In such a case you need to acquire and practise those skills in preparation of the presentation of the work.

How much knowledge do I need? What depth of knowledge is required?

At level one of your law studies you will be given assessments that test your basic knowledge and understanding of the law, the institutional framework and basic legal concepts. In addition, the assessments will test your ability to write in a way that is consistent with you being an undergraduate, including showing skills expected of a law student – handling of legal materials, proper citation and referencing skills. At this level you will not be expected to display enhanced academic skills or an advanced knowledge or appreciation of the law. Also, you will not be expected to conduct extensive research.

- Ensure that you display an awareness of the basics.
- Try to give the impression that you have understood what you have learnt in lectures and seminars.
- Be sure to employ basic writing and legal skills.
- Ensure that you make good use of legal sources such as cases, statutory provisions and secondary sources.
- Be prepared to conduct some research beyond the main textbook – other texts, articles and primary sources.
- Avoid esoteric or advanced arguments and articles unless you fully understand them and can comment on them in a constructive manner. It is better to answer the question soundly, rather than risking failure by including material and arguments that you do not understand.

You will be expected to display greater skills at levels two and three of your studies (**see Chapter 8**), but for the time being you are learning the fundamentals so concentrate on the simple things, especially in your first assessments of the year.

- generally accurate and well-informed;
- reasonably comprehensive;
- well organised and structured;
- provide evidence of general reading;
- demonstrating a sound grasp of basic principles;
- demonstrating a good understanding of the relevant details;
- succinctly and cogently presented;
- displaying some evidence of insight.

The answer must deal competently with the question; in problem questions all the major issues and most of the minor issues must have been spotted; the application of the legal rules must be accurate and comprehensive; the application of the legal rules must be insightful.

You will notice that the guidance stresses comprehensiveness, accuracy and clarity, but in addition requires in-depth research, a very sound appreciation of the law and evidence of insight and originality. To gain enhanced marks you will need to practise the skills identified in this and the next chapter; you will also need to show that you truly understand the issues that are raised in the question and evince an ability to assimilate and utilise the various primary and secondary sources necessary to address those issues.

Critical reasoning

Legal reasoning and critical thinking are explored in detail in Chapter 3. For present purposes one of the essential keys to first-class and upper-second marks is critical reasoning – the ability to read a source or piece of information, under-stand its logic, and then apply and/or criticise that principle in your work.

You can identify these skills by reading varied and appropriate secondary sources, written by authors who are expert in their field, have read and digested the available sources and arguments, and who have the ability to understand those sources and arguments, to place them in the context of their work, and, most importantly, to add to those arguments by bringing new data and perspectives to the discussion.

Students are not expected to provide the same level of knowledge and insight, but to be awarded top marks they are expected to appreciate those arguments and any relevant theories and to make relevant observations in their work; suggest at least some modest criticisms and proposals for reform.

The main difference between sound answers and very good and excellent ones is very often reflected in this extra research and a willingness and ability to think about the issues and engage in critical reasoning and analysis. This will involve getting to grips with sometimes complex rules and concepts and proving not only that you have understood what an author is saying, but that you can appreciate that view in the wider context of the subject area or legal theory.

TIPS FOR GETTING HIGHER GRADES

- Go beyond the basic required reading and seek out other sources – specialist texts and journal articles.

- Before you write your essay, clearly identify the main issues and theories raised by the question.

- Stress these issues and theories when you are making your points so as to display to the marker that you appreciate them and the context in which you are raising them.

- Show that you understand and appreciate the various arguments even though you might favour a particular approach or viewpoint.

- If there is no 'correct' or definitive answer to the question, show that you understand all the arguments.

- Show that you have read and appreciated the relevant sources before arriving at your conclusion.

- Importantly, your arguments and conclusions must be logical, displaying skills such as **deductive and inductive reasoning** (see Chapter 3).

- When using case law or other primary sources to illustrate your answer, select the most appropriate extracts from the judgment or statute, ones that highlight the dilemmas posed by the question

In short, the first-class or upper-second answer displays confidence with the subject matter, the various theories and the wide primary and secondary sources.

It is also expertly and professionally constructed, raising and stressing the essential issues in a succinct yet critical manner. Such answers are the product of hard work, in-depth research and reflection and natural academic ability. Keep reading quality texts and commentaries and note how those authors tackle and explain the law.

SUMMARY OF WRITING AND PRESENTATIONAL SKILLS

At the end of Chapters 1 and 2 you should have learnt or enhanced a wide range of basic academic and writing skills to assist you with your general law study, but most specifically with the writing of your law assessments.

- Engage with the course and the relevant module and get the most out of the lecturer and the teaching sessions.
- Research your assessments as early as possible and get to know the legal area thoroughly.
- There is no substitute for knowing your law, although your work will be enhanced by good writing skills.
- Start learning how to cite and reference legal sources.
- Ensure that you have understood the question and that you know what the lecturer is after.
- At the very least, show that you have understood the basics.
- Avoid any possible claim of plagiarism.
- Avoid complicated legal jargon and esoteric and too advanced sources.
- Check your work thoroughly before you submit it.
- Take note of any comments made on your work and address any shortcomings before submitting further work.
- Begin to understand the importance of legal reasoning and critical thinking and writing.

2

Writing good
essays and
answering
problem questions

Part 2 of the text looks at the particular skills required of the student in answering essay and problem-type questions in law.

Chapter 3 builds on the skills outlined in Chapter 2 on addressing and answering the set question, and concentrates on critical reasoning and and to ensure the best possible marks in essay questions.

Chapter 4 then takes the student through some bad, then good essays, contract and constitutional law. This will allow the student to observe poor practice and learn from those errors, before observing good practice and enhanced essay writing.

Specifically, Chapter 5:

- Provides simple advice on how to plan answers to problem questions.
- Enables students to identify central issues raised in such questions.
- Provides advice on how to apply the relevant law to the facts of any given scenario.
- Advises students on how to avoid bad practice when tackling such questions, such as ignoring the scenario and writing general essay answers, failing to give advice to the parties (or allowing for a number of possible answers and solutions).

NOTE

Chapter 5 contains two examples of problem-type questions and a poor and sound answer to each question. It also contains an appraisal of each answer, highlighting the strengths and weaknesses of each and providing hints as to how they could have been improved, and what marks each answer might receive.

2

Writing good essays and answering problem questions

Part 2 of the text looks at the particular skills required of t...
answering essay and problem-type questions in law. ...udent in

Chapter 3 builds on the skills outlined in Chapter 2 on addre...
answering the set question, and concentrates on critical reasoning and and
to ensure the best possible marks in essay questions.

Chapter 4 then takes the student through some bad, then good essays,
contract and constitutional law. This will allow the student to observe poo...
practice and learn from those errors, before observing good practice and
enhanced essay writing.

Specifically, Chapter 5:

- Provides simple advice on how to plan answers to problem questions.

- Enables students to identify central issues raised in such questions.

- Provides advice on how to apply the relevant law to the facts of any given
  scenario.

- Advises students on how to avoid bad practice when tackling such questions, such as ignoring the scenario and writing general essay answers,
  failing to give advice to the parties (or allowing for a number of possible
  answers and solutions).

NOTE

Chapter 5 contains two examples of problem-type questions and a
poor and sound answer to each question. It also contains an appraisal
of each answer, highlighting the strengths and weaknesses of each
and providing hints as to how they could have been improved, and
what marks each answer might receive.

3

Legal reasoning and critical thinking in assessments

The purpose of this chapter is to introduce the student to the essential skills of legal reasoning and critical thinking. The chapter is not intended to provide an exhaustive account of the rules and theories of logic, legal reasoning and critical thinking and writing; there are other texts (some referred to in the reading list at the end of the text) which can provide you with that.

The chapter will provide you with the basic rules relating to these skills and, more importantly, examples of how to employ those skills in your law studies and assessments.

NOTE

Two essential keys to first-class and upper-second marks in your assessments are the use of **legal reasoning** and the adoption of **critical thinking**.

LEGAL REASONING

This involves the ability to read a legal source or other piece of information, to understand its logic and relevance, and then to apply that source or information in your answer. Importantly, your arguments and conclusions must be logical, displaying skills such as deductive and inductive reasoning.

- **Deductive reasoning** involves a situation where it is only logical to argue X instead of Y, because the conclusion must be based on uncontested facts. For example, if an Act of Parliament stated that only people over the age of 18 at the time of dismissal can apply for unfair dismissal, and John is only 17 at that time then the conclusion must be (by deduction) that John is not entitled to claim unfair dismissal. Thus, all you require for a logical and correct conclusion is knowledge of the rule and the uncontested facts. Note that only very rarely will this answer the question for you, because the question will not simply test knowledge of the rule.

- **Inductive reasoning,** however, requires further evidence and further analysis of that evidence in order for you to draw a conclusion. As opposed to deductive reasoning, therefore, the conclusion is open-ended and admits of more than one answer, depending on your enquiries and your assessment of that evidence. For example, if the basic legal rule is that consultation with affected parties before passing legislation is required where a lack of consultation would cause undue unfairness to those affected, although you need to be aware of that rule (as with deductive reasoning), further enquiry and reasoning is necessary before you can conclude logically. You need to look at various facts, such as the context and nature of the legislation, who it affects, what unfairness would be caused by a lack of consultation etc. Only after understanding the general rule, and asking the relevant questions, can you then make a logical conclusion.

NOTE

Even then it might not necessarily and inevitably be 'correct' as the question is open-ended; however, if you misunderstand the rule, or do not consider all the relevant evidence (including supporting cases), and fail to appreciate their meaning and sense, then your conclusion will lack authority and logic. You may come across this principle when studying judicial review in constitutional law: that the courts will interfere when the decision-maker gets the law wrong or where their decision is illogical (irrational).

Logic is essential in law as it is in any other discipline. A question can be answered by adopting simple logic and if logic is not employed then the answer will be wrong:

All humans are mortal (they will, eventually, die).

1   Jack, a man, is a human being, therefore he will die.

2   Judy is a human being, therefore, like Jack, she is a man.

The main statement is inescapable fact. The first statement is correct because it is a logical consequence of the main statement of fact – Jack *is* human and he will die because all humans die. However the second statement is wrong because it is based on flawed logic – the fact that Judy is a human being, and that she will die, does not make her a man. The logic is flawed because we have misinterpreted the first statement to mean that to die you have to be a man (i.e. that 'humans' in the main statement means man, or that all humans are men – both conclusions are wrong and illogical).

Equally, it is easy to adopt flawed logic in legal arguments. Imagine that you are asked the question: '*Is there a right to die in UK law?*'

Naturally you examine the relevant statue and case law and you find s.1 of the Suicide Act 1961, which decriminalises suicide, and s.2 which makes it unlawful to assist another's suicide. You conclude that there is a right to die because of s.1, and that s.2 is overridden by the general right to die contained in s.1.

Your answer is wrong! Firstly, it is based on the flawed logic that as it is no longer an offence to commit, or attempt, suicide then one automatically has a legal right to die (and get someone's assistance). Immunity from legal action is not necessarily the same as having a legal right to do something and you are wrong in suggesting that it is the same thing. Secondly, even if s.1 was to be interpreted as containing a right to die, by concluding that s.2 is overruled by (your interpretation) of s.1 you are ignoring the reality that Parliament has created two sections, and that s.2 clearly makes it an offence to assist in another's suicide. The second mistake, therefore, shows a lack of awareness of the basic principles of statutory interpretation and of the court's powers to challenge legislation – a legal skill required of you as a lawyer and a law student.

- Logic and legal reasoning are essential to all lawyers and law students – anyone can read a legal source and copy it out. Consider the question: '*In what circumstances does a person require planning permission?*' Most people could access the relevant statutory rules and provide that basic information. But it would require a lawyer, employing legal knowledge and skills, to give advice on the interpretation of those rules, whether they apply in particular circumstances, whether those circumstances are similar or different to previous cases, and whether those rules are affected by established legal principles and rules of interpretation. Being a lawyer provides you with those skills and as a law student you will be expected to employ those skills in coming to your answers.

- This skill is particularly important in law because very often the answer to a legal question is not clear and there may not be a clearly *right* answer. This is very frustrating for students, who want to be assured that they are getting it right. But although there might not be a definitely right answer, there is certainly a *right way* of going about providing an answer to the question, and certainly a *wrong* answer – because you have either ignored or misinterpreted the law or applied flawed legal logic.

An example of the need to use legal reasoning is where the student has to decide whether an individual has entered into a contract. The student is provided with the facts of the scenario and the basic legal principles of offer and acceptance, but that is not enough to provide clear advice. The student needs to examine whether those rules and any relevant cases apply to the scenario and that will involve legal reasoning:

- What is the purpose of that rule?
- What was the ratio of that case?
- Are the facts different in our scenario and are those differences relevant?

For example, you are given a problem question which says that X has placed an advert in the newspaper saying that anyone who comes to their shop and buys their goods, and then finds those goods cheaper, can have their money back and £50 from their next purchase. You are asked to advise the shopkeeper as to whether that advert is binding. Naturally you refer to previous case law on adverts – most of which state that adverts are not to be construed as contractual offers, but others (most notably *Carlill*) that an advert can be an offer, and was in that case.

You have to decide which category your scenario comes into and come to a legally correct and logical answer. Assuming you consider and understand all the relevant cases, your conclusion will still be wrong if it lacks logic:

- That this advert cannot be binding as no money was deposited in the shopkeeper's bank as it was in *Carlill* (that was not the basis of *Carlill*, simply further evidence of intent).
- That this case is different from *Carlill* because in that case there was a medical issue (that factual difference is irrelevant to the question of intent and the legal status of the advert).

in coming to a decision on a judicial review case. Of course the answer may have already been provided by previous case law (by a judge employing legal reasoning) and the assessment is merely testing your knowledge of that case, but an awareness of the rules of legal reasoning is essential in your law studies and in your assessments.

- **Does the Act apply to UK citizens?** Logically, and in principle, no. The use of the phrase 'their home country' suggests that the individual will not be a UK citizen. Although it is possible to have dual citizenship, provisions relating to deportation have traditionally not been used against UK citizens and it would be presumed by the courts that this section did not introduce such a radical change to such policy. There would also be constitutional and human rights arguments against interpreting the section in that way.

- **Must the Home Secretary provide reasons and a fair hearing?** On the face of it either answer could be correct. The section does not say either way. But to conclude that as the section does not give a right to reasons or a hearing it is then not possible for the court to allow one is fundamentally wrong. Courts *do* imply such rights and indeed presume that such hearings will be given. An ignorance of these rules and of the court's powers and practice will make your answer wrong.

- **Must the individual have committed a specific criminal offence?** The phrase 'where their presence is not conducive to public safety' does not suggest that a specific offence has to be committed; the question appears to be whether they are, in some way, a danger to public safety. Thus, a person could be such a danger without having committed a specific offence, and again you, or a judge, would look at similar provisions in other legislation to see whether a specific offence needs to have been committed. However, having concluded that a specific offence need not be committed, it would be wrong to reason that the absence of such an offence was irrelevant – it might well be relevant as it might provide stronger evidence of a threat to public safety. Equally, it would be wrong to conclude that committing a specific offence will always constitute stronger evidence, as the offence may not have had anything to do with public safety.

Before we move on to critical thinking, which of course is related to logic and logical legal thinking, the golden rule is **always be prepared and able to support the logic of your legal argument or assertion in the face of questioning and alternative theories**. Let us imagine this scenario in a seminar.

Lecturer: So who thinks prisoners should have the right to vote?

Student: Not me, they are prisoners and have no rights, they have given them up.

Lecturer: So you agree that they can be tortured, denied family visiting rights?

Student: No, that is not what I said (he did actually), I mean that the right to vote is lost when they are in prison.

Lecturer: But why? Why can they have family visiting rights, but not be able to vote?

Student: Because their family is free to visit, but prisoners are not free to leave prison to vote.

Lecturer: Good point, to a degree. But we could let them vote in prison.

Student: Suppose so. But, surely if they have committed a crime serious enough to be incarcerated then they have given up their democratic right to vote?

Lecturer: But not their right to family visits?

Student: Losing your democratic right to vote whilst in prison is the consequence of your breach of society's rules; it is a form of punishment for acting in an undemocratic way, it is part of the prisoner's sentence. And punishing the family for the prisoner's acts is unfair.

Lecturer: Those are good points. In fact the European Court of Human Rights accepts that that may indeed be the basis of prisoner disenfranchisement.

Student: Then I was right all along? Prisoners should not be able to vote.

Lecturer: Well, you certainly have a valid point about sentencing and punishment. But does that mean we have to use it as a reason to disenfranchise? Isn't social inclusion by allowing them to vote a better alternative? Why don't other countries have a similar ban to the UK?

Student: Because that is part of the state's discretion – the margin of appreciation given to each state. Just because some states allow prisoners to vote, does not mean that the UK have to allow its prisoners to vote.

Lecturer: Ah, good point! But neither does it mean that the UK should disallow *every* prisoner the right to vote, irrespective of the original crime and sentence. Surely that is not proportionate?

Student: But I think it is proportionate, given that the individual has committed a crime that is serious enough to justify a custodial sentence. And the right to vote is resumed on release from prison.

Lecturer: Perhaps we will have to agree to disagree on that one.

The argument can, of course, continue, with both parties providing stronger legal and moral evidence. But the thing to note is how the student moved from an inflexible and illogical approach to one where his argument was convincing and sustainable. That transition was achieved by adopting a logical approach (and by recalling some sound legal principles that he had studied on the course).

CRITICAL THINKING AND WRITING

This is related to legal reasoning and involves the student appreciating the various dilemmas and arguments arising from the interpretation and application of the law, and legal writing, and then taking a critical approach in providing their answer. This does not necessarily mean criticising or being critical of the law or of legal writers; you need to show an awareness of the various legal, moral, political, constitutional or social issues, and then be able to construct your answer around those issues. It may well be that you end up agreeing with the law, or a decision, or an academic opinion – nevertheless you can take a critical approach to law by analysing it in the light of various, accepted, ideals. The thing is not to take the law at face value and then simply state what the law is, or what the court held, or what an author's view is. If you do this you are in danger of the marker saying *'A sound, but largely descriptive answer. 55%'*.

A critical thinker, therefore, does not have a closed mind, and nothing is fixed or certain; they are always prepared to consider alternative views, even though

To answer this essay you need to be conversant with the recent case law and to appreciate the constitutional arguments surrounding the enforcement of human rights and the challenge to legislation which impacts on such rights. In particular you need to appreciate what is meant by the phrase 'democratic legitimacy' and why the courts are accused of lacking it. You might have been referred to a chapter in your legal system or constitutional text on the appropriate role of the judiciary, and a recent short article on terrorism and human rights.

You will not be able to tackle this question by referring solely to your standard text, and researching more specialist sources will expose you to more complex and stimulating ideas. This may also require you to get to grips with theories in disciplines other than law – political, socio-legal, criminological – which will require patient research and reading.

A **fair answer** to the question will examine the cases and what has been held, and then make some general observations about judges not being elected or democratically accountable and Parliament and politicians being the most suitably qualified to maintain the appropriate balance. However, there are a number of possible reasons why an answer will fail to achieve **higher marks**:

- because too much time is spent detailing the facts and decisions in the cases without drawing out the necessary principles;
- because it fails to appreciate and thus stress the relevant theories and principles;
- because it fails to appreciate and consider all possible arguments;
- because it only consults one very general source (a chapter in the set text) and thus the student has confined their arguments to opinion gathered from limited and uninspiring sources.

In short, although there is nothing wrong with the answer, there is nothing to distinguish it from the majority of answers, which are based on limited reading and a bare appreciation of the vital issues. The student is thus repeating what they have been told in the guided reading without really thinking about what the issues are and what the essay is asking for.

To achieve a higher grade, you need to display an appropriate level of individual and further research and an enhanced understanding of the issues raised by the question.

TIPS FOR ACHIEVING A HIGHER GRADE

- Go beyond the basic required reading and seek out other sources – specialist texts on the role of the judiciary in a legal and constitutional system; texts and articles on human rights law; articles on terrorism and human rights. This will provide you with an essential grasp of principles and substantive law that will allow you to address the specific issues raised in the question.

- Before you write your essay, clearly identify the main issues and theories raised by the question – separation of powers; limited role of the judiciary; parliamentary sovereignty, the rule of law and fundamental notions of justice and liberty; domestic and international human rights standards; judicial deference and emergency situations.

- Stress these issues and theories when you are making your points so as to display to the marker that you appreciate them and the context in which you are raising them.

> 'Although responsible and accountable democracy is achieved by upholding parliamentary sovereignty and respecting the limited role of unelected judges, equally adherence to international human rights law and basic tenets of the rule of law demand that there should be some judicial supervision of government policy. Thus, in this context, the courts should show appropriate deference to legislation passed by Parliament, and to relevant government policy which executes such provisions. However, as Lord Bingham stressed in *A v Secretary of State for the Home Department*, (provide appropriate reference) the courts would be failing in their democratic duty if they were to refuse to uphold the rule of law and to supervise such legislative and executive actions accordingly.'

- Show that you understand and appreciate the various arguments even though you might favour a particular approach or viewpoint. Thus, you may favour judicial deference in this type of case, but you must appreciate the need for some judicial supervision.

- If you appreciate both arguments, you may be able to identify a compromise – perhaps some form of 'democratic dialogue' between Parliament, government and the courts whereby certain decisions are left to the appropriate organs of government.

- Very often there is no 'correct' or definitive answer to the question that is being posed. Provided you understand all the arguments and have read and appreciated the relevant sources, then you can come to your own (now informed) opinion or conclusion. You will not be penalised unless your arguments are not supported by the relevant legal rules, or are unsustainable in the light of existing argument and theory.

- Remember, if your conclusion is based on misunderstanding of the law, or essential facts, it will be flawed, however eloquently it is argued and presented.

- It is important, therefore, to distinguish between a fact (legal or otherwise) and an opinion: you cannot deny a legal fact – that the courts have upheld the rights of prisoners – but you can, to a limited extent, put forward your opinion that they have taken human rights too far in doing so.

EXAMPLE

'For example, it is possible to argue legally that suspected terrorists should have their human rights compromised in times of emergency, but not that suspected terrorists, or indeed convicted terrorists, should be tortured to gain evidence. The former argument is not popular with civil libertarians but is arguable, whereas the latter argument cannot be supported in international law. Even morally, the latter argument is popularly dismissed as indefensible, so must be approached very cautiously.'

- Importantly, your arguments and conclusions must be logical, displaying skills such as **deductive and inductive reasoning**; see earlier. This will allow you to show the examiner that you understand the rules and cases, their scope, and the limits of any potential arguments.

- When using case law to illustrate your answer, select the most appropriate extracts from the judgments, ones that highlight the constitutional dilemmas faced by the courts, and how they resolved them in a particular case. You will also be required to identify analogous cases, and cases which justify drawing a distinction between those that support a particular theory or trend. This skill will be explored in Chapter 5 on providing answers to problem questions.

In short, the first-class or upper-second answer displays confidence with the subject matter, the various theories and the wide primary and secondary sources. It is also expertly and professionally constructed, raising and stressing the essential issues in a succinct yet critical manner. Such answers are the product of hard work, in-depth research and reflection and natural academic ability. Keep reading quality texts and commentaries and note how those authors tackle and explain the law.

USING CRITICAL REASONING AND ANALYSIS

We will now provide a more detailed example of how to use critical reasoning and analysis in your work, and how to increase your marks by doing so. We have chosen the area of assisted suicide – a topical and controversial area, involving medical, ethical, moral, constitutional and legal issues.

It is possible to construct **a sound answer** to the question below by understanding the legal issues that were before the Supreme Court, and clearly explaining the decision of the Court (together with any dissenting judgments). However, to receive **a very good mark** you need to understand the various issues raised by the question (other than the bare claims made by the parties) and construct your answer in a manner which tackles those issues in a critical way (having researched and understood various academic and other opinion on these issues).

Let us return to the question, 'Is there a right to die in UK law?'

EXAMPLE COURSEWORK QUESTION

'Critically analyse the Supreme Court's decision in R (Nicklinson) v Ministry of Justice (2013) with respect to the question of whether there should be a right to die.'

NOTE

The content of your analysis will differ depending on which module the work was set for Medical Law, Criminal Law, Constitutional and Human Rights Law. The case has ramifications in all those areas and the module leader will expect you to concentrate your analysis on the points that are relevant to the module; you need to be careful with your research and ensure that the secondary sources you use are relevant to the specific points that are applicable to that module. On the other hand, some of these issues will overlap, and you may be given the question in a more general module, which expects you to consider all those issues.

When tackling a question in this controversial area – the right to die – you obviously need to access the relevant law – statutes, human rights treaties, case law. This question has been the subject of many legal challenges, proposed legislation, public opinion and academic commentary (from lawyers, medics, religious groups, politicians and others).

You could provide a **sound answer** by examining the relevant domestic statute and the various legal challenges (in domestic courts and before the European Court of Human Rights, both before and after the decision in *Nicklinson*), and then summarising the formal legal situation – there is no legal right to die either under the Convention or in domestic law and the relevant statute is not incompatible with any of the individual's Convention rights. There is currently a Bill before Parliament, which proposes a modest change to the law. Assuming that you deal with all the sources clearly and tackle the main points you will provide a sound answer – around 55%.

To provide a **very good** or **excellent answer** the marker is looking for something more:

- You should examine the law in the context of ongoing debates on this question. Don't simply provide a black letter answer to the question '*Is there a right to die . . . ?*' Instead, recognise that this area is controversial in your answer – legally and morally – and that there are many opinions on whether a person *should* have the right to die. You are not changing the nature of the question, but simply recognising the context in which the question is being asked: legal questions are not asked in a vacuum and judges, politicians and doctors always answer questions in the context of all those surrounding issues.

- When explaining the legal position, you should appreciate the reasons *why* the law exists in its present state: *Why* does the statute criminalise assisted suicide? *Why* did the courts reject the right to die? *Why* didn't the courts declare the legislation incompatible with human rights? *Why* does the Bill propose only modest changes? The answers to all these questions reflect an awareness of the various moral, political and constitutional issues underlying the strict legal answer to those questions.

- You should comment critically on all of these decisions, employing an appreciation of various theories and opinions – for example, comment on whether the courts were right in showing respect to Parliament in this area.

Now, to **critically analyse** the Supreme Court's decision you need to be aware of the claims made by the parties and the Supreme Court's decisions on those claims:

- Will the Supreme Court alter the criminal (common) law to allow a defence of necessity where a person who wishes to die requests another person to end their life? (No)

- Will the Court declare the relevant law – s.2 Suicide Act 1961 – incompatible with the individual's Convention rights (Article 8 European Convention on Human Rights)? (No)

- Will the Court require the DPP to clarify their policy on prosecutions in this area, so as to provide clearer guidance to the medical profession? (No)

The above information is essential to *any* answer to the question that has been set – you cannot begin to critically analyse a decision unless you know what the court was required to decide and what its decision was in respect of those claims. A mistake as to the claims and the decision at this stage – that the Court was required to decide whether the domestic law was consistent with EU law – will be fatal.

Yet this answer has not begun to even **analyse** the decision, yet alone **critically analyse** it. To **analyse** the decision, you have to understand and explain, *why* the Supreme Court came to the decision it did. So let us re-visit the decision:

- The Court would not change the criminal law because there is no right to die at common law and in any case such a change would directly conflict with the plain words of s.2 of the Suicide Act 1961 (unanimous decision).

- The Court had the power to consider incompatibility, but would not declare the section incompatible with article 8 ECHR because the European Court of Human Rights had ruled that the section was not inconsistent with the Convention, and in any case the domestic courts would be reluctant to declare it incompatible if it reflected the current will of Parliament on a controversial area; and where Parliament was currently considering reform of the law (two judges would have declared the provision incompatible; some judges dissented on the issue of whether it had the power to issue a declaration in this case).

- The Court would not require the DPP to alter and clarify their prosecution policy as it would be inappropriate for the court to interfere with and dictate the content of that policy (unanimous).

We are beginning to get to grips with the decision, but the answer has still not begun to (critically) analyse the decision, or even to explain clearly *why* the decision was made:

- Why is there no right to die at common law?
- Why can't a court declare such a right in preference to a statutory ban on assisted suicide?
- Why did the Court consider the decisions of the European Court of Human Rights?
- Why did the majority of the Court consider it inappropriate to declare the statutory provision incompatible with Convention rights?
- Why was it inappropriate for the Court to require the DPP to change and clarify the policy?

A closer examination of the various opinions of the judges will allow you to at least partially answer those questions – and to explain why certain judges dissented. You will now have the basis for analysis, for it is now becoming clear what was the **legal reasoning** of each judge, and the majority and minority. Yet to provide a **critical analysis** you require at least two further things:

- An understanding and appreciation of the moral, ethical and constitutional issues raised by the case.
- An understanding and use of critical opinion on these matters (from texts, journal articles, current political, moral and medical opinion).

Armed with these, you can then begin to contribute to the debate that the answer expects and to provide your own critical analysis. Thus to engage in that debate you need to appreciate the following:

- That assisted suicide is a controversial topic, raising **ethical, religious and moral issues** – the courts (domestic and European) are bound to tread carefully in this area; they will be reluctant to rule definitively in the area, perhaps leaving such matters to public opinion, or to Parliament.

- That legal and other practice in this area may vary from state to state and thus the courts will allow a **margin of appreciation** (the European Court) or show **judicial deference** (domestic courts) to the domestic legislature.

- That the case raises a variety of **constitutional issues** for the domestic courts to consider: would a change in the common law clash with the legislative will and thus be inconsistent with **parliamentary sovereignty**; would a declaration of incompatibility be inconsistent with the **separation of powers and parliamentary sovereignty**; would a failure to provide a remedy be inconsistent with the **courts' role of upholding basic human rights**; must and should the domestic courts follow the decisions of the European or should they develop their own jurisprudence in this area (**supremacy of domestic over European Convention law**); would a change or clarification of the prosecution policy be inconsistent with the courts' judicial function (**judicial law-making**), or is it necessary to uphold certainty and the **rule of law** and **basic rights**?

We can see, therefore, that the Supreme Court's decision involves not only the application of complex legal issues, but is surrounded by moral, medical and constitutional issues, which help us to understand, and **critically analyse**, the decision.

A **sound answer** will take for granted that the Supreme Court's decision on these issues is correct, but **a good, critical answer** will question (not necessarily disagree with) the decision in the light of various academic opinions in this area. Reading academic journals on this topic will assist you in this respect, as those authors will raise these views and take a critical approach to the decision. However, you must use these sources to inform *your* views in *your* assessment:

> Although Professor Foster is critical of the Supreme Court's decision not to make a declaration of incompatibility – accusing the Court of undue judicial deference and of failing to carry out its constitutional role of upholding basic rights (provide reference) – it should be noted that other academic opinion is in favour of the Court's decision. Thus Professor Forrester believes that the dissenting view that a

declaration was appropriate and should have been made in this case was a clear breach of the separation of powers and paid too little attention to parliamentary sovereignty and the inevitable element of discretion that should be allowed in this delicate area (provide reference). Both arguments have validity, but it is suggested that the majority decision paid appropriate respect to Parliament and the court's constitutional role. Although the domestic courts have been given a mandate to uphold Convention rights, such a task does not disturb the basic principles relating to the separation of powers and to the constitutional role of the courts. Thus, although the domestic courts may in these cases be tempted to provide a remedy to those whose basic rights are being interfered with, it is suggested that the Supreme Court took the most appropriate approach by allowing Parliament to decide whether the existing law struck an appropriate balance between the protection of life and an individual's right to private and family life. This is particularly so where Parliament is currently considering a change to the law (reference to Parliamentary Bill); to issue a declaration of incompatibility in such a case would, it is suggested, be a usurpation of the legislative role, putting undue pressure on Parliament to change the law in line with the court's decision and thus obstructing the parliamentary process.

The above extract achieves a good, critical approach to the decision because the author understands the underlying issues and controversies as well as the legal principles, has read and understood various academic opinions, and has thought about those conflicting views before offering a personal conclusion. The marker will appreciate these efforts and award higher marks to students who can display these skills.

TIPS FOR APPROACHING CRITICAL ANALYSIS

- Always start from your knowledge of the law: do not attempt to critically analyse something that you know nothing about and have not researched and understood.

- Always get the law right; a critical analysis based on a misunderstanding or misstatement of the law will always be flawed.

- Be prepared to ask questions about the law that raise legal, moral, constitutional or ethical issues: every law essay has a legal dilemma that needs addressing.

- Appreciate the potential and limits of the law, the dilemmas facing law makers, how it is applied and interpreted, and the powers and duties of the courts in making decisions.

- Appreciate the qualities of the law – certainty, justice (as opposed to fairness), openness etc., this will allow you to judge the law and its application in a critical manner.

- Use leading academic opinion as a framework for your analysis, but ensure you have your own understanding of the issues.

- Do not use others' academic opinions if you do not understand them and do not use experts to answer the question for you.

- Do not criticise the law or academic opinion until you are certain of your ground and have a logical argument.

This exercise is then repeated with respect to Question 2 – a question on the Human Rights Act 1998, which tests knowledge and appreciation of both constitutional law and the English legal system.

This question is used primarily to illustrate the relevant techniques in how to address and answer the question that has been set by the module leader. Section A contains a poor answer to the question, although the mistakes and style will not be as abject as that employed in Question 1.

Again, you are invited to identify any shortcomings and mark them on the essay before consulting the author's criticisms and recommendations. A much improved answer is then provided in section B, together with observations and recommendations for further improvement.

It is hoped that at the end of this chapter, you will have a clear idea of how – and how not – to write an essay and what qualities are needed for a sound answer. You should then be able to employ those skills in your law assessments for the remainder of the course, although it may take some time before you perfect these skills.

NOTE

These (good) essays should not be used as up-to-date and authoritative sources for researching your own assessments; they are intended for guidance on style and structure and referencing and are not reproduced as academic sources to be used or cited in your work. You also risk a charge of plagiarism if you use them in your work.

QUESTION 1: CONTRACT LAW ESSAY

EXAMPLE QUESTION

By the use of case law explain the distinction between an offer and an invitation to treat. Why is the distinction so important?

This question could appear on a variety of undergraduate and sub-degree courses, although some undergraduate institutions might not offer such a basic question.

The area should be familiar to most law students, and the question is a relatively straightforward one, although it does require the student to grasp the rationale of the legal area as well as the substantive rules.

The word limit given for the question is 2,000 words, but such questions may give a lesser word limit depending on the level of the course and the particular institution.

The student is on the first year of his LLB degree and is submitting this work as part of a module entitled '100 LAW – Law of Obligations (Contract)'. The module leader is Maureen Williams.

The following guidance is given to all students.

Students are expected to display the legal and other study skills outlined in their student handbook. In relation to the particular question, the student must:

- Show an appreciation of the distinction made in the law of contract between offers and invitations to treat.
- Use case examples to illustrate how the courts make that distinction.
- Explain and appreciate the factors that are considered by the courts in distinguishing between offers and invitations to treat.
- Explain why the distinction is important in relation to that legal area.

A: A poor essay

This essay highlights bad practice in writing legal essays. We then suggest how that practice might be improved so as to reflect the standard of skills and knowledge one is expected to display at undergraduate level.

Imagine that you are the module leader who set this question.

- What is wrong with the following essay? To what extent has the author addressed the question?
- Point out any irrelevant information and indicate where he has failed to clearly explain cases or concepts.

Another illustrative case was that of Harvella Investments v Royal Trust of Canada 1985 2 all ER 966. In this case the vendors of a plot of land sought a single offer for the whole plot from each of the two interested parties, promising to accept the highest offer provided it made other conditions stipulated. Both parties submitted bids complying with the conditions, but while one merely stated a price it was prepared to pay, the other stated both a concrete sum and a referential bid. The court held that the referential bid broke an implied condition of the offer and thus there was no contract. So we can see from this case that sometimes a request for a tender can be held to be an offer: see also the case of Spencer v Harding [1870] LR5CP561 which tells us that averts for tenders are not offers.

So where does that leave us with the question of whether there is a differnce between an offer and an invitiation to treat? It is quite clear that there is a diffenrce, and that the courts have adopted a variety of conceptual tools in order to assist them in their enquiry. However space precludes a full expalanation.

Why then is the distinction important? An offer is an expression of willingness to be bound by contractual relations if the offeree (the one who the offer is made towards) is willing to accept the essential conditions laid down in the offer (made by the offerror who makes the offer). An invitation to treat (made by an invitor to the invited) however is not an offer and can never form the basis of contractual relations because it is only an invitation to treat. It is merley inviting people to enter into a contract and cannot be an offer, the cases above clearly show this. Thus it is very important to make the distinction and that is why the courts want to make the distinction.

Obviously on many occcasions offers and invitations to treat are easy to distinguish, like in the case of Carill which was obviously an offer because the woman smoked the smoke ball. On the other hand, the distinction is a very fine one and whilst some commentators prefer to speak in terms of rules, the courts tend to look at the individual facts of each case. In conclusion therefore it is probably safer to proceed on the basis of the single principle that an offer must be sufficiently specific and comprehensive to be capable of immediate acceptance and also as well made with an intention to be bound by the mere fact of acceptance.

If all things were offers then there would be absolute chaos, so the courts have to make a distinction. This is shown in the case of Crainger v Gough (see the page before) where the court held that it was only an invitation to treat and never an offer, otherwise the wineseller would have run out of wine. And in Gibson the council would have run out of houses. So adverts can never be invitations, but in Carlill it was different because they hade made an offer.

Again in conclusion a hidden element of discretion permits the courts to label the facts with the terminology of offer and acceptance, whenever they believe it is fair and reasonable to impose contractual liability. Consider for example the purchase of goods in a self service store. At what point is an agreement completed. Does the customer accept the offer when he or she places the goods in the wire basket? Or does acceptance take place when the customer presents the goods in the wire basket, or when they present the goods to the assistant, or when the assistant accepts the offer by ringing up the price? Or is that merly the offer? Each interpretation is plausible and thus we can see the distinction clearly.

In this essat I have told you how the courts make the distinction between offers and invitations to treat and why they want to make the distinction. In conclusion then an offer is an offer which can be accepted, like in Mrs Carlills' case, wheras an invitation to treat does exactly that – it invites and it is not an offer. The difference is negligible and easy to make in every case apart from some difficult cases like in Gibson. An offer cannot be revoked after it has been accepted, see the very important case of Dikensian v Dodo (1840). An invitation can be revoked because it is not an offer, but merly an invitation. There would be commercial chaos if it was not so. An offer can crystallise in to a contract without further ado, but an invitation can't because it isn't an offer, although sometimes adverts can be offers as illustrated in Carlill.

To conclude therfore there is a clear difference, and indeed distinction between an offer and an invitation to treat and the courts have shown this to be true on a number of occassions. A contract needs an offer, an acceptance, consideration and an intention to create

→

5 What needs to be done now **(clumsy – 'we can now consider')** is to look at some of the cases where the court **(courts)** have made the distinction between an offer and an invitation to treet. **(should be 'treat')** We will then be able to see how they make the distinction and how important it is to make a distinction between an invitation and an offer. **(repetitive – 'to make such a distinction')** As I have said before **(clumsy – 'as mentioned earlier/above')** it is difficult to make a distinction and the courts find it very difficult as well, even though they do this sort of thing for a living. **(an immature and inappropriate remark. Some students believe they are being witty, but such comments are likely to irritate the marker – rather like saying, 'All judges are old and out of touch with real life')**

6 Let us look at **(clumsy – 'Now let us examine')** the case of Fisher and **('v' not 'and')** Bell (1961). **(full reference needed)** Here a flicknife **('flick knife')** was displayed in a window and the shopkeeper was done **('prosecuted'/'charged')** under the Flicknife Act **(wrong legislation – he has made it up)** for trying to sell a flicknife without a licence. **(not correct – he was charged with offering for sale)** In court **(clumsy – if you are going to mention the court, state which court it was and which judge passed judgment)** he was founf **(typo)** not guilty because he hadn't offered **(what is an offer?)** the flicknife but merley **(incorrect spelling)** invited **(what is an invitation?)** a man (or woman) **(awkward – 'customers')** to buy it. Similarly in Pharmaceutical Society of Great Britain v Boots Cash Chemists Ltd (1952 QB 765) **([1952] QB 765)** goods were dispayed **(typo)** on a supermarket shelf and the customer picked them upand **('up and')** took them to the cash desk. The Boots company **(the company)** were charged with selling drugs under the drugs law **(name the act and offence)** but again they were not convicted because they had never offered them for sale, only invited them to be sold. **(that merely tells us what was decided; it does not tell us why it wasn't an offer and why it was an invitation)**

7 So in cases of adverts **(non sequitur – he has been talking about shops)** there can never be an offer, only an invitation to treat. **(this is wrong, as we will soon find out)** However the case of Carlill (1983] 1kb at page 256 (*Carlill v Carbolic Smoke Ball Co*

[1893] 1 KB 256) is different. **(he has contradicted himself because he said adverts can never be (as opposed to are usually not construed as) offers)** (See also the very important case of Bowerman versus (v) ABTA [1995] 145 NLJR 1815.) **(he does not explain why we should see it or given any impression that he has read it)** In that case **(which, Carlill or Bowerman?)** a woman smoked a smokeball **('smokeball' – what is that?)** and still caught the flu, even though the Carbolic Smoke Ball Company said she would not. **(poor explanation of the facts)** When she sued for the £100 **(what £100?)** the company said she had never accepted the offer **(it first pleaded that it was not an offer)** because they had only invited her to smoke the ball and not offered her to smoke the ball. **(confusing – what is the difference?)** The judge **(Bowen LJ)** held that there was an offer **(why, and what is an offer?)** and she had accepted it by smoking the ball. The company had deposited money in the bank **(first mention of this)** and sothey **('so they')** hade **(typo)** made an offer to smoke balls.

8 From this case we can see **(not from his explanation of the case)** that the distinction between an offer and an invitation to treat is a very difficult one to make, **(it wasn't that difficult in that case)** but nevertheless it is an important one. **(a pointless statement – why was it, and why is it, generally, important?)** But why should the courts have to make a distinction and does it matter if they don't **(clumsy English – 'But why is it important for the courts to make this distinction?')** make a disticnction **(typo)** between an offer and an invitation to treat? In answering this we may wish to look at the case of Gibson V **(v)** Manchester Council(1979) 1aLLer. **([1979] 1 All ER, page number)** In this case it was held that the Council had not made an offer, but only an invitation to treat therefore the council were **(was)** not bound. **(confusing and incomplete account of the facts and decision – what had the Council done or said?)** Another illustrative **(his account of Gibson was not illustrative)** case was that of Harvella Investments v Royal Trust of Canada 1985 2 all ER 966. **([1985] 2 All ER 966)** In this case the vendors of a plot of land sought a single offer for the whole plot from each of the two interested parties, promising to accept the highest offer provided it made other conditions stipulated. Both parties submitted bids complying

→

with the conditions, but while one merely stated a price it was prepared to pay, the other stated both a conctrete **(typo)** sum and a referential bid. The court held that the referential bid broke an implied condition of the offer and thus there was no contract. So we can see from this case that sometimes a request for a tender **(what is a request for a tender? In any case the account of the case does not address this issue. The student has explained another aspect of the case which is not relevant to our present discussion)** can be held to be an offer: see also the case of Spencer v Harding [1870] LR5CP561 **(LR 5 CP 561)** which tells us that averts **(adverts)** for tenders are not offers. **(the student should have looked at this case first as a simple illustration of invitations for tender)**

9 So where does that leave us with the question of whether there is a differnce **(typo)** between an offer and an invitiation **(typo)** to treat? It is quite clear that there is a diffenrce, **(typo)** and that the courts have adopted a variety of conceptual tools in order to assist them in their enquiry. **(that same plagiarism from Collins again)** However space precludes a full expalanation. **(incorrect spelling, and space does not preclude a full explanation. He has seen the phrase used in academic journals when an author is writing on a specific issue, but has not the time to cover some aspect of the basic law. He falls short of the word limit by 700 words so he had plenty of space to explain it)**

10 Why then is the distinction important? An offer is an expression of willingness to be bound by contractual relations if the offeree **(the one who the offer is made towards) (clumsy – 'to whom the offer is addressed')** is willing to accept the essential conditions laid down in the offer **(made by the offerror who makes the offer). (he asks the second question in the essay and then gives us the answer to the first question. He has in fact given us a decent definition of an offer here, but this is more than halfway through the essay – this should have appeared in the first paragraph)** An invitation to treat (made by an invitor to the invited) **(inappropriate words)** however is not an offer and can never form the basis of contractual relations because it is only an invitation to treat. **(why can't it? – he must define an invitation and explain what it is, not just say it is not an offer)** It is merley

(incorrect spelling) inviting people to enter into a contract **(that is quite a decent point, but it needs expanding)** and cannot be an offer, the cases above clearly show this. **(the cases might, but his account of them does not)** Thus it is very important to make the distinction and that is why the courts want to make the distinction. **(again, this does not explain how and why the courts make the distinction)**

11 Obviously on many occassions **(incorrect spelling)** offers and invitations to treat are easy to distinguish, **(clumsy – 'it is relatively simple to make the distinction')** like in **('as in')** the case of **(delete the words 'the case of')** Carill **(Carlill)** which was obviously an offer because the woman smoked the smoke ball. **(a confusing explanation of the ratio of that case – does this mean to say that there can only be an offer when someone smokes a smoke ball? Anyway, the use of the ball was the acceptance)** On the other hand, the distinction is **('can be'?)** a very fine one **(he has contradicted his first sentence – is it easy or is the distinction fine?)** and whilst some commentators **(which? – cite particular authors)** prefer to speak in terms of rules, the courts tend to look at the individual facts of each case. **(quite a good point, but plagiarised – it needs crediting and explaining)** In conclusion therefore it is probably safer to proceed on the basis of the single principle that an offer must be sufficiently specific and comprehensive to be capable of immediate acceptance and also as well **(repetitive – delete 'as well')** made with an intention to be bound by the mere fact of acceptance. **(another good point, but plagiarised and not expanded)**

12 If all things were offers then there would be absolute chaos, **(inappropriate expression – 'there would be a good deal of disruption in the commercial world')** so the courts have to make a distinction. **(an obvious point that adds nothing)** This is shown in the case of Crainger **(Grainger)** v Gough (see the page before) **('see above', or if using footnotes, 'supra note x'. In fact, when we do 'see the page before', it tells us nothing about the case so he never explains the significance of that case)** where the court **(which court?)** held that it **(what is 'it'?)** was only an invitation to treat and never **(not)** an offer, otherwise the wineseller would have run out of wine. **(what wine seller, and what wine?)** And in

→

Gibson the council would have run out of houses. **(what houses?)** So **(consequently)** adverts **(non sequitur)** can never be invitations, **(in fact they are normally invitations so of course they can be)** but in Carlill it was different **(contradiction because he used the word 'never')** because they hade **(typo)** made an offer. **(he is confused – he should have said adverts are normally invitations but in *Carlill* it was an offer, then explained why the advert in that case was an offer)**

13 Again in conclusion **(another conclusion?)** a hidden element of discretion permits the courts to label the facts with the terminology of offer and acceptance, whenever they believe it is fair and reasonable to impose contractual liability. **(clear plagiarism and a failure to explain what this sentence means)** Consider for example the purchase of goods in a self service **(should be hyphenated)** store. At what point is an agreement completed. **(?)** Does the customer accept the offer when he or she places the goods in the wire basket? Or does acceptance take place when the customer presents the goods in the wire basket, or when they present the goods to the assistant, or when the assistant accepts the offer by ringing up the price? Or is that merly **(spelling)** the offer? Each interpretation is plausible and thus we can see the distinction clearly. **(because each interpretation is plausible does not mean that we can see the distinction clearly, particularly if he has not explained it to us. What he has done is pose a number of (relevant) questions, but then failed to provide the answers)**

14 In this essat **(typo)** I have told you how **(clumsy – 'I have attempted to explain how')** the courts make the distinction between offers and invitations to treat and why they want to **(they need to/it is necessary to do so – in fact he has not explained this)** make the **(such a)** distinction. In conclusion **(yet another conclusion)** then an offer is an offer **(that does not tell us what it is)** which can be accepted **(that tells us the consequence of it being an offer, but does not tell us what it is)**, like **(as)** in Mrs Carlills' case **(Carlill)**, wheras **(incorrect spelling)** an invitation to treat does exactly that – it invites **(invites what? – explain)** and it is not an offer. **(but why? – explain)** The difference is negligible and easy to make in every case apart from

(contradiction because he has used the word every) some difficult cases like in (such as) Gibson. (he does not explain why *Gibson* was a case where the distinction was difficult) An offer cannot be revoked after it has been accepted, (this is a consequence of a proposition being an offer and in any case revocation is irrelevant to the question) (see the very important case of Dikensian v Dodo (1840). (*Dickinson v Dodds*, with full reference) An invitation can be revoked (one does not revoke invitations; offers can be revoked) because it is not an offer, (why?) but merly (incorrect spelling) an invitation. (why?) There would be commercial chaos if it was not so. (explain what this means) An offer can crystallise in to (into) a contract without further ado, (casual phrase) but an invitation can't because it isn't an offer, (what is it then?) although sometimes adverts (non sequitur) can be offers as illustrated in Carlill. (because . . . ?)

15 To conclude (another conclusion!) therfore (incorrect spelling) there is a clear difference, and indeed distinction (there is no difference between difference and distinction) between an offer and an invitation to treat and the courts have shown this to be true (clumsy – 'have been called upon to make that distinction') on a number of occassions. (spelling – and the courts might have, but he hasn't told us how, or why, they did it) A contract needs an offer, an acceptance, consideration and an intention to create legal relations. (this is not relevant to the question and is merely taking up a few more words) Invitations don't need any of these as they are not offers. (he is confused as to the context of making the distinction between offers and invitations) Terms can be implied into offers, (irrelevant) but not invitations and Carlill displays this perfectly. (that case does not illustrate anything of the sort)

Autobibliography (Bibliography)

Lecture notes from Maxine Williamson (never quote lecture notes during the essay or in your bibliography; also the lecturer's name is wrong)

The Law of Contract by Hugh Collins (wrong citation – author's full name, title of the text, publisher, year, edition; also, he should never

→

have used this text when he has not yet grasped the basics of the subject)

Textbook on Contract by Terry Downs (ditto regarding citation, the book is now written by Jill Poole)

The Transformation Thesis and the Ascription of Contractual Responsibility by Collins (wrong citation – author, title of article, year, volume and title of the article (*Law Quarterly Review*, LQR) and page number)

Hanson's Law of Contract, BY Hanson (it is Anson, not Hanson – in fact it is now written by Jack Beatson. There is also no proper citation)

Various articles in the New Law Journal, the Oxford and Cambridge Law Journal and International and Comparative Law Quarterly. (all articles must be specifically and separately cited – he is trying to give the impression that he has read so many that it would be futile to cite them all; in addition, some of these journals are not relevant to the legal area and the 'Oxford and Cambridge Law Journal' does not exist – does he mean the *Oxford Journal of Legal Studies* and the *Cambridge Law Journal*?)

Summary of errors

- The student does not appear to have any knowledge of the subject matter, of what has been taught during the academic session or of the module itself.
- The piece lacks any of the legal skills necessary to tackle a law essay.
- The introduction is irrelevant and garbled.
- The writing style is too casual and the grammar is very poor.
- The piece is repetitive and unstructured (caused mainly by ignorance of the subject matter).
- The essay is full of typographical and spelling mistakes.
- The student is careless with his choice of words and, as a consequence, confuses the reader and contradicts himself.
- The student does not know how to cite and refer to legal authorities and shows inconsistency in style.

- The student does not know how to use cases and other legal materials to support his answer; they never explain the significance or ratio of the case and give a confused account of the facts and decision. Instead of enhancing the answer, the use of cases makes the essay worse.

- The student is guilty of plagiarism on several occasions and tries to use words and ideas that he/she simply does not understand.

- The student makes about four attempts to conclude, and the conclusion(s) contains new information.

- The bibliography is not properly cited and contains lecture notes as a source; furthermore, the author attempts to mislead the marker into believing that they have actually read a number of sources.

This is an essay written by a student who lacks strong academic skills and who has an insufficient grasp of the demands of undergraduate study in law. He clearly has not (for one reason or another) engaged with the module and the subject and has not in any sense acquired any of the necessary legal and academic skills to write law essays or survive on the course.

What is it worth?

- The piece would struggle to pass at sub-degree level, but is clearly a very bad fail at undergraduate level. Many students might feel aggrieved by this as they have at least attempted to answer the question and have included some relevant information; you are given little reward for referring to relevant concepts and cases if you do not understand them, or are incapable of explaining them.

- The student would lose substantial marks for the poor grammar and the typographical and spelling mistakes, but essentially it is muddled and unstructured – because he is completely confused on (or indifferent to) the relevant law.

- A mark of between 10% and 20% could be suggested, but certain lecturers would give even less.

What could be done to improve it?

- The student needs to go back to the textbooks and note and learn the basics of the subject.

- He needs to learn how to cite and refer to legal materials and how to compile a bibliography.
- He needs to plan the answer and to know exactly what he is going to say before he puts pen to paper.
- He needs to read the cases properly and use them to illustrate the answer.
- He needs to learn how to write in a clear and formal style – reading texts, law reports and articles and listening to how the lecturer talks will be of the greatest assistance in this respect.
- He should check his piece for typographical, spelling and grammatical errors.
- The introduction and conclusion need rewriting so that they exclude irrelevant information and relate to the relevant legal area.
- The student needs to begin engaging with the module and his law studies and to realise that he cannot write an essay without first learning the subject matter.

B: A sound essay

Below is a reworking of the poor essay. Examine this essay and consider the remarks made at the end of each paragraph and at the conclusion of the essay itself.

Answer with commentary

> *By the use of case law explain the distinction between an offer and an invitation to treat. Why is the distinction so important?*
>
> 1 To answer this question one has to appreciate the basic rules relating to the formation of a contract. A contract is a legally binding agreement[1] and in most cases results from the agreement of the parties.[2] This agreement usually takes the form of a specific offer made by one person (the offeror) to another (the offeree), which that other person accepts. An offer has been defined as an expression of willingness to be bound, made with the intention that it shall become binding as soon as it is accepted.[3] To constitute an offer, therefore, the proposition needs to be firm enough

to be capable of acceptance, and there needs to be sufficient evidence that the offeror is ready, at that stage, to accept liability should the other accept his proposition.

(In paragraph 1 the student has made a good start, first by identifying what area of law the question is concerned with, and second by giving the reader a clear and useful definition of an offer. As the question directs the student to make a distinction between an offer and an invitation to treat, his definition provides him with a reference point whenever he has to make the distinction or explain why a particular case was decided as it was. The student also makes good use of secondary sources and footnotes and writes in a clear, uncomplicated and appropriate way. He shows quite clearly that he has read and understood the texts and appreciates what the question is asking.)

2 In this area the courts attempt to draw a distinction between an offer, which is capable of creating a contract on its acceptance, and an invitation to treat, which merely invites the other person (or persons in general) to make an offer, and which in turn can be accepted or rejected by the other party. This essay will seek to illustrate how the courts make this distinction, identifying some guiding principles that they use in making the distinction. It will then explore *why* such a distinction is important, although, as we shall see, the two questions may be linked as the importance of the distinction will often be relevant to the actual outcome of a particular case.

(The second paragraph is useful for two reasons: first, it explains what the legal dilemma is all about and what effect the distinction between offers and invitations means in contractual practice; and, second, it informs us what he is going to tell us in the essay – how he is going to approach it and in particular how he is going to split and interrelate the two parts of the question.)

3 As mentioned above, an offer has two characteristics: it is capable of acceptance; and the offeror's intention is that he or she should be bound at the point of acceptance by the person to whom the offer was addressed. Thus, Poole states that an offer must be (i) sufficiently specific and comprehensive to be capable

of immediate acceptance; and (ii) made with an intention to be bound by the mere fact of acceptance.[4] If the court is not satisfied that the proposition in question has these characteristics then it will decide that there exists no offer capable of being transformed into a contract.

(There is some repetition in paragraph 3, and had he not been given 2,000 words as a limit, this paragraph might have had to be deleted. In any case, some of the material could have been merged within the second paragraph. However, he does stress the essential issues, and this paves the way for a discussion on the cases.)

4 To assist the courts in this function the law may presume that certain actions are not to be treated as formal offers. This presumption may be made on the basis that the proposition simply lacks the certainty so as to constitute an offer. Thus, in *Harvey* v *Facey*,[5] in reply to a question whether the defendant was willing to sell certain property and a request to telegram his lowest price, the defendant replied that the lowest price would be £900. It was held that the defendant had not made an offer. He had responded to the plaintiff's question, but showed no willingness to be bound should the plaintiff find the price acceptable. Presumably, he was saying that that was the price with which he would begin negotiations, should he wish to sell the property.

(In paragraph 4, the student begins by making a good and relevant point that goes a long way to explaining how the courts make the distinction in practice (which is the whole point of the question). He also makes very good use of the case – by making a relevant point to introduce the case, by giving the briefest account of facts and the decision and, finally, by concluding on its relevance and its ratio. In particular, he uses italics to stress the real rationale of the case, giving the strong impression that he understands the case and the way it was decided.)

5 Applying this principle, the courts may in similar cases conclude that the person making the initial proposal was looking for a more concrete proposition from the other party. This can be seen in the area of tenders. A company, or local authority, might wish certain work to be done, or goods delivered. It will invite people

to make offers (tenders) and then accept only the tender that it finds most attractive. In most cases this invitation for tenders is considered as just that. Thus, in *Spencer* v *Harding*[6] it was held that a circular distributed to potential customers offering the defendant's stock for sale was not in fact an offer, but merely an invitation to buyers in general to make their offers, which could then be accepted or rejected by the defendant. This was despite the defendant using the word offer in the circular. However, certain requests for tenders may be regarded as offers. In *Harvella Investments Ltd* v *Royal Trust Co of Canada (CI) Ltd*[7] the defendants had invited two persons to make a bid for a certain plot of land. They had instructed them to make a sealed bid and had intimated that the highest offer would secure the shares. It was held that the invitation to apply for the shares was an offer capable of acceptance. Here the defendants had *clearly indicated* that they were prepared to accept the highest bid and the general rule was thus displaced.

(Paragraph 5 follows on neatly from the preceding one and provides a good, clear illustration of the principle in action. He uses the area of tenders to explain the rationale of the law and how the courts approach the problems in hand, giving us just enough detail on the facts and the decision of each case. The use of *Harvella* as an exception to the rule clearly shows his understanding, and he stresses the real ratio by putting the relevant words in italics.)

6 A similar rationale is used in the case of auctions. The seller of the goods, via the auctioneer, does not, by putting the goods in an auction, offer to sell the goods to the highest bidder, and can normally withdraw the goods before the bidder's firm offer is accepted by the auctioneer.[8] The courts have thus concluded that the offer is made by the bidder, and can be accepted or rejected by the auctioneer.[8A] This type of case, and others such as those involving bus and train timetables,[9] can be explained either on the basis that the placing of goods in an auction is too vague an act to constitute a firm offer – in other words, the terms of the contract are, as yet, too vague – or that the vendor does not *at that stage* wish to commit him/herself to selling the goods at an

unknown price. This presumption, however, can be rebutted by a clear indication that the auctioneer will accept the highest bid.[10]

(In paragraph 6, the student gives the reader further illustrations of the principle, drawing on examples that he has found in textbooks and in lectures. He gives us a number of illustrations and makes good use of authority and his footnotes to give the impression that he could have provided much more detail had time allowed. Equally importantly, he tells us the rationale of this general principle and uses italics to stress that he fully understands the cases and the rules. Note that he does not have the space to devote an equal amount of time to all these examples, instead using tenders as his main example. He could as easily have chosen auctions as the main vehicle, but chose tenders – this generally will be a matter of personal choice and the student should choose an example that he or she understands and can explain simply and fully.)

7 In making the distinction the courts may presume that a person wishes to avoid the harsh or absurd consequences of his or her proposition being held to be an offer. Thus, in the following cases there is a presumption that the proposition is not an offer, but simply an invitation for offers. This is the case even though the proposition is, theoretically, capable of immediate acceptance. One example is the advertising of goods for sale in a newspaper or catalogue. Thus, in *Partridge* v *Crittenden*[11] it was held that a notice placed in a periodical that a person had bramblefinch cocks and hens for sale at 25 shillings each was not an offer so as to constitute an offence of offering for sale a wild live bird under the Protection of Birds Act 1954. Explaining the decision Lord Parker said:

> 'I think that when one is dealing with advertisements and circulars, unless they indeed come from manufacturers, there is business sense in their being construed as invitations to treat and not offers.'[12]

(In paragraph 7, the student moves the essay on by looking at how commercial sense might dictate the outcome of the law and the cases. This explains the second requirement of an offer – that the offeror wishes to be bound at that stage if the other party accepts. He makes good use of the decision in *Partridge* and uses a quotation from the case to illustrate its ratio. This quotation shows that he has read the case properly, perhaps in a law report (or at least in a good textbook or cases and materials book). The quotation is relevant and neatly explains the principle in question. (It is also properly referenced, displaying good referencing and citation skills.)

8 In this type of case, the proposition might have one of the characteristics of an offer – certainty of terms – yet not possess the other characteristic: a willingness to be bound once someone accepts the proposition. For instance, an advert in the newspaper that I wish to sell my specific car for a specific price and on specific terms might have the characteristics of a firm offer, yet still be classed as an invitation to treat because, presumably, I do not intend to be bound by every person who purports to accept that proposition. If I were to be so bound, I would be bound to *everyone* who accepted that proposition, and would, somehow, have to notify all the other interested parties of the concluded contract.

(Paragraph 8 follows neatly on from the last, pursuing the relevant argument. More importantly, the author uses a hypothetical example in illustration. This displays his understanding by proving that he is confident enough to use his own examples to explain the law and its rationale. Note that if the student has seen this specific example in a textbook, he should credit the author with the idea by citing and referencing the source. Alternatively, as in this case, if the example is the student's own, he or she can use it as such even though it has been inspired by one noticed in lectures or texts. In such a case, the student may wish to create a footnote and say something like 'Treitel gives a similar example', citing the text and the page number.)

9 Another example is the display of goods in a shop window. Here the courts have concluded that (generally) the display of goods is merely inviting offers, and is not an offer in itself. For example, in *Fisher* v *Bell*,[13] when a flick-knife was displayed in a shop window and the shopkeeper was charged with offering for sale an

offensive weapon, it was held that the defendant had not *offered* the flick-knife for sale as required by the statute. The display merely invited the potential customer to make an offer to the shopkeeper, who could then accept or reject it. Otherwise, the shopkeeper would be bound to sell the goods even though, for example, the display item had already been sold, or had been incorrectly priced. This principle was applied to self-service supermarkets in *Pharmaceutical Society of Great Britain v Boots Cash Chemists (Southern) Ltd*.[14] Here goods were displayed on a supermarket shelf, and the customer was invited to pick them up and take them to the cash desk. A registered pharmacist had been placed at the cash desk, but not at the shelf where the customers were able to help themselves to the goods. The company was charged with selling listed drugs without the supervision of such a pharmacist. It was held that the point of sale was the cash desk. The display of goods on the shelf was not an offer capable of acceptance and merely invited the customer to place the goods in their basket and make an offer at the cash desk. The court reasoned that to hold otherwise would prevent the customer from changing their mind after they had taken the step of placing goods in the basket.

(In paragraph 9, the student works through other, well-known examples in which the law presumes that certain actions are merely invitations. He makes good use of this well-established case law and is careful to explain the rationale of each case rather than merely reciting the facts and decision. Note that, had he been given a shorter word limit, he would have to provide this information in brief and in footnotes, although he has the choice of which illustrations to use and could have spent more time on circulars and adverts.)

10 In the above cases, therefore, the courts seem to be ruled by some form of commercial sense and presume, generally, that the person making the proposal did not intend to be bound at that point in time. This presumption can, of course, be rebutted. As a consequence it is wrong to conclude that adverts or circulars (or indeed shop window or supermarket displays) can *never* be offers. The famous case of *Carlill v Carbolic Smoke Ball Co*[15] illustrates this in the area of advertisements. In this case the

company placed an advert in a newspaper stating that they were prepared to pay £100 to any person who used their product (a smoke ball) and yet still contracted influenza. The company stated that it had deposited £1,000 in its bank as a mark of its sincerity. The plaintiff tried the product yet still contracted influenza and sued the company for the promised £100. In rejecting the company's claim that its advert was a mere invitation to treat, and not intended to be legally binding, the court held that the advert was clearly an offer. It was couched in clear terms, was capable of acceptance, and the company had shown its intention to be bound by depositing the money in its bank account. Thus there is no rule of law that adverts, invitations for tenders or shop (window) displays are merely invitations to treat. Provided they are certain enough, and there is a clear intention to be bound at the point of acceptance, then the courts will declare that the (advert) was indeed an offer.

(The student begins paragraph 10 by stressing the importance of commercial sense in this area and then makes it clear that this presumption is only that, and not a hard and fast rule. He has allowed himself to do this and to bring in exceptions to the general rule because he has been careful in the words that he has employed and has never presented this presumption as a rule without exception (as the bad essay writer often did). He then makes extensive use of the decision in *Carlill* to make his point. This case is always a good one to use, as almost every student knows the facts and decision and, more importantly, understands the ratio. It makes much more sense to use examples that one understands – only use more complicated ones if the nature of the question asks for it (for example, 'Explain how the traditional rules of agreement have been modified to meet complex and modern commercial relationships') or if it is necessary (because of the level at which you are studying or to ensure a higher grade) to show more than a basic understanding of the traditional cases.)

11 With regard to the question *why* such a distinction is important, it will have become clear that the finding of the court in each of the above cases was significant to the parties involved in the legal action. In cases such as *Fisher* v *Bell*, the court had to

decide whether an offer had been made for the purposes of determining criminal liability for making an offer to sell certain prohibited products. Here the defendant was found not guilty because the offence was to make an *offer*, and *inviting* persons to offer did not, therefore, attract liability.[16] In the context of contractual liability, the court's decision will be important in establishing the point, if any, at which the contract came into existence. Thus in cases such as *Harvey* v *Facey*, above, the court will have to decide whether one party had made an offer to another, or whether the parties were still at the stage of preliminary negotiations. If the court concludes that an offer exists, then the other party may accept the offer at that juncture; if not, then that other party needs to put forward a firm proposition which in turn is then capable of acceptance. The finding that the proposition is an offer means that the offer can be accepted immediately, whereas a finding that the act was merely inviting offers will at the very least delay liability until the time when the firm offer is accepted. We have also seen that the court's decision *whether* an offer has been made is also tied to the *consequences* of them holding such. In other words, the courts presume that a person does not wish to suffer the harsh consequences of his or her actions, unless they have made it clear by specific words or actions.

(In paragraph 11 the student begins to tackle the second part of the question and appears to have left himself little time to do it. However, he explains that the two questions are interrelated and that in fact by answering the first part he has been addressing the issues raised by the second part. This is an acceptable tactic provided the student gives advanced warning of this (which he does in the second paragraph of the essay) and the two parts are indeed interrelated (which in this case they are). He then proceeds to illustrate why the distinction is important by referring to case examples employed in the first part of the question, making some good observations about how the courts use the reason for the distinction as the basis of their decision.)

12 In conclusion, the courts appear to make the distinction between an offer and an invitation to treat by looking at the

essential elements of an offer and considering whether the parties' actions are consistent with such a definition. Thus, in those cases where it has been held that the proposition was not in fact an offer but only an invitation to treat, it is apparent that the proposition either lacked the certainty of an offer, or failed to display a sufficient intention to be bound at that stage of negotiations. Although the courts may presume that certain acts are invitations, their minds are not closed on this issue; adverts and invitations for tenders, for example, may be construed as offers provided there is sufficient evidence of the party's intention. The contractual or criminal consequences of the court's finding make the distinction between an offer and an invitation important, and in general the courts have devised guidelines in order to make that distinction sufficiently clear and predictable.

(The student's conclusion is neat and relevant. It recaps the main points made during the main body of the essay. It does not introduce any fresh information (as the bad essay attempts to do) and concludes with a suitably intelligent and open-ended comment with respect to the current state of the law.)

Bibliography

Adams, J and Brownsword., R. *Understanding Contract Law* (5th edition, Sweet & Maxwell, 2007)

Beatson, J. *Anson's Law of Contract* (28th edition, Oxford, 2002)

Poole, J. *Textbook on Contract* (9th edition, OUP, 2010)

Treitel, G. *The Law of Contract* 13th edition (Sweet & Maxwell, 2011)

(The bibliography is properly cited and there is evidence throughout the essay that he has actually read and understood some of the texts. However, he has not used all the texts cited in the bibliography and could have shown off his reading to better effect in this respect. The bibliography is also missing one or two good academic articles and could have referred to a more theoretical textbook such as Hugh Collins's *Law of Contract* (a book that the bad essay writer plagiarised from).)

[1] See Gunter Treitell, *The Law of Contract* (13th edition, Sweet & Maxwell, 2011), 1: an agreement giving rise to obligations which are enforced or recognised by law.

[2] Some contracts are explainable on a basis other than pure agreement. See *Clarke v Earl of Dunraven and Mount Earl; The Satania* [1897] AC 59, where a contract came into existence by implication – a person entering his ship for a race impliedly entered into a contract to be bound by the rules.

[3] Gunter Treitel, *The Law of Contract*, note 1 above, 8.

[4] Jill Poole, *A Textbook on Contract*, 9th edition, OUP (2010), 64.

[5] [1893] AC 552. See also *Gibson v Manchester City Council* [1979] 1 All ER 972. Here the council's invitation to local people to buy their council houses by completing an application form was held not to be an offer.

[6] (1870) LR 5 CP 561. See also *Grainger and Sons v Gough* [1896] AC 325: a wine merchant's catalogue with price list held to be an invitation to treat, inviting offers via customer orders.

[7] [1985] 2 All ER 966. However, it was held on the facts that the offer had been improperly accepted.

[8] See *Harris v Nickerson* (1873) LR 8 QB 286: an advertisement that an auction was to take place was not an offer to hold the auction and to sell to highest bidder.

[8A] *Payne v Cave* (1789) 3 Term Rep 148.

[9] *Wilkie v London Passenger and Transport Board* [0947] 1 ALL ER 258.

[10] See *Warlow v Harrison* (1859) 1 E and E 309, where it was held (obiter) that an auction advertised 'without reserve' imposes an obligation to sell to the highest bidder once the auction begins. See also the more recent case of *Barry v Davis (Heathcote Ball Co)* [2001] 1 WLR 1962, which upholds this principle.

[11] [1968] 2 All ER 421.

[12] *ibid*, at page 424.

[13] [1961] 1QB 394

[14] [1953] 1 QB 401.

[15] [1893] 1 QB 256.

[16] The particular legislation had to be amended so as to make it an offence to *display* offensive weapons; see now s. 1 Restriction of Offensive Weapons Act 1961.

Summary of good points: hints on how to write good essays

- It is clearly written, employing a simple yet legal style that one would find in most good textbooks.

- The introduction is direct and to the point and contains useful legal definitions of relevant legal concepts.

- The student makes it clear what the question is about and how he is going to tackle it.

- Having done that, he follows the plan and format he has set out.

- It is clear that the student has researched the area and has planned the answer to the question *before* writing out the answer.

- The student makes good use of case authority, always introducing the reader to the relevance of the case, its facts and decision (where relevant).

- The student also displays an appreciation of the cases and their rationale and application to the question.

- The piece is professionally constructed, contains good reference and citation skills and makes good use of footnotes.

- The conclusion is direct and related to the most salient points he has made in the main body of the answer.

- The bibliography displays reasonably wide research and is properly cited.

In general, it is a very competent piece of work written by a student who has paid attention to the lectures, has attended seminars, has read the books and cases and has ensured that he understood the area before attempting to provide an answer.

What is the essay worth?

Given that the essay was directed at a first-year law student and that the area of law and the title was fairly basic, we might consider that he has done as well as he possibly could in providing this answer.

Consequently, *some* markers might regard this as a first-class answer, albeit with some reservations. This might be the case particularly if the course is sub-degree.

Other teachers might regard the answer as lacking academic rigour and any theoretical analysis – it lacks one or two meaty articles and does not make use of the more theoretical texts such as Hugh Collins's *Law of Contract*; in which case a mark of between 60 and 68 might be more appropriate.

It is a very competent, although rather functional, piece, and the mark might depend on what particular contract lecturers are looking for from the student.

How could the essay have been improved?

- For a degree-level student, the piece might be regarded as a little pedestrian and functional, and some teachers might see it as lacking real academic rigour.

- The student could have employed a more theoretical approach, looking at authors such as Hugh Collins. The student could have used sources such as this to explore various views and arguments in this area, then adding his own views.

- There is some repetition in the essay, particularly in the early part.

- The essay does not refer to some of the sources quoted in the bibliography; including these in the answer itself would display greater research and analytical skills.

QUESTION 2: LEGAL SYSTEM AND CONSTITUTIONAL LAW ESSAY

> **EXAMPLE QUESTION**
>
> *The passing of the Human Rights Act 1998 has had a profound effect on both the British Constitution and the English legal system. Discuss.*

This question is likely to appear in one form or another on most undergraduate courses, either on a public (constitutional and administrative law) course, or one on legal system or legal process; although many questions in this area will concentrate on the possible reform of the Act.

The question is relatively straightforward and requires the student to possess a sound knowledge of the Act and its central provisions as well as an appreciation of the impact of the Act on both the constitutional system and certain aspects of the English legal system.

The main difficulty with the question is that it requires a lot of issues to be raised and for the student to have a very broad knowledge of the Act, its provisions and any relevant case law. The student must focus on the actual question and find room to include a lot of information in the answer without omitting relevant points. The answer requires very careful planning.

The word limit given for the question is 2,000 words (excluding the front page, all references and citations and the bibliography), but other word limits are possible, depending on the particular institution.

The student is on the first year of her LLB degree and is submitting this work as part of a module entitled Legal and Constitutional System.

The following guidance is given to all students:

Students are expected to display the legal and other study skills outlined in their student handbook. In relation to the particular question, the student must:

- Display a sound knowledge of the provisions of the 1998 Act as they affect both the British Constitution and the English legal system.

- Appreciate the potential impact of those provisions on the central features of both the British Constitution and the English legal system.

- Analyse the truth of that statement by reference to relevant case law or other evidence.

A: A poor essay

Below is a poor answer to the question. It does not suffer from the very poor grammar and style witnessed in the bad essay in Question 1; most of the defects are related to the problem of not answering the question. For this reason, there is no detailed marked-up essay to examine as with the preceding question. Read through the essay and make criticisms as you are doing so. Then you can compare your notes with the appraisal at the end.

The answer

The passing of the Human Rights Act 1998 has had a profound effect on both the British Constitution and the English legal system. Discuss.

1 The Human Rights Act 1998 was passed to incorporate the European Convention on Human Rights into domestic law. Before the Act was passed the European Convention had no role to play in domestic law and if an individual's human rights were violated the only redress was to take the case to the European Court of Human Rights in Strasbourg. Since October 2000[1] an individual may bring a claim for breach of their human rights in the domestic courts and thus they do not have to take the long journey to Strasbourg.

2 The European Convention contains a list of human rights which can be described as civil and political rights, and these rights are incorporated into domestic law by the Human Rights Act 1998.[2] These rights include the right to life (Article 2), freedom from torture (Article 3), liberty and security of the person (Article 5), the right to a fair trial (Article 6), the right to private and family life (Article 8), freedom of expression (Article 10), freedom of peaceful assembly (Article 11) and the right to marry (Article 12). We can see, therefore, that these rights are civil and political rights and that the Convention does not include any social, economic and cultural rights. This has been criticised and it has been proposed that the Human Rights Act be expanded to include such rights.[3]

3 These rights are enforced by the European Court of Human Rights who hear cases of human rights violations by member states to the Convention. Thus under Article 34 to the Convention it may hear applications from individuals claiming to be a victim of a violation of the Convention and may award just satisfaction to that person under Article 41 of the Convention. Many cases have been brought under this process against the United Kingdom and the Court has ruled in favour of individuals with respect to matters such as censorship of prisoners' correspondence (*Golder v United Kingdom*),[4] freedom of expression (*Sunday Times v United Kingdom*),[5] corporal punishment (*Tyrer v United Kingdom*)[6] and the right of peaceful assembly (*Steel v United Kingdom*).[7]

4 The rights are either conditional, in which case they can be violated if there is a legitimate reason for their interference, or absolute, in which case there can be no justification for their violation. For example, freedom of expression (under Article 10) can be compromised provided the restriction is prescribed by law, and necessary in a democratic society for the protection of things such as public safety, health or morals, or national security. Thus, in R v *Shayler*[8] it was held that a prosecution under the Official Secrets Act 1989 was not in violation of Article 10 of the Convention. On the other hand, in *Chahal v United Kingdom*,[9] the European Court held that Article 3 could not be violated whatever the circumstances and whatever risk the individual posed to society.

5 The passing of the Human Rights Act has been described as having great constitutional significance.[10] For the first time individuals will be able to seek a remedy for violation of their human rights before the domestic courts. Thus, if an individual is tortured by the police he or she will be able to bring an action before the domestic courts under the Human Rights Act and the courts can, under section 8 of the Act, provide just satisfaction for that breach. No longer will the individual have to take an action under the European Convention. Thus, in *Napier v Scottish Ministers*,[11] a prisoner brought a successful claim under Article 3 when he was subjected to 'slopping out' in prison. Also, in *Campbell* v *MGN*,[12] the House of Lords held that a model's privacy had been invaded when the newspapers printed stories about her drug habit, and thus she was awarded compensation. More significantly, in *A* v *Home* Secretary[13] the House of Lords held that the power to detain persons suspected of terrorism under the Anti-Terrorism, Crime and Security Act 2001 was incompatible with Article 5 of the Convention and thus declared the Act incompatible under section 4 of the Human Rights Act 1998.

6 As we can see from the above cases, the Act has had a substantial effect on both the legal and constitutional system of the United Kingdom. Under section 2 of the Act the courts can now take into account the case law of the European Court and Commission of Human Rights when adjudicating upon human rights disputes in domestic law. In addition, they have the power to interpret legislation in line with the European Convention (under section 3 of the Act), and the power to declare both primary and secondary legislation as incompatible with the Convention (under section 4). Thus, in R v A *(Sexual History)*[14] the House of Lords held that the Youth Justice and Criminal Evidence Act 1999 could be interpreted so as to allow a defendant to cross-examine a rape victim wherever that was necessary to ensure the right to a fair trial under section 6 of the Act. The courts have also used their new power under section 4 of the Act to declare legislation incompatible with the European Convention. For example, in *A* v *Home Secretary* (above), section 26 of the Anti-Terrorism, Crime and Security Act 2001 was declared incompatible with Article 5

→

of the European Convention, which guarantees the right to liberty and security of the person.

7 Before the Act was passed domestic courts could not take the European Convention into account. For example, in *Malone v Metropolitan Police Commissioner*[15] it was held that the plaintiff could not rely on Article 8 of the European Convention when the police had tapped his telephone because it was pointed out that the Convention had not been incorporated into domestic law and that any remedy the plaintiff had under the Convention would have to be pursued before the European Court of Human Rights. In that case *Malone* took his case to Strasbourg (*Malone v United Kingdom*)[16] and the European Court held that the telephone tapping was in violation of his right to private life and correspondence. As a consequence Parliament enacted the Interception of Communications Act 1985, which put telephone tapping on a statutory footing, and this power is now contained in the Regulation of Investigatory Powers Act 2000. In another case, *R v Ministry of Defence, ex parte Smith*,[17] the Court of Appeal held that Article 8 of the Convention could not assist armed forces personnel who had been expelled from the armed forces because of their sexual orientation. On appeal, the European Court of Human Rights held that such expulsions were contrary to Articles 8 and 14 of the Convention and that the expulsions were disproportionate.[18] Following that decision the armed forces replaced the blanket ban with a conduct-based policy so as to comply with the judgment of the European Court.

8 Under the Act the courts have got the power to interpret legislation compatibly with the European Convention, although this does not mean that they can refuse to apply clear legislation that is in breach of the Convention. In *Mendoza v Ghaidan*[19] the House of Lords held that the words 'living together as husband and wife' could be interpreted as 'as if they were living together as husband and wife'. Accordingly, same-sex partners were given equal treatment and this was re-enforced by the Civil Partnership Act 2004. On the other hand, in *Bellinger v Bellinger*[20] the House of Lords refused to interpret the words man and woman to include a person who had undergone gender reassignment. This was despite the European Court's decision in *Goodwin v*

United Kingdom[21] that discrimination against transsexuals was in violation of Articles 8 and 14 of the Convention. As a result of the decision in *Goodwin* Parliament has enacted the Gender Reassignment Act 2004, which recognises the rights of transsexuals to change their sexual identity and to marry a person of their choice.

9   The courts have also got the power under the Act (section 4) to declare primary and secondary legislation incompatible with the European Convention, although again this does not empower the courts to overrule legislation. For example, in R (*Anderson and Taylor*) v *Home Secretary*[22] the House of Lords held that the Home Secretary's power to fix the minimum terms of life sentence prisoners was incompatible with Article 6 of the European Convention, which guarantees the right to a fair trial, including the right to a fair sentence. This decision followed the decision of the European Court of Human Rights in *Stafford* v *United Kingdom*,[23] where it was held that the Home Secretary's powers were inconsistent with the rule of law and the separation of powers and thus in breach of the Convention. Interestingly, the Court of Appeal in *Anderson* refused to declare the power of the Home Secretary as incompatible until the European Court had made its decision in *Stafford*, because before that decision the European Court had held that such a power was lawful with respect to mandatory life sentence prisoners.[24]

10 The Human Rights Act 1998 may also have a horizontal effect and thus apply to disputes between private individuals. Normally the Act only applies between individual victims and public authorities (as defined in section 6 of the Act). However, because the courts are public authorities under section 6 they have the duty to safeguard and uphold Convention rights and as a consequence the Act has been applied horizontally in the law of confidentiality in cases such as *Campbell* v *MGN*[25] and *Douglas* v *Hello!*[26] However, the House of Lords has held recently that the Act cannot be used to create a separate law of privacy, and that the decision in *Hello!* was confined to the law of confidentiality. Nevertheless the courts have gained extensive powers under the Act and can now apply the principles of proportionality when adjudicating upon disputes that raise Convention rights. →

Thus, any interference with a Convention right must now be necessary in a democratic society and be proportionate to any legitimate aim being pursued (R *(Daly)* v *Home Secretary*).[27] Furthermore, this test of proportionality is stricter than the previous test of *Wednesbury*[28] unreasonableness and will require the courts to take a more active approach to defending civil liberties.

11 Since the Act came into force there have been a number of cases brought against public authorities claiming that Convention rights have been violated. For example, in R v *DPP, ex parte Pretty*[29] it was held that the European Convention was not violated when domestic law (the Suicide Act 1961) outlawed assisted suicide. The House of Lords held that the right to life guaranteed by Article 2 of the Convention did not include the right to die with dignity. This decision was upheld by the European Court of Human Rights in *Pretty* v *United Kingdom*[30] where it was confirmed that Article 2 was principally concerned with preserving life. Another example of the Act's use was in A v *Home Secretary* (above) where the House of Lords held that the indefinite detention of a foreign person suspected of acts of terrorism was in breach of Article 5 of the European Convention. The House of Lords held that although there was an emergency threatening the life of the nation within Article 15 of the Convention, the measures within the Anti-Terrorism, Crime and Security Act 2001 were both discriminatory and disproportionate and thus incompatible with the Convention. As a result the government introduced the Terrorism Bill 2005 into Parliament.

12 In conclusion, the Human Rights Act 1998 has had a profound effect on the protection of human rights and has thus impacted on both the legal and constitutional system in the United Kingdom. The courts can now take the Convention and its case law into account and thus must apply European principles to human rights cases. Further, the courts have new powers of interpretation under section 3 of the Act and under section 4 can declare legislation incompatible with the Convention. Since the implementation of the Act the courts can use the Convention in domestic law and the individual no longer has to make use of the procedure under the European Convention. This will save considerable time and expense, although it should be pointed

out that the victim can still make use of that procedure if they are unsuccessful under the Human Rights Act. These new powers, therefore, have had a profound effect on the legal system and the constitution in the United Kingdom, bringing rights home to domestic law.

Bibliography

Ewing, K. and Bradley, A. *Constitutional and Administrative Law,* 16th edn. (Longman, 2014)

Foster. S. *Human Rights and Civil Liberties,* 3rd edition (Longman, 2011)

Van Beuren, G. 'Including the excluded: the case for an economic, social and cultural Human Rights Act' [2002] PL 456.

---

[1] The Act's implementation was delayed to allow for fuller training of the judiciary and thus came into force on that date.

[2] See section 1 and Sched. 1 of the Human Rights Act 1998.

[3] Geraldine Van Beuren, 'Including the excluded: the case for an economic, social and cultural Human Rights Act' [2002] PL 456.

[4] (1975) 1 EHRR 524.

[5] (1979) 2 EHRR 245.

[6] (1978) 2 EHRR 1.

[7] (1999) 28 EHRR 603.

[8] [2002] 2 WLR 754.

[9] (1997) 23 EHRR 413.

[10] See Keith Ewing and Anthony Bradley, *Constitutional and Administrative Law,* 16th edn (Longman, 2014), at page 420.

[11] *The Times,* 13 May 2004.

[12] [2004] 2 AC 457.

[13] [2005] AC 68.

[14] [2002] 1 AC 1546.

[15] [1979] Ch 344.

[16] (1984) 7 EHRR 14.

[17] [1996] 1 All ER 257.

[18] *Smith and Grady* v *United Kingdom* (2000) 29 EHRR 493.

[19] [2004] 2 AC 557.

[20] [2003] 2 AC 467.

[21] (2002) 35 EHRR 18.

[22] [2002] 3 WLR 1800.

[23] (2002) 35 EHRR 32.

→

24 *Wynne* v *United Kingdom* (1994) 19 EHRR 333.

25 See above, note 12.

26 [2001] 2 WLR 992.

27 [2001] 2 WLR 1622.

28 *Associated Provincial Picture House Ltd* v *Wednesbury Corporation* [1948] 1KB 223.

29 [2002] 1 AC 800.

30 (2002) 35 EHRR 1.

Poor answer with commentary

The passing of the Human Rights Act 1998 has had a profound effect on both the British Constitution and the English legal system. Discuss.

1 The Human Rights Act 1998 was passed to incorporate the European Convention on Human Rights into domestic law. Before the Act was passed the European Convention had no role to play in domestic law and if an individual's human rights were violated the only redress was to take the case to the European Court of Human Rights in Strasbourg. Since October 2000[1] an individual may bring a claim for breach of their human rights in the domestic courts and thus they do not have to take the long journey to Strasbourg.

(In the introductory paragraph the student uses the word incorporate rather than the phrase 'give further effect to', which is technically correct. She makes an incorrect statement about human rights before the Act, suggesting that there were no remedies at all apart from the Convention machinery. The introduction does not refer to any of the constitutional and legal issues highlighted in the question.)

2 The European Convention contains a list of human rights which can be described as civil and political rights, and these rights are incorporated into domestic law by the Human Rights Act 1998.[2] These rights include the right to life (Article 2), freedom from torture (Article 3), liberty and security of the person (Article 5), the right to a fair trial (Article 6), the right to private and family life (Article 8), freedom of expression (Article 10), freedom of

·peaceful assembly (Article 11) and the right to marry (Article 12). We can see, therefore, that these rights are civil and political rights and that the Convention does not include any social, economic and cultural rights. This has been criticised and it has been proposed that the Human Rights Act be expanded to include such rights.[3]

(The second paragraph simply lists some of the Convention rights given effect to by the Act rather than addressing the Act's provisions. The student does not explain the difference between the two sets of rights or the consequence (if any) of that distinction on the impact of the Act.)

3 These rights are enforced by the European Court of Human Rights who hear cases of human rights violations by member states to the Convention. Thus under Article 34 to the Convention it may hear applications from individuals claiming to be a victim of a violation of the Convention and may award just satisfaction to that person under Article 41 of the Convention. Many cases have been brought under this process against the United Kingdom and the Court has ruled in favour of individuals with respect to matters such as censorship of prisoners' correspondence (*Golder* v *United Kingdom*),[4] freedom of expression (*Sunday Times* v *United Kingdom*),[5] corporal punishment (*Tyrer* v *United Kingdom*)[6] and the right of peaceful assembly (*Steel* v *United Kingdom*).[7]

(This information relates to the role of the European Court of Human Rights under the Convention, rather than to the terms and impact of the Human Rights Act 1998. The cases mentioned towards the end do not appear to be relevant in answering the question and thus can be regarded as background information at most.)

4 The rights are either conditional, in which case they can be violated if there is a legitimate reason for their interference, or absolute, in which case there can be no justification for their violation. For example, freedom of expression (under Article 10) can be compromised provided the restriction is prescribed by law, and necessary in a democratic society for the protection of things such as public safety, health or morals, or national security.

→

Thus, in R v *Shayler*[8] it was held that a prosecution under the Official Secrets Act 1989 was not in violation of Article 10 of the Convention. On the other hand, in *Chahal* v *United Kingdom*,[9] the European Court held that Article 3 could not be violated whatever the circumstances and whatever risk the individual posed to society.

(The explanation that some rights are absolute and some conditional does not appear to be relevant to the question and the issues it raises. Thus, whilst the information is true, without some explanation of the provisions of the Act itself the content of the paragraph is largely irrelevant. The fact that some rights are conditional and some absolute will impact on the domestic court's role, but the student does not identify this.)

5 The passing of the Human Rights Act has been described as having great constitutional significance.[10] For the first time individuals will be able to seek a remedy for violation of their human rights before the domestic courts. Thus, if an individual is tortured by the police he or she will be able to bring an action before the domestic courts under the Human Rights Act and the courts can, under section 8 of the Act, provide just satisfaction for that breach. No longer will the individual have to take an action under the European Convention. Thus, in *Napier* v *Scottish Ministers*,[11] a prisoner brought a successful claim under Article 3 when he was subjected to 'slopping out' in prison. Also, in *Campbell* v *MGN*,[12] the House of Lords held that a model's privacy had been invaded when the newspapers printed stories about her drug habit and she was awarded compensation. More significantly, in *A* v *Home Secretary*[13] the House of Lords held that the power to detain persons suspected of terrorism under the Anti-Terrorism, Crime and Security Act 2001 was incompatible with Article 5 of the Convention and thus declared the Act incompatible under section 4 of the Human Rights Act 1998.

(The student does not explain why the Act has been described as having great constitutional significance, or what that constitutional, rather than legal, significance might be. She repeats the error about the Act providing a remedy for the first time, ignoring the pre-Act position. She mentions section 8 but has not put

that section into any context because she has not yet explained the central provisions of the Act (including sections 6 and 7, which allow Convention rights actions against public authorities to be brought in legal proceedings). The case examples she uses would then have been useful had they been placed in that context.)

6 As we can see from the above cases, the Act has had a substantial effect on both the legal and constitutional system of the United Kingdom. Under section 2 of the Act the courts can now take into account the case law of the European Court and Commission of Human Rights when adjudicating upon human rights disputes in domestic law. In addition, they have the power to interpret legislation in line with the European Convention (under section 3 of the Act), and the power to declare both primary and secondary legislation as incompatible with the Convention (under section 4). Thus, in R v A (*Sexual History*)[14] the House of Lords held that the Youth Justice and Criminal Evidence Act 1999 could be interpreted so as to allow a defendant to cross-examine a rape victim wherever that was necessary to ensure the right to a fair trial under section 6 of the Act. The courts have also used their new power under section 4 of the Act to declare legislation incompatible with the European Convention. For example, in A v *Home Secretary* (above), section 26 of the Anti-Terrorism, Crime and Security Act 2001 was declared incompatible with Article 5 of the European Convention, which guarantees the right to liberty and security of the person.

(The paragraph opens with a claim that the previous paragraphs have addressed and illustrated the relevant legal and constitutional issues, which they have not. The student then gives information relating to some provisions of the Act that do have such an impact, but she does not explain the significance of those sections vis-à-vis issues such as precedent, the separation of powers and parliamentary sovereignty. Consequently the information via the cases adds little to the debate and does not assist in answering the question.)

7 Before the Act was passed domestic courts could not take the European Convention into account. For example, in →

Malone v *Metropolitan Police Commissioner*[15] it was held that the plaintiff could not rely on Article 8 of the European Convention when the police had tapped his telephone because it was pointed out that the Convention had not been incorporated into domestic law and that any remedy the plaintiff had under the Convention would have to be pursued before the European Court of Human Rights. In that case *Malone* took his case to Strasbourg (*Malone* v *United Kingdom*)[16] and the European Court held that the telephone tapping was in violation of his right to private life and correspondence. As a consequence Parliament enacted the Interception of Communications Act 1985, which put telephone tapping on a statutory footing, and this power is now contained in the Regulation of Investigatory Powers Act 2000. In another case, R v *Ministry of Defence, ex parte Smith,*[17] the Court of Appeal held that Article 8 of the Convention could not assist armed forces personnel who had been expelled from the armed forces because of their sexual orientation. On appeal, the European Court of Human Rights held that such expulsions were contrary to Articles 8 and 14 of the Convention and that the expulsions were disproportionate.[18] Following that decision the armed forces replaced the blanket ban with a conduct-based policy so as to comply with the judgment of the European Court.

(This paragraph contains some useful content, but again it is not put into context. The case examples could have been used early on to illustrate how the Act now allows the Convention to be used directly in domestic law, thus illustrating the change brought about by the Act to the old system. Instead, the student concentrates on the facts and the measures taken by the domestic authorities in response to the judgments, failing to mention the significance of the absence in domestic law of substantive human rights and doctrines such as proportionality.)

8 Under the Act the courts have got the power to interpret legislation compatibly with the European Convention, although this does not mean that they can refuse to apply clear legislation that is in breach of the Convention. In *Mendoza* v *Ghaidan*[19] the House of Lords held that the words 'living together as husband and wife' could be interpreted as 'as if they were living together as husband and wife'. Accordingly, same-sex partners were given

equal treatment and this was re-enforced by the Civil Partnership Act 2004. On the other hand, in *Bellinger* v *Bellinger*[20] the House of Lords refused to interpret the words man and woman to include a person who had undergone gender reassignment. This was despite the European Court's decision in *Goodwin* v *United Kingdom*[21] that discrimination against transsexuals was in violation of Articles 8 and 14 of the Convention. As a result of the decision in *Goodwin* Parliament has enacted the Gender Reassignment Act 2004, which recognises the rights of transsexuals to change their sexual identity and to marry a person of their choice.

(This is the first mention of section 3 and the courts' new interpretative powers. The section and its scope and wording are not properly examined, and there is no real mention of the legal and constitutional issues that might arise from that provision – for example, whether it gives the courts the power to legislate. Thus, the cases, which are very relevant, are simply presented as bald examples and reference is made to the background and the follow-up to the cases without exploring the legal and constitutional impact of the cases.)

9 The courts have also got the power under the Act (section 4) to declare primary and secondary legislation incompatible with the European Convention, although again this does not empower the courts to overrule legislation. For example, in *R (Anderson and Taylor)* v *Home Secretary*[22] the House of Lords held that the Home Secretary's power to fix the minimum terms of life sentence prisoners was incompatible with Article 6 of the European Convention, which guarantees the right to a fair trial, including the right to a fair sentence. This decision followed the decision of the European Court of Human Rights in *Stafford* v *United Kingdom*,[23] where it was held that the Home Secretary's powers were inconsistent with the rule of law and the separation of powers and thus in breach of the Convention. Interestingly, the Court of Appeal in *Anderson* refused to declare the power of the Home Secretary as incompatible until the European Court had made its decision in *Stafford*, because before that decision the European Court had held that such a power was lawful with respect to mandatory life sentence prisoners.[24]

(Section 4 is very relevant to the question, but the student does not highlight the relevant constitutional problems associated with it – for example, does it impact on parliamentary sovereignty? Instead, she provides a paraphrased account of the section's wording. This is followed by a rather long-winded account of the *Anderson* case, which does not really assist in addressing the relevant issue. The case is useful in illustrating parliamentary sovereignty and the status of European Court decisions, but the student doesn't really explain these points, providing instead some unnecessary detail about life sentences.)

10 The Human Rights Act 1998 may also have a horizontal effect and thus apply to disputes between private individuals. Normally the Act only applies between individual victims and public authorities (as defined in section 6 of the Act). However, because the courts are public authorities under section 6 they have the duty to safeguard and uphold Convention rights and as a consequence the Act has been applied horizontally in the law of confidentiality in cases such as *Campbell* v *MGN*[25] and *Douglas* v *Hello!*[26] However, the House of Lords has held recently that the Act cannot be used to create a separate law of privacy, and that the decision in *Hello!* was confined to the law of confidentiality. Nevertheless the courts have gained extensive powers under the Act and can now apply the principles of proportionality when adjudicating upon disputes that raise Convention rights. Thus, any interference with a Convention right must now be necessary in a democratic society and be proportionate to any legitimate aim being pursued (*R (Daly)* v *Home Secretary*).[27] Furthermore, this test of proportionality is stricter than the previous test of *Wednesbury*[28] unreasonableness and will require the courts to take a more active approach to defending civil liberties.

(The student mentions section 6 of the Act for the first time; this provision is absolutely central to the scope of the Act and the effect of the Act on the legal system! Because those issues are not properly explored, she loses the impact of mentioning some of the relevant cases under that heading. There is then a non sequitur when she moves on to the doctrine of proportionality (again mentioning it for the first time). She fails to define proportionality and explain its significance and also fails to distinguish it from the Wednesbury test. Consequently, she finishes the paragraph by making a general and unsupported statement about civil liberties protection.)

11 Since the Act came into force there have been a number of cases brought against public authorities claiming that Convention rights have been violated. For example, in R v DPP, *ex parte Pretty*[29] it was held that the European Convention was not violated when domestic law (the Suicide Act 1961) outlawed assisted suicide. The House of Lords held that the right to life guaranteed by Article 2 of the Convention did not include the right to die with dignity. This decision was upheld by the European Court of Human Rights in *Pretty v United Kingdom*[30] where it was confirmed that Article 2 was principally concerned with preserving life. Another example of the Act's use was in A v *Home Secretary* (above) where the House of Lords held that the indefinite detention of a foreign person suspected of acts of terrorism was in breach of Article 5 of the European Convention. The House of Lords held that although there was an emergency threatening the life of the nation within Article 15 of the Convention, the measures within the Anti-Terrorism, Crime and Security Act 2001 were both discriminatory and disproportionate and thus incompatible with the Convention. As a result the government introduced the Terrorism Bill 2005 into Parliament.

(This paragraph contains some useful cases, but the student wastes them by not explaining their significance and by failing earlier to explain the basic provisions of the Act and its constitutional and legal scope and impact. The decision in A has now been used three times, but the student doesn't really explore the significance of that decision with respect to the question.)

12 In conclusion, the Human Rights Act 1998 has had a profound effect on the protection of human rights and has thus impacted on both the legal and constitutional system in the United Kingdom. The courts can now take the Convention and its case law into account and thus must apply European principles to human rights cases. Further, the courts have new powers of interpretation under section 3 of the Act and under section 4 can declare legislation incompatible with the Convention. Since the implementation

➔

of the Act the courts can use the Convention in domestic law and the individual no longer has to make use of the procedure under the European Convention. This will save considerable time and expense, although it should be pointed out that the victim can still make use of that procedure if they are unsuccessful under the Human Rights Act. These new powers, therefore, have had a profound effect on the legal system and the constitution in the United Kingdom, bringing rights home to domestic law.

(The conclusion presumes that the student has covered the central issues raised by the question, which she has not. Thus, there is no firm basis for any of her conclusions, and she ends up summarising the provisions of the Act and making an unsupported and vague statement that the Act has had a profound effect in those areas.)

Bibliography

Ewing, K. and Bradley, A. *Constitutional and Administrative Law*, 14th edn (Longman, 2014)

Foster, S. *Human Rights and Civil Liberties*, 3rd edition (Longman, 2011).

Van Beuren, G. A. 'Including the excluded: the case for an economic, social and cultural Human Rights Act' [2002] PL 456.

(The bibliography is limited and did not contain any texts on legal system or recent articles on the relevant legal and constitutional issues.)

---

[1] The Act's implementation was delayed to allow for fuller training of the judiciary and thus came into force on that date.

[2] See section 1 and Sched. 1 of the Human Rights Act 1998.

[3] Geraldine Van Beuren, 'Including the excluded: the case for an economic, social and cultural Human Rights Act' [2002] PL 456.

[4] (1975) 1 EHRR 524.

[5] (1979) 2 EHRR 245.

[6] (1978) 2 EHRR 1.

[7] (1999) 28 EHRR 603.

[8] [2002] 2 WLR 754.

[9] (1997) 23 EHRR 413.

[10] See Kevin Ewing and Anthony Bradley, *Constitutional and Administrative Law* 16th edn (Longman, 2014), at page 420

[11] *The Times*, 13 May 2004.

[12] [2004] 2 AC 457.

[13] [2005] AC 68.

[14] [2002] 1 AC 1546.

[15] [1979] Ch 344.

[16] (1984) 7 EHRR 14.

[17] [1996] 1 All ER 257.

[18] *Smith and Grady* v *United Kingdom* (2000) 29 EHRR 493.

[19] [2004] 2 AC 557.

[20] [2003] 2 AC 467.

[21] (2002) 35 EHRR 18.

[22] [2002] 3 WLR 1800.

[23] (2002) 35 EHRR 32.

[24] *Wynne* v *United Kingdom* (1994) 19 EHRR 333.

[25] See above, note 12.

[26] [2001] 2 WLR 992.

[27] [2001] 2 WLR 1622.

[28] *Associated Provincial Picture House Ltd* v *Wednesbury Corporation* [1948] 1KB 223.

[29] [2002] 1 AC 800.

[30] (2002) 35 EHRR 1.

Summary of errors

- The student did not address or answer the question, and the information that they did provide was sometimes irrelevant. Thus, although it includes some reasonable information on the Act, the European Convention and the protection of human rights, little of it addresses the issue of whether and to what extent the Act has impacted on the constitutional and legal system. In addition, when the author does mention information that is relevant to those issues, they do not take the opportunity of highlighting the significance of that information, or case, to the question.

- The student does not appear to have understood the question or the issues that it raises, or seem able to identify the potential impact of the Act on the legal system and the Constitution; and perhaps is confused on how the two issues can be distinguished or might overlap.

- A lot of the information relates to the machinery and case law of the European Convention on Human Rights, rather than the provisions and effect of the Human Rights Act itself.

- The student deals with some relevant cases but rarely makes the relevant point, failing to extract the real issue of the case and providing instead unnecessary detail on the facts of and decision in the case.

- The student omits discussion of some provisions of the Act that are relevant to the question, such as the effect of the Act on the legislative process (sections 10 and 19 of the Act).

- Many of the points the student makes are repetitive, such as that there is no longer the need to go to Strasbourg.

- Most of the cases are not explained clearly, and some of the explanations of the Act's provisions are general and vague.

- The content (where relevant) would have been improved by a closer reading of the Act, the cases and the secondary sources.

- The bibliography is limited and did not contain any texts on legal system or recent articles on the relevant legal and constitutional issues.

- In the conclusion, the student professes to have covered the constitutional and legal issues raised by the question, but in truth has not done so.

What is the essay worth?

The marker might reply with comments such as the following.

Marker's feedback

The essay is reasonably well written, although a little vague and general at times. You have raised some relevant points about the Act and the Convention, but you do not address the question. What legal and constitutional issues *are* raised by the Act, and *how* has the Act impacted on those issues? You need to explore the scope of the Act's provisions and the powers of the courts under the Act, and then assess their impact on the legal and constitutional system. For example, how has the Act impacted on matters such as precedent, the public/private law divide, the separation of powers, the constitutional role of the courts, sovereignty of parliament and the provision of legal remedies for human rights violations? You do not really address any of these issues, but rather provide some unfocused information about the Convention, the Act and some case law under both.

You have wasted a lot of your research and some very useful case law by not discussing the law in the context of the question. **Read the question** and address the issues raised by that question!! **40%**

How could this essay be improved?

The student needs to look at the question carefully and to make a careful plan of her answer, identifying the central thrust of the question, the issues that she is going to raise and the specific provisions of the Act and any case law that she is going to use in support of her answer. She should have identified the following:

- The question suggests that the Act has had a profound constitutional and legal effect; therefore, the answer should concentrate on either substantiating or refuting that suggestion.

- The question mentions the impact on both the British Constitution and the English legal system, so the answer must identify the potential and actual impact on both. To do this, the student must appreciate the difference between the legal system and the Constitution and be able to identify relevant statutory provisions and case law that may have, or have had, an impact on both.

- To examine whether the Act has had a profound effect, the student must examine the pre-Act as well as the post-Act situation and consider carefully the aims of the 1998 Act.

A plan for the answer would, therefore, look something like this:

- A general explanation of the role of human rights protection in a constitutional and legal system.

- An examination of the reasons why the Act was passed, including a summary of the pre-Act position and any defects of that system.

- An examination and explanation of the central provisions of the Act as they affect the British Constitution and any of its basic principles (e.g. the separation of powers, the rule of law, sovereignty of power and the constitutional role of the courts), along with an examination of any statutory or case developments to support the contention that the Act has had a profound impact.

- An examination of the same with respect to the impact of the Act on various aspects of the legal system (e.g. judicial precedent, judicial law-making, the parliamentary law process, statutory interpretation, the development of the common law).

- General conclusions as to the truth of the statement in the question.

B: A sound essay

Answer with commentary

NOTE

This answer is provided as a sound and appropriate answer to the question – it should *not* be used as an up-to-date and definitive research source of your own assessments in this area.

The passing of the Human Rights Act 1998 has had a profound effect on both the British Constitution and the English legal system. Discuss.

1 The protection of human rights and civil liberties is a principal function of any state's legal system, providing an effective method of redress when fundamental rights are transgressed. In addition, such protection will impact on the state's constitution, addressing questions such as the constitutional role of the courts, the separation of powers and, particularly within the British Constitution, the sovereignty of Parliament.[1] The passing of the Human Rights Act 1998 ('the Act'), under which rights are to be brought home, and the European Convention on Human Rights is to be given further effect in domestic law,[2] appears to raise a number of legal and constitutional questions, some of which, as we shall see, overlap. This essay will examine the Act's content and operation in order to assess the impact of it on the United Kingdom's constitutional and legal system.

(The student has identified the central thrust of the question and the relevant aspects of the 1998 Act that should be concentrated on. The student has identified that the Act gives rise to issues with respect to both the constitutional and the legal system and tells the reader how she is to tackle those issues and the extent to which they might overlap.)

2 According to the long title, the Act was passed to give further effect to the rights and freedoms guaranteed by the European Convention on Human Rights 1950. As this will involve the partial incorporation of the Convention into domestic law, the Act is bound to have some effect on the constitutional arrangements for the protection of human rights in domestic law, which in turn will impact on both the constitutional role of the courts as well as the sovereignty and autonomy of, respectively, Parliament and executive government.[3] The 'incorporation' of the Convention into domestic law questions whether the United Kingdom would follow many other states in establishing an entrenched and supreme bill of rights, which will protect fundamental rights from the general law. This would indeed fundamentally alter the traditional common law system of rights protection, favoured by writers such as Dicey, whereby such rights were protected within the traditional law.[4] Furthermore, the idea that these rights could be upheld by the courts despite conflicting legislation would be contrary to the doctrine of the sovereignty of Parliament, thereby clashing fundamentally with the central principle of the British Constitution.[5]

(The student begins to identify and address the potential impact of the Act on the Constitution by explaining the traditional constitutional position and by identifying the potential constitutional changes brought about by the passing of the Act. There are also good references to secondary sources.)

3 However, both of these fears remain largely unfounded. First, the Act does not create a domestic bill of rights as such, but instead allows the traditional domestic law to be informed by the rights contained in the Convention, and for the domestic courts to enforce the Convention in legal disputes which raise Convention rights. Second, the Act makes it quite clear that the new powers of the courts to enforce Convention rights do not disturb the

→

validity and application of conflicting legislation, where such provisions are clearly in conflict with the Convention.[6] Thus, the sovereignty of legislation passed and authorised by Parliament is preserved under the Act and the domestic courts do not have the general power to overrule legislative and executive acts that violate human rights, as does, for example, the US Supreme Court.[7] This principle is also reflected with respect to the potential supremacy of the European Convention over domestic law. Whilst the European Communities Act 1972 incorporates relevant European Community law into domestic law and attempts to give supremacy of such law when it is in conflict with domestic law, the Human Rights Act does not create a direct conflict, and instead preserves parliamentary sovereignty when compatibility with the Convention cannot be achieved by the domestic courts via interpretation.[8] Thus, the constitutional principle whereby international law does not override domestic law is maintained, despite the duty of the courts, under s. 2 of the Act, to take into account the case law of the European Court and Commission of Human Rights when adjudicating upon disputes that raise Convention rights.

(The student displays a keen awareness of the true nature of the Act and its potential impact on the Constitution, clearly explaining the nature and scope of the Act and the cautious method of incorporation adopted by the Act. Relevant references are made to key provisions of the Act to illustrate these observations.)

4 Despite the retention of parliamentary sovereignty, the Act does provide the courts with powers to enforce Convention rights, which might create a shift of power from the legislative and the executive to the courts. Thus, s. 3 of the Act empowers the courts, *so far as it is possible to do so,* to interpret both primary and secondary legislation in a manner which is compatible with the European Convention. This section allows the courts to find a Convention-friendly interpretation even where the legislation in question is not truly ambiguous.[9] Although the section makes it clear that this power does not affect the validity of legislation (primary or secondary) which is incompatible with the Convention,[10] this new power of interpretation, if abused by the courts, might lead them to giving a strained interpretation to clear

legislative provisions and thus blur the distinction between interpretation and law-making. In the post-Act era, although the courts have stressed that their role is one of interpretation, and does not entitle them to legislate, there have been instances where the courts have taken a robust and inventive approach. For example in *R v A (Sexual History)*[11] the House of Lords held that the niceties of statutory language could be subordinated in the desire to achieve a Convention-compliant result, thus making it possible to read up or read down legislation which appeared on its face to be in conflict with the Convention. Similarly, in *Mendoza v Ghaidan*[12] the House of Lords held that it was possible to depart from the traditional meaning of the Act so as to make it compliant with Convention rights. On the other hand, the courts have been reluctant to reinterpret legislation when to do so would clearly conflict with the aims and policy of the Act, and where repeal or amendment of such legislation would be more appropriately carried out by Parliament.[13] Further, s. 3 cannot be used where that would amount to 'judicial vandalism' of clear legislative provisions.[14]

(The student now balances the observations made in the previous paragraph with some discussion of the courts' increased powers under the Act, as well as an appraisal of their likely and actual impact on issues such as the constitutional role of the courts. The student uses several good case examples to illustrate the points she makes and provides a balanced account of the cases with respect to their constitutional impact.)

5 Further, s. 4 of the Act allows the higher courts to issue a declaration of incompatibility with respect to both primary and secondary legislation that cannot be read consistently with Convention rights. Although this does not allow the courts to strike down or refuse to apply such legislation, it does allow them to pass judgment on the compatibility of legislation passed or authorised by Parliament.[15] For example, the courts have issued declarations of incompatibility with respect to legislation which imposed disproportionate criminal penalties,[16] which denied transsexuals the right to marry,[17] and which gave the Home Secretary the right to fix sentences for mandatory lifers.[18] It should be noted, however, that in such cases the relevant

legislation remains in place and that Parliament is left with the power to amend or repeal such legislation,[19] or, indeed, to ignore the court's ruling altogether.

(Again, the student explains a central provision of the Act in a manner that provides the basis for a balanced argument as to the likely effect of that provision on the Constitution. She offers a range of case examples, which illustrate their impact without giving unnecessary detail of their facts and decisions.)

6 In particular, the Act, by allowing the domestic courts to take into account the jurisprudence and principles of the European Convention on Human Rights, has impacted on the separation of powers and the level of deference expected of the judiciary towards both the executive and Parliament.[20] Since the Act's coming into force the courts are free to apply the principle of proportionality when assessing the balance between the achievement of a legitimate aim (such as national security or public safety) and the protection of Convention rights. In R *(Daly)* v *Home Secretary*[21] Lord Steyn warned that proportionality allowed the courts to conduct a more intensive review of acts that infringe fundamental rights, going beyond the traditional *Wednesbury* unreasonableness test,[22] which only allowed the courts to interfere if there was strong evidence of irrationality. Although Lord Steyn stressed that this did not allow a merits-based review, subsequent case law shows that the courts will be prepared to take a robust approach in the defence of human rights. For example, in A v *Home Secretary*[23] the House of Lords declared detention powers under the Anti-Terrorism, Crime and Security Act 2001 incompatible with the right to liberty of the person, despite the powers being authorised by Parliament, and despite the government lodging a derogation under the Act to accommodate the threat of terrorism. Such an approach appears radically different from the traditional principles of judicial review, although, as Lord Bingham stated in that case, this approach has been sanctioned by Parliament itself, bypassing the 1998 Act.

(The student places greater emphasis on a central aspect of the courts' new powers – the use of proportionality. The student is careful to explain the significance of this power and to contrast it with the traditional position before the Act. She also uses the

'Belmarsh' case as a stark example of the courts' new approach and justified the use of such power in the context of the aims of the Act itself.)

7 In addition to the constitutional ramifications, the Act also impacts on the general legal system in areas such as precedent, legal process and remedies. For example, the court's duty to take into account the case law of the European Court and Commission of Human Rights (under s. 2), coupled with its new powers of statutory interpretation under s. 3 (above), affects the traditional principles of judicial precedent. Accordingly, if a previous decision of a higher court is now inconsistent with a ruling of the European Court of Human Rights, that decision can now be departed from, even by a lower court. This reflects Parliament's intention that the domestic courts should follow the Convention case law, although it has been held that unless the European decision deals specifically with the domestic law issue, the courts should wait until the House of Lords rules on that point before departing from earlier authority.[24] Similarly, with respect to s. 3 of the Act, domestic courts are now allowed to depart from previous interpretations of primary and secondary legislation. This again reflects Parliament's intention that statutory provisions are, wherever possible, to be compatible with the enjoyment of Convention rights.

(The student now begins to address the effect of the Act on the legal system and identifies a number of aspects of the system that might be so affected. The student then moves swiftly to the first aspect (judicial precedent), clearly and succinctly explaining the effect of ss. 2 and 3 on the traditional doctrine of precedent and providing clear general examples; also making an effort to explain the rationale of those provisions.)

8 The Act also addresses the duty of the legal system to provide redress for violations of human rights. Formerly, the legal system provided redress thorough traditional private law remedies,[25] but the 'incorporation' of the Convention into domestic law means that specific procedures and redress will be available for human rights cases in addition to existing public and private law remedies. Under s. 6 of the Act it is now unlawful for a public authority to act in a way that is incompatible with a Convention right, and

→

under s. 7 the victim of any violation may either bring proceedings for such under the Act or rely on the Convention rights in any legal proceedings. This will affect how the traditional criminal and civil courts deal with cases which raise Convention rights, because whether the Convention issue is raised in direct proceedings under the Act or in other public, criminal or civil proceedings, the court will need to consider its powers under the Human Rights Act. This will include its power under s. 8 of the Act to grant just and equitable orders for the commission of unlawful violations by public authorities, including the power to award just satisfaction in the form of compensation, and in this respect the courts must be informed by the case law of the European Court of Human Rights.[26]

(The student now moves to the next issue, summarising the main effect of the Act on the provision of legal remedies for human rights violations, contrasting it with the previous position and explaining how such remedies will be addressed and provided in practice. Again, good use is made of references to either case examples or statutory provisions.)

9 More specifically, the Act creates a further public/private law divide with respect to the bringing of legal actions against public bodies. In general, the Act only applies to violations committed by 'public authorities' (s. 6) and this has required the courts to apply the distinction previously employed in determining the availability of judicial review proceedings.[27] Thus, in the post-Act era, the courts have had to distinguish between pure public authorities, which are liable under the Act, and bodies which, despite carrying out functions affecting the public, are nevertheless essentially private.[28] However, as the courts are public authorities under the Act,[29] it is possible for the Act to have a 'horizontal' effect and thus inform disputes in the private law domain. Thus, the case law and principles of the Convention have been used to develop the law of confidentiality,[30] although the House of Lords has stressed that the Act largely applies to public authorities and that it is not necessary to develop a private common law action in privacy.[31]

(This aspect of the Act follows on neatly from the previous paragraph and deals with a more specific concern – the effect of the

Act on the public/private law divide. Having identified the particular concern, the student refers to relevant case law with respect to the definition of public authorities and then introduces the possibility of the Act applying in the private sphere, again referring to relevant authority. The paragraph provides a good and balanced account of the legal position in this area.)

10 Finally, the Act has impacted on the general legislative process.[32] For example, under s. 19 of the Act the relevant Minister must, before the Second Reading of any Bill, either make a statement of compatibility of the Bill with the Convention, or make a statement that the Bill is incompatible, but that nevertheless he wishes the House to proceed with the Bill.[33] This seeks to ensure that Parliament passes compatible legislation, although such a declaration of compatibility would not stop the courts using its powers under ss. 3 and 4 of the Act (above). In addition, s. 10 of the Act provides a fast track procedure for the amendment of incompatible legislation, thus reiterating that the ultimate power of legislative amendment lies with the government through Parliament.

(The student now winds up her discussion of the Act and the legal system by considering the impact on the legislative process, identifying two central provisions of the Act in this respect. The description of the provisions is coupled with a balanced and intelligent commentary on their rationale and potential impact.)

11 In conclusion, the Act has provided the courts with new powers of interpretation and review, and allows victims a more structured system for redressing human rights violations. The 'incorporation' of the European Convention allows European Convention case law and principles to inform domestic law and for individuals to seek redress more akin to the system applied by the European Court of Human Rights. However, the Act simply gives 'further effect' to the Convention, and retains the essential constitutional and legal structure of the United Kingdom, in particular the concept of the sovereignty of Parliament. Accordingly, given the method of incorporation adopted by the Act, together with the relatively cautious approach taken by the judiciary in enforcing the Act, it would be incorrect to suggest that the Act has had a *profound* effect on the constitutional and legal system.

(The conclusion reflects the approach taken by the student in the main body of the essay. Thus, it neatly summarises the central issues raised in the main text and contains a reasoned and balanced conclusion on the truth of the statement within the question. Note that the student stresses the word profound to display the careful conclusion, illustrating that the student is always addressing the question.)

Bibliography

Bradley, A. and Ewing, K. *Constitutional and Administrative Law*, 16th edition (Longman, 2014)

Feldman, D. *Civil Liberties and Human Rights in England and Wales*, 2nd edition (OUP 2002)

Feldman, D. 'The Human Rights Act and Constitutional Principles' (1999) LS 195.

Foster, S. *Human Rights and Civil Liberties*, 3rd edition (Longman, 2011)

Lester, A. 'The Art of the Possible: Interpreting Statutes under the Human Rights Act' [1998] EHRLR 665.

Nicol, D. 'The Human Rights Act and Politicians' (2004) LS 451.

Slapper, G. and Kelly, D. *The English Legal System*, 15th edition (Routledge, 2015)

Stychin, K. and Mulcahy, D. *Legal Method: Text and Materials*, 4th edition (Sweet & Maxwell, 2010)

Wadham, J., Mountfield, H. and Edmundson, A. *Blackstone's Guide to the Human Rights Act 1998*, 7th edition (OUP 2015)

(the bibliography includes a sound selection of texts and articles and displays wide reading)

---

[1] See Steve Foster, *Human Rights and Civil Liberties*, 3rd edition Pearson 2011), 12–14.

[2] Home Office, *Rights Brought Home: The Human Rights Bill*, Cm 3782. See also John Wadham, Helen Mountfield and Anna Edmundson, *Blackstone's Guide to the Human Rights Act 1998*, 4th edition (OUP, 2007), pages 6–11.

[3] See David Feldmam, 'The Human Rights Act and Constitutional Principles' (1999) LS 195.

[4] A.V. Dicey, *Introduction to the Law of the Constitution* (Macmillan, 1965).

[5] For general discussion on the constitutional effect of the Act, see Keith Ewing and Anthony Bradley, *Constitutional and Administrate Law*, 16th edition (Longman, 2014), Chapter 19.

[5] See ss. 3 and 4 of the Act.

[7] See David Feldman, *Civil Liberties and Human Rights in England and Wales*, 2nd edition (OUP, 2002), at page 60.

[8] See ss. 3 and 4 of the Act, discussed below.

[9] See Anthony Lester. 'The Act of the Possible: Interpreting Statutes under the Human Rights Act' [1998] EHRLR 665, and Carl Stychin, and Linda Mulcahy, *Legal Method: Text and Materials*, 3rd edition (Sweet & Maxwell, 2007) 218–251

[10] Section 3(2)(b) and (c) of the Act.

[11] [2002] 1 AC 1546.

[12] [2004] 2 AC 557.

[13] *Bellinger* v *Bellinger* [2003] 2 AC 467. See also Lord Millett in *Mendoza* (above), who felt it was inappropriate to interpret a statute inconsistently with its original aim when its amendment was a matter for Parliament.

[14] *R (Anderson and Taylor)* v *Home Secretary* [2002] 3 WLR 1800.

[15] See, in particular, the decision of the House of Lords in *A* v *Home Secretary*, discussed below.

[16] *International Transport Roth GmbH* v *Home Secretary* [2002] 3 WLR 344.

[17] *Bellinger* v *Bellinger*, above, note 13.

[18] *R (Anderson and Taylor)* v *Home Secretary*, above note 14.

[19] The Minister will probably use the procedure under s. 10 of the Act, discussed later.

[20] See Richard Edwards, 'Judicial deference under the Human Rights Act' (2002) MLR 859.

[21] [2001] 2 WLR 622.

[22] *Associated Provincial Picture Houses Ltd* v *Wednesbury Corporation* [1948] 1 KB 223.

[23] [2005] 2 AC 68.

[24] *Price* v *Leeds County Council* [2005] 1 WLR 1925.

[25] For example, in the law of trespass: see *Entick* v *Carrington* (1765) St Tr 1030.

[26] See section 8(4) of the 1998 Act and Article 41 of the European Convention on Human Rights (1950).

[27] *O'Reilly* v *Mackman* [1983] 2 AC 237.

[28] Contrast the decision in *Heather, Ward and Callin* v *Leonard Cheshire Foundation* [2002] 2 All ER 936 with *Poplar Housing Association* v *Donogue* [2001] 2 WLR 1546.

[29] See s. 6(3) of the Act.

[30] See *Douglas* v *Hello!* [2001] 2 WLR 992 and *Campbell* v *MGN Ltd* [2004] 2 AC 457.

[31] *Wainwright* v *Home Office* [2004] 2 AC 406.

[32] See, in particular, Danny Nicol, The Human Rights Act and Politicians' (2004) LS 451.

[33] Thus far, the Communications Bill 2003 has been the only Bill stated to be incompatible with the European Convention, with respect to its ban on political advertising.

Summary of good points

- The student has looked at the question very carefully and has decided which issues need to be raised with respect to the Act. The answer is well structured and appears to correspond to a clear plan.

- The student has distinguished between issues relating to the constitution and those relating to the legal system, whilst identifying where the issues may overlap.

- Given the word limit and the wide scope of the question, she covers a wide range of issues in the essay, choosing the most controversial and pressing concerns relating to the Act and its impact.

- The student displays a sound understanding of the relevant law and confidence with the various legal and constitutional issues raised by the question.

- The student refers to a variety of statutory provisions and relevant case law, being careful to exclude unnecessary detail.

- The consideration of each issue is reasoned and balanced, always addressing the question and making way for any conclusions.

- The conclusion is neat and covers the salient points that have been made during the essay. It concludes with an intelligent and reasoned comment on the truth of the statement contained in the question, which is backed up by the content of the essay.

- Her bibliography contains a sound selection of texts and articles and displays wide reading in the area considering the level at which she is studying. **Please note: the sources used in this essay are not up to date and there are more topical issues about the Act that are not covered by the question or in the answer.**

What is it worth?

Given the broad range of the question and the amount of issues that needed to be raised and addressed by the student, the answer is a very good one.

It shows evidence of a wide knowledge of, and wide reading in, the area and is well written and very well structured. In particular, it shows expertise in including so much information in the answer whilst retaining a critical and analytical approach.

It could, perhaps, have been a little more critical, and the student could have made more use of some of the academic opinion contained in her bibliography, as well as some further extracts from judges.

All in all, it is a very good essay and may be regarded as a 'bare first'. **Note, a student answering that question today would include more recent cases and academic arguments and would include more topical discussions, such as the reform of the Act.**

TIPS FOR GOOD ESSAY TECHNIQUES

- Read the question thoroughly the moment you get it so that you are sure that you understand the question and that you can pick up on any clues in lectures and seminars and do your basic research and reading as soon as possible.

- Always ensure that you know the legal area thoroughly before attempting to write out your answer; this will help you understand the question and locate relevant sources. Read the set text very carefully and then advance to further and more specialist texts and articles.

- Never leave the research and planning of your answer until the last minute, even though you may write it up at the eleventh hour.

- Always plan your answer to ensure that you are answering the set question. Carefully plan what you are going to say and how it is to be structured in individual paragraphs.

- Always follow the three-stage pattern: say what the question is about and what you are going to say, say it and then conclude by saying what you have said.

- Follow the academic *style* (not the actual content) adopted in good textbooks and journals and adopt that general style in your essays, but ensuring that you develop and use your own personal writing style.

- Make sure that when you include legal authority in the form of statutes, cases and so on that they enhance your answer.

- Make the most of your research and ensure that you use the appropriate parts of books, articles, cases and statutes in your essay: avoid plagiarism and over-reliance on secondary sources and ensure that you have displayed your own understanding.

- Ensure that you are sufficiently analytical and critical and that you use those skills with respect to addressing and answering the question – do not just copy from texts and other sources.
- Always ensure that you read through your answer to check for typographical and spelling mistakes, to ensure that the essay makes sense and to confirm that you have answered the question.

Remember, it is much easier to apply these skills if you engage with your law studies and with the individual modules. By undertaking regular and in-depth study you will witness and then acquire the necessary writing skills in addition to substantive legal knowledge in that area.

5

Answering problem questions

UNDERSTANDING PROBLEM QUESTIONS

What are problem questions?

Problem questions are based around a hypothetical scenario that raises a number of legal issues that require the student to give advice to the parties affected by the situation. They are set in almost all legal subjects but are particularly evident in subjects such as contract, tort, criminal law and property law, although they can often appear in constitutional and administrative law assessments, particularly in the areas of human rights and administrative law.

Why are they set?

- Problem questions are set to test your ability to *apply* the relevant legal principles that they have studied to a set of facts.

- They test your knowledge and appreciation of the law that they have been taught, but more specifically require them to explain how the law will be applied in a given factual situation.

- Such questions thus test your ability to identify the relevant legal issues, digest legal material including case law, and decide whether and how that law can be applied to the given facts.

- By setting problem questions, the lecturer will be able to identify whether you have fully appreciated the law and cases that have been explained to you. The questions also test your ability to explain the law and its application to another person (usually a layperson) in a simple, clear and professionally legal style.

NOTE

These skills are central to an undergraduate law student and their success in assessments: most people can copy out legal facts, but a good law student needs skills of assimilation and application – it is that ability to apply the law in a given situation that will be expected, and rewarded with higher marks.

How are problem questions different from essay questions?

Unlike essay questions, problem questions do not simply ask you to explain and analyse the relevant legal principles and case law in a given area. Specifically, they ask you to advise the parties as to how the law will apply to them.

Thus, although you will need a thorough knowledge of the law and the cases, you will not be expected to give a detailed account of those principles or to supply an academic analysis or critique of the law (although you will have to be aware of any controversial or unresolved issues in the law when giving advice).

Rather, you must concentrate on giving advice to the parties after explaining the law in as simple a fashion as possible and only in respect of the specific issues raised by the scenario.

Why are they more difficult than essay questions?

Basically they are more difficult because they not only test your ability to learn legal principles and cases, but also require you to apply that law to a factual situation.

To do this you need to:

- appreciate and understand what you have learned;
- identify which legal issues are raised by the given scenario;
- decide which cases and other materials are relevant to the given scenario;
- identify possible legal arguments so as to apply established law to the facts, or to distinguish such law on the facts;
- explain the law clearly to the interested parties;
- consider all possible arguments and to assess their respective strengths;
- draw sensible, logical and supportable conclusions.

With some essay questions, some students can provide a reasonable answer simply by learning the relevant law, even where they do not really appreciate what they are saying. Even where the essay question asks for a critical analysis, the germ of the answer can usually be located in the student's text or other sources.

With problem questions, however, you are to a great extent on your own. You will need to know the law, but to advise someone as to how it applies requires you to truly understand what that law is saying and what its significance is. Consequently, students who have gone through the course without truly engaging with the subject will find problem questions especially difficult because they do not provide you with anywhere to hide. You cannot simply write about the general legal principles and the cases you have read about in the book; you must be able to identify the relevant legal area (essay titles at least give you that clue) and then apply this general knowledge to the facts.

However, do not go away with the idea that answering problem questions is impossible and that they should be avoided if at all possible.

- Some students prefer problem questions to essay questions, perhaps because they like the constraints of a specific scenario and often cannot determine what an essay question is getting at.

- In addition, the problem question tests different skills that some students might excel at, such as the structuring and ordering of legal issues, the ability to explain the law to a layperson and the ability to spot potential legal arguments within the factual scenario.

- Although problem questions do not allow them to waffle, some students pick up valuable marks by identifying a particular legal argument and by putting together a cogent argument in favour of one of the parties. Thus, while some students are good at remembering large amounts of legal information and providing academic commentary and criticism, others have more practical skills and prefer to apply the law to the facts of a hypothetical problem.

Whatever skills you have as a student – and you may have both – you must acquire the basic skills in order to answer problem questions; you are not going to survive on your law course if you cannot do this. Below are a number of points about tackling problem questions that you should find useful when faced with this type of question. But remember, you cannot exercise these skills before you learn the relevant legal principles. A sound knowledge of the legal principles and the cases is a prerequisite of tackling problem questions, so do not go away with the idea that they are the type of question you can answer with pure common sense and good problem-solving skills.

NOTE

The main reason why students fail these questions is that they fail to provide legal authority to support their findings: giving sound common sense advice is not enough to pass.

HOW TO TACKLE PROBLEM QUESTIONS

The following offers advice for how to answer problem questions successfully.

Identify the legal areas and the specific problems

This aspect of answering problem questions is perhaps the one that students experience most difficulty with. Many students will look at a factual scenario and fail to identify what legal issue and area it raises. Inevitably, therefore, the student will provide an inappropriate answer by including the wrong law and cases and missing out the central issues.

There is no easy mechanism for solving this issue other than saying that you must know your law before you attempt any problem question. If you have engaged with the lectures (and particularly the seminars), the likelihood is that you *will* recognise the legal issues in the scenario.

The chances are that you will have gone through similar scenarios in seminars; in addition, there are a number of self-test questions included in your textbooks and examples given in question-and-answer books that will be reasonably similar to the scenario you are now faced with. This will help you identify the specific issues raised in the question and, along with a good knowledge of the cases studied on the module; you should now be ready to start answering the question.

You should thus identify the legal areas immediately and include these in your plan and, briefly, in your introduction. You can then begin your answer by saying something like:

'This question is concerned with the area of misrepresentation and whether a person can avoid a contract when a misrepresentation has been made to her during negotiations leading up to the conclusion of the contract.'

Note that at this stage you should avoid launching into a long explanation of the law (of misrepresentation); the preceding introduction merely identifies the area of law and explains the importance of that area to the parties concerned. More importantly, you must identify the specific legal arguments that will need to be raised in the answer. Again, you need to make a plan of these points:

1 Did X make a statement of fact, rather than future intention?

2 Was Y induced to enter into that contract because of that statement?

3 More specifically, did Y rely on X's statement, or rather on his own investigations and experience?

4 If he did, can he recover the loss that he is claiming?

In addition, in your plan, but not necessarily in your introduction, you can include the cases and other legal sources that you are going to use when answering these specific points. These points can then form the basis of the introduction to your answer, and such questions can be asked every time you begin addressing each issue in turn. Such an introduction will provide a focus for your answer and a guide for you as to which point to deal with next.

NOTE

For these answers you will be expected to adopt and apply the principles of deductive and inductive reasoning (see Chapter 3).

Give clear, simple but full advice

Remember, with problem questions you are giving advice to the interested parties. They want to know what the relevant law is but are only interested in the specific legal issues that are raised in their dispute. Ensure that your advice is:

Clear

Your answer must deal with the relevant points in a structured and ordered manner. You also need to take the parties through the law and its application clearly. If your answer lacks this cohesion and structure, the person you are advising will become confused and, more importantly, the marker will think that *you* are confused as to the law, the relevant issues and the application of the law to the facts.

Simple

This does not mean that your client is simple, or that you can use a casual and unprofessional style. Rather, it means that the interested parties do not want a complicated and academically analytical answer that you might write in an essay question.

You will often be asked to advise laypersons (e.g. a businessperson, a consumer) as to the law, and they will not appreciate it if your answer is riddled with academic jargon.

You should write in plain and simple English, avoiding overly complex legal language wherever possible. However, the lecturer will expect you to write like a lawyer (or at least a law student) and not a layperson. Your style should combine clarity that would appeal to the layperson and legal professionalism.

In other words, you are writing the answer for *both* the parties involved and the marker. Study the following styles.

EXAMPLES

1 **'Your problem is about the law of misrepresentation, which is where one party tells the other a lie and the other is tricked to enter into a contract.'**

(This is far too informal and unprofessional.)

2 **'The scenario raises the possibility that the apparent agreement has been vitiated by misrepresentation, a factor which will allow the innocent party to rescind the contract. Professor Treitel has noted that the difference between a misrepresentation and a contractual term is often an illusory one and . . . '**

(This is too academic and complex. Your client does not want an academic analysis or the views of academic authors on conceptual matters that do not really concern them. If you are going to use words such as 'rescind' and 'vitiated', provide a simple translation and, perhaps, an example to illustrate.)

3 **'The scenario faced by John concerns the law of misrepresentation, whereby a person may seek to avoid a contract if during the negotiations a false statement of fact has been made, which then**

> induces that person to enter into that contract. **An actionable misrepresentation therefore consists of** . . . [a simple definition]'.
>
> (This introduction is both simple and legally professional. It avoids academic jargon or complex conceptual arguments and issues, and provides the person to be advised with a straightforward explanation of the legal area involved. It also shows the marker that you are familiar with relevant and appropriate legal phrases and concepts, but that equally you can explain them simply to the layperson.)

Full

The client will want you to cover every angle and to provide as many feasible solutions as possible. A good answer will think of a number of possible interpretations and outcomes, but at the very least you need to cover the essential arguments.

Do not just state the law

Many students fill out their answers with a general account of the law and then not address the facts of the given scenario or apply the law to those facts. Thus, they show that they understand the law, or at least that they are able to locate the relevant legal issues and cases in their texts, but fail to address the facts and apply those principles and cases to the given facts.

Many students fail problem questions because they simply state the relevant law (and often include some irrelevant law) and do not make any real effort to address the issues or to give advice. As a consequence, students can receive low marks even though they have a good knowledge of the law and have written a well-structured answer, displaying sound research and writing skills.

Use only relevant cases and statutes and apply them to the facts

Remember, the person you are advising has no interest in the general law, how it is developing and what people think about it, *unless* it has a bearing on the outcome of their dispute. Thus, discuss legal principles or cases to assist you in giving advice on the particular facts, and concentrate on those principles and cases as they affect the possible outcome of that dispute.

Students tend to give a general explanation of the law or of a specific area because the information is contained in their notes or textbooks. Avoid this mistake and only include principles and cases if they are relevant to the factual situation.

Once you have raised a relevant legal point, apply it (and the case law) to the facts and consider its possible application to those facts *before* you move on to the next point.

Choose and use cases whose facts, outcome and ratios are of relevance to the scenario: do not use every case (on misrepresentation) but use cases that are analogous to, or can be contrasted with the facts of your scenario.

Do not give vague and open advice

You will not be expected to give the definitive answer to the legal issues raised by the scenario. Often the law and its application are unclear, and it will not be certain whether the rules apply to a given set of facts.

However, you will be expected to come to a logical and feasible conclusion on the facts based on your knowledge and appreciation of the law and its potential application.

Do not avoid giving advice by either ignoring the possible application of the law to the facts altogether or by providing vague or open advice. Look at the following example.

EXAMPLE

'In conclusion, whether Jack's exclusion clause is valid and reasonable depends on whether it has been incorporated into the contract and whether it is reasonable within the terms of the Unfair Contract Terms Act 1977.'

(This fails to inform Jack as to the likely outcome of his dispute. In effect, the student is saying, 'Well, I have given you the law and the cases, now sort the rest out yourself.' This is not only unhelpful to Jack, but it also shows that the student is unable to apply the relevant law and cases to the facts and that they do not really appreciate the law and its application. The student is thus failing in the central task, even though their knowledge of the general law may be sound.)

Always read the facts carefully

It is amazing how many students, when asked in a seminar 'Do you think Jack intended to accept John's offer in the seminar question before us?' start looking for the answer in their lecture notes or textbooks! The notes and books will give you information on the general law, but that question can only be answered by looking carefully at the facts of the scenario in the seminar question and discovering whether what he said or did amounts to acceptance in the legal sense.

You must, therefore, look at the facts very carefully before answering the question: make a list of factual as well as legal problems raised in the scenario (see the plan to the sound answer in the next section) and ensure that you address those factual issues. You will then be able to offer constructive advice on the basis of the similarity, or otherwise, of the facts in the case with previous cases.

Don't repeat the facts

Too many students pad out their answers by reciting the facts of the scenario. This is not helpful and is taking up time better spent on addressing the issues raised by those (already established) facts. On the other hand, you can refer to the facts so as to give relevant advice:

> 'As we are told that Colin did not read the advertisement, it may be argued that he cannot take advantage of any offer that has been made.'

Consider all options

Your advice should include your consideration of all the legal possibilities and solutions to the problem. You must address all possibilities, even if you ultimately opt for one conclusion and reject the others.

EXAMPLE

If the question is whether X has accepted Y's offer, you should consider both possible arguments – that his conduct was evidence of acceptance, or that his reply was too conditional to be regarded as an acceptance. Problem questions are usually phrased in a way which admits of alternative constructions and you will gain extra marks by considering both possibilities.

Furthermore, you must consider the legal effect of alternative conclusions.

EXAMPLE

If the question is whether an advertisement was an offer or merely an invitation to treat, you need to consider the effect of either construction. Thus, you would say:

'If the advert was an offer, then Y was at liberty to accept that offer and thus X would be bound to supply the goods to Y. If, on the other hand, the advert was an invitation to treat, it appears Y has made an offer and X can reject that offer and thus no contract will have come into existence.'

You can then consider the most likely construction and conclude accordingly.

Do not invent facts, but consider every possibility

You should not introduce hypothetical facts in order to consider other possibilities. Generally, therefore, you must stick to the established facts given to you in the problem.

However, if the facts are unclear, you should consider all the factual possibilities, followed by the legal consequence of each.

EXAMPLE QUESTION

Fred is serving a prison sentence and is sharing a cell with Peter. Peter threatens to attack Fred because he discovers that he has burgled Peter's mother's house. Fred asks the prison warden to move Fred to another cell and this request is refused. The next day Peter attacks Fred, causing him head injuries. Discuss.

From the facts it is not clear whether Fred informed the warden of the reason for his request. If he did, the warden should have appreciated the risk of attack and moved him; if he didn't, the warden might have no reason to appreciate such a risk. This will have an effect on the liability of the prison in negligence (or human rights law), and you must consider the legal effect in either contingency.

Moreover, it is not made clear why the request was refused. Whether it was for a sound operational reason or for an unsatisfactory reason impacts on the liability of the prison, and again you must consider

---

the legal impact in both possible scenarios, in addition to providing examples of satisfactory or unsatisfactory reasons.

Consequently, because the facts are unclear, you have the task of asking further questions, rather like a lawyer advising a client.

Ensure that your conclusions are as clear and full as possible

After you have considered all the possible factual and legal permutations, you should provide clear and full advice, considering all *possible* conclusions (disregarding highly unlikely answers), and settling on the most likely solution.

Do not simply state several possible outcomes and leave the client to choose the most likely.

EXAMPLE

'The advert could be an offer, or indeed it could be construed as an invitation to treat. Equally, Y's conduct might suggest that he accepted the offer (if indeed it was an offer), but his actions could also be construed as a counter offer.'

(This is largely unhelpful and again shows the student's uncertainty as to the law and its application to particular facts.)

If the state of the law is uncertain, or the potential decision of the court on the facts is difficult to predict, then warn the client of that fact, but still comment on the most likely outcome.

EXAMPLE

'This area of law (the privacy of public figures) is still being developed and the case law is far from consistent. However, given the fact that the celebrity in our case had a high public profile, had admitted committing certain anti-social or criminal acts in the past, and had indicated a desire to become a Member of Parliament, it is submitted that it is unlikely that he could successfully sue for the disclosure of his past sexual activities by a public newspaper.'

NOTE

Your answer can still be a good one even if the conclusions are not the same as other students or the marker – it is the reasoning that matters, provided your conclusions are logical and based on an understanding of the law. Equally, your answer will not necessarily be a good one simply because you have arrived, by chance, at the right conclusion.

QUESTION 1: CONTRACT PROBLEM

Below is a fairly straightforward problem question on the formation of a contract. The topic is dealt with at the beginning of any contract law module and thus should not be beyond the ability of any first-year law student. The word limit for the answer is set at 1,500 words, indicating that the answer should be succinct and simple and will not require extensive or in-depth analysis. First, we will look at how to tackle the question. Then we will examine both sound and poor answers.

EXAMPLE QUESTION

Easy Sell Ltd, a company selling various household goods, placed the following advertisement in the local newspaper:

> 'Exclusive Offer! Hundreds of fridges to be sold at discount prices. For example, we have 200 ElectroBest 250s at just £150 each. All you have to do is to telephone in your order and we will deliver the next day.'

Sam saw the advertisement and immediately telephoned the company, ordering 150 ElectroBest 250s, but was told that that product was now out of stock.

The next day Ella telephoned the company and asked whether they had any BSV fridges and was told that there were 100 left in stock priced at £125 each. Ella said that she would have 50 of them, and was then told to fill in an application form at the company's office,

---

in which case the fridges would be delivered to her the next day. When she travelled to the office to complete the form she was told that the company had sold out of that particular product.

Advise Sam and Ella as to whether they can sue Easy Sell Ltd for breach of contract.

How to tackle this question

Identifying the legal area and the relevant legal issues

- Formation of a contract – offer and acceptance. The scenario is clearly about whether a contract has come into existence, which of the parties has made an offer and whether any offer has been accepted. The student thus needs to be aware of the basic rules on offer and acceptance and the relevant case law in this area.

- Nature and status of advertisements. The answer must assess the legality and status of the company's advertisement and decide whether it is an invitation to treat or a true offer. The student must be aware of the relevant case law in this area.

- Study the words of this particular advert. The student will need to look at the wording of the advert and the surrounding circumstances to decide its true status.

- Was the advert an offer or an invitation to treat? By answering this question the student can then assess the significance of the parties' subsequent actions in deciding whether or at what point a contract came into existence.

- Was Sam's order an offer or acceptance? The answer to this question is determined by whether the student feels the advert is – *in law, not just their opinion* – an offer or an invitation to treat.

- Was Ella's order an offer or acceptance, or neither? Again, the answer will depend on how the student has classified the advert, but in addition it needs to be asked whether Ella's initial inquiry is an offer or indeed a preparatory inquiry, whether the company's reply is an offer or merely the supply of information, or whether the offer is made when she says that she will have 50 fridges.

- Did the company accept Ella's offer on the telephone? Assuming Ella has made an offer for the fridges, it must be considered whether that offer is accepted on the telephone, or whether the company has postponed the formation of the contract until Ella fills in an order form and they accept that order.

- Was the requirement to complete the application form a condition of formation, or a mere formality? The essential issue is whether the agreement on the telephone is subject to contract, or whether the subsequent written order is a mere formality confirming the already existent contract.

Giving legal advice to Sam and Ella

- Identify the central legal arguments (see the preceding section) and explain the relevant law clearly and simply, explaining the significance of any findings.
- Apply the relevant legal principles and case law to the facts of each situation, carefully considering the facts and the actions of the parties and deciding whether such actions are consistent with established principles and any previous case law.
- Give advice on the basis of such principles and on the likely outcome. Do not simply give an account of the law and cases, but rather provide clear and direct advice to the parties as to the probable, or possible, legal outcome. Be careful to consider all possible outcomes, but stress the most likely result.

Use of relevant legal authority

Students need to use relevant case law with respect to:

- Advertisements and circulars – *Spencer* v *Harding, Partridge* v *Crittenden, Carlill* v *Carbolic Smoke Ball Company.*
- Certainty of offers – *Harvey* v *Facey, Carlill.*
- Fact of acceptance – *Brogden* v *Metropolitan Railway Co, Gibson* v *Manchester City Council, Branco* v *Cabarro.*

A: sound answer

Below is a good and appropriate answer to the question, displaying all relevant problem-solving skills and identifying the essential issues as previously outlined. **Note: this answer should not be used as a research tool for your assessments in this legal area.**

Introduction

The scenario raises the question of whether Easy Sell Ltd has entered into a valid contract with Sam and/or Ella. For a contract to come into existence, a valid offer must be made by one person, which is then accepted by another person. An offer must be firm and capable of acceptance and must imply that the person making it intends to be bound if that offer is accepted, whereas an acceptance must accept the terms of the offer unconditionally,[1] and then be communicated to the person making that offer.[2] If both an offer and acceptance are found to exist then the contract will be complete and both parties will be bound to fulfil their respective promises.

Sam

Sam will argue that the company made an offer when it placed an advert in the newspaper, and that he accepted that offer when he placed an order for 150 named fridges. On the other hand, the company will argue that the advert was not an offer, but merely an invitation to treat, inviting people such as Sam to make an offer by placing an order and leaving the company free to accept that order.

In law, advertisements, and circulars distributed by traders, are usually construed as invitations to treat. This is because they usually lack the certainty of terms necessary to make them offers; for example, they may not contain specific terms (such as price and description) and require the customer to provide such details on making the order. Thus in *Spencer* v *Harding*[3] it was held that a circular advertising the defendant's goods for sale and distributed to the general public was an invitation to treat rather than an offer. Equally in *Partridge* v *Crittenden*[4] it was held that an advertisement placed in a magazine that certain birds were for sale was held to be an invitation to treat and in that case Lord Parker CJ held that there was business sense in construing such advertisements as invitations to treat. This would reflect business practice and hence allow the company to inform the customer that the goods are out of stock or have already been sold. Consequently, there is a presumption that the advert in our case is merely an invitation to treat and that Sam has made an offer, which has been rejected by the company.

However, this is merely a presumption and if the court finds that the terms of the advertisement are clear enough to constitute an offer, then they will construe the advert as an offer capable of acceptance by Sam. For example, in *Carlill* v *Carbolic Smoke Ball Company*[5] it was held that the defendant's advert, stating that it would pay £100 to anyone who contracted flu after they had used its herbal remedy, was not an invitation to treat but indeed a clear offer, made to anyone who was capable of and willing to perform the conditions of the offer. In that case it was stated that the terms of the offer were certain and capable of clear acceptance by anyone who wished to perform the conditions.

Thus, whether the advert in our case is an offer or an invitation to treat depends on whether the company intended, by the words it used, to make a certain offer capable of acceptance. On one interpretation, it could be concluded that by stating that all that the customer had to do was to telephone in their orders, the company had indeed made a clear offer and that Sam had accepted the offer by placing his order. Sam would thus argue that the company had made a unilateral contract, which was binding on the company if Sam followed the instructions in the advert and binding on Sam only when he placed such an order. However, on another interpretation, it could be concluded that the advert was only an invitation to treat and that the use of the words 'Exclusive offer' and the instructions to simply telephone your order were not sufficiently certain to rebut the normal commercial rule that such adverts merely invite offers in the form of orders. The wording of the advert is not as clear as the one in *Carlill*, and in *Carlill* the finding of the court that the advert was an offer appeared to be the only sensible explanation of the company's actions (particularly as they had deposited £1,000 as a mark of the company's good faith).

In our case, although the company has stated that all the customer needs to do is to telephone his or her order, and promised that it will deliver the next day, the most likely interpretation of the advert is that the company is inviting people to make an offer over the telephone and then promising in good faith that delivery will be made the next day once that offer is accepted. It is suggested that this is the case even though the goods ordered by Sam have been identified and priced in the advert. Thus, although the terms of the agreement between Sam and the company appear certain, it is likely that the courts will construe the advert as a general invitation for potential customers to make their offers.

Ella

In Ella's case, if a court was to construe the original advert as an open and definite offer, then Ella's order could be regarded as an acceptance of that offer and the contract could have been concluded the moment she placed that order. However, as has been stated above, it is unlikely that the advert will be construed in that manner and that the more likely possibility is that a court will find that the company has merely invited Ella to make an offer. In addition, even if the words used in the advert did intend to bind the company, the fact that the advert did not contain any details of the particular fridges that Ella was interested in would preclude a court from labelling the advert as a firm offer in her case.

Consequently, the negotiations begin with the telephone call and Ella's inquiry regarding the BSV fridges will be regarded as merely a preliminary inquiry, which will bind neither her nor the company. The company's response that it had 100 of the fridges left and that they were priced at £125 per machine would appear to be no more than the provision of essential information, rather than any definite offer to supply those goods to Ella. Thus, in *Harvey* v *Facey*,[6] when the claimant asked the defendant what was the lowest price he would accept for his property and the defendant replied £900, it was held that the defendant had not made an offer, but had merely indicated a price at which he might sell, should he sell at all. Using that case in our scenario, it is likely that a court would conclude that the company is still awaiting a definite offer from Ella.

If that is the case, the next question is whether the contract came into existence over the telephone, or whether the contract's formation was suspended until Ella made a formal offer via the official application form. In this case the company would argue that Ella had been asked to make a formal offer via the application form at the office, and that until that formal offer was made, and accepted by

→

the company, then no contract would come into existence. Thus, in *Gibson* v *Manchester City Council*[7] it was held that the council had not made an offer to the claimant when it had requested him to fill in an order form if he wished to buy. On the other hand, Ella would argue that her offer had been impliedly accepted by the company,[8] and that the request to fill in an application form should be regarded as a mere formality or a formal record of an already completed bargain. Thus, in *Branco* v *Cabarro*,[9] where the parties had described a contract as a provisional agreement, to be replaced by a more formal arrangement, the court held that the contract was already in existence, and that the more formal agreement was not a condition of the contract's formation.

Ella's claim could be supported by the fact that the advert stated that all one had to do was to place an order and the goods would be delivered the next day. Thus, although the advert is probably not a clear offer in itself (see above), its terms could be used to discover the intention of the parties. Ella could argue that the terms of the advert led her to believe that the company was willing to complete the contract over the telephone, and that the completion and acceptance of the order form were to act as a formal record of that agreement. However, the company would claim that it had made a clear counter offer to Ella by insisting on new conditions of acceptance,[10] and that because the majority of terms had not been settled over the telephone, a formal order form was needed to clarify the exact terms of their agreement. On balance, it is likely that the courts would conclude that the completion of the order form was a prerequisite of the formation of the contract and that no contract was completed between Ella and the company.

Conclusion

In conclusion, Sam would probably fail in any action for breach of contract. The advert is likely to be construed as an invitation to treat, and his offer appears to have been rejected by the company by stating that the goods are no longer in stock. In Ella's case, although there are grounds for arguing that Ella's specific offer has been accepted by the company's conduct, and that the filling in of the order form is a mere formality to act as a record of an already concluded agreement, the court is more likely to find that no agreement was reached over the telephone and that the company had notified Ella of the fact that they had sold out in good time.

---

[1]*Hyde* v *Wrench* (1840) 3 Beav 334.
2*Entores* v *Far Eastern Miles Corp* [1955] 2 QB 327.
[3](1869–70) LR 5 CP 561.
[4][1968] 1 WLR 1204.
[5][1893] 1 QB 256.
[6][1893] AC 552.
[7][1978] 1 WLR 520.
[8]See, for example, *Brogden* v *Metropolitan Railway Co* (1876–87) LR 2 App Cas 666, where one party accepted the terms by placing an order for the goods.
[9][1947] KB 854.
[10]see *Brogden* (above, note 8).

What was good about this answer?

- The introduction immediately identifies the general legal area and the specific legal issues that are relevant to resolving any dispute.

- Separate advice is given with respect to both potential contracts so that the author can deal specifically with each dispute.

- The student identifies the arguments that would be put forward to both parties before applying the relevant legal principles and coming to any conclusion.

- The student uses relevant and useful authority before attempting to reach any conclusions.

- Cases are explained briefly and simply and are illustrated in the context of the dispute.

- The student at least considers all possible arguments before coming to a conclusion.

- The conclusion is sufficiently certain and appropriately guarded, and is based on sound reasoning and a knowledge and appreciation of the case law.

- It is written in a style that could be readily understood by a business client, but with appropriate legal skills expected of those giving legal advice.

What is it worth?

The marker might make the following comments:

> **Marker's feedback**
>
> The piece is well written and structured and you deal with the points in a logical and clear fashion. You also make good use of relevant legal authority, and consider a number of alternatives. However, some of the possibilities you considered were not entirely feasible and could have been dismissed at an earlier stage, leaving you more room to discuss the relevant legal principles and cases in detail. In addition, try to use more recent commercial cases in your answer
>
> Overall, a good effort – **65%**

B: poor answer

Below is an inappropriate and poor answer to the problem involving Sam, Ella and the company. Identify the mistakes that the author has made throughout the answer and advise him as to how he could improve the answer. **Do not consult the guidance points discussed in the text after the essay before you carry out the exercise yourself.** You can check your comments with the text afterwards to see whether you have spotted the same errors.

> Easy Sell Ltd have not made an offer by putting the advert in the paper so Sam and Ella cannot accept by telephoning the company and placing their order. Consequently it is unlikely that either of them can sue the company for breach of contract. If they can sue the company then they can either sue for damages, which would be the difference between the price that they would have to pay in the open market and the price that they had contracted to pay Easy Sell Ltd. Alternatively, they could bring an action for specific performance, ordering Easy Sell Ltd to deliver the goods. This would be unlikely because the goods are not unique, and in any case the company no longer has them in stock.
>
> A contract is a legally binding agreement that must contain the following elements. First, there must be agreement between the parties

in the form of an offer and acceptance. Secondly, the parties must intend the agreement to have legal effect. Thirdly, both parties must show consideration.[1] Fourthly, the agreement must be legal and, finally, the parties must have the capacity to enter into the contract in the first place. In our case only the first element – offer and acceptance – appears relevant.

An offer is a firm proposition put by one person (an offeror) to another person (the offerree) that is intended to be legally binding if the other person accepts that proposition. For an offer to be valid, therefore, it must be firm in the sense that it contains sufficient certainty. Thus if the proposition lacks information on the fundamental terms of the contract it will not be considered an offer. For example, if X said that he was willing to sell a car, that proposition could not be an offer as we do not know what car he is selling and so if Y said 'yes' to that proposition it could not result in a contract as X and Y would not know which car was being referred to. There would be no meeting of the minds, no *consensus ad idem*. Similarly, in *Harvey* v *Facey*,[2] there was held to be no offer because when the plaintiff asked what the lowest price for Bumper Hall Pen was and the defendant said £900 it was held that the defendant had not made a certain offer but had only indicated a price at which he might start negotiating.

In contrast to a firm offer, the law regards some propositions to be mere invitations to treat. These invite a person to make an offer, rather like the advert in our case, and do not amount to offers themselves. Examples of these invitations to treat are shop window displays and the placing of goods on a supermarket shelf. In these cases the law says that a shop window display is an invitation to treat, so in *Fisher* v *Bell*[3] it was held that the display of a knife in a shop window was not an offer but merely an invitation to treat. Similarly, in *Pharmaceutical Society of Great Britain* v *Boots Cash Chemists*[4] it was held that the display of goods on a supermarket shelf was not an offer and that the customer makes the offer when he or she goes to the checkout and places the goods on the belt for the cashier to accept. Other examples of invitations to treat are invitations for tenders and, as in our case, general advertisements, where the courts have held that the person placing an advert does not intend

→

to make a definite offer, but rather wants to invite others to make offers.[5]

The company's advert in our case is very similar to this as it is merely inviting Sam and Ella to make an offer by placing their order. When the order is placed, therefore, Sam and Ella make an offer and the company can accept or reject the offer. It would only be different if the company had made a clear offer to Sam and Ella, which was capable of acceptance by them placing the order with the company. This happened in *Carlill* v *Carbolic Smoke Ball Company*.[6] In this case a company had placed an advertisement in a newspaper promising everyone that if they sniffed their product and still caught influenza the company would pay £100. Mrs Carlill used the product as instructed and still caught influenza and then claimed the £100 from the company. The company claimed that it had not made an offer, and that Mrs Carlill had not accepted that offer, that there was no intention to create legal relations, and that Mrs Carlill had not provided any consideration for the £100. The court rejected all the company's claims and held that the company had made a firm offer to the whole world, that Mrs Carlill had accepted that offer by using the product, which was also her consideration, and that the company did intend to create legal relations as the advert was not a mere advertising puff but was on the other hand a firm proposition capable of acceptance.

This case shows that an advert can be an offer if there are exceptional cases. However, in *Carlill* the company had placed £1000 in the bank as a mark of its sincerity and thus were bound by its advert. In our case the company has not done anything like that, they have simply said all you need to do is to telephone your order, which will then be the offer, and we will deliver. It does not suggest that they intend to be bound. Thus, the company have made an invitation to treat and not an offer and Sam and Ella cannot claim that they accepted when they telephoned the company with their orders.

A contract also requires an acceptance for it to be binding. First of all there must be a fact of acceptance, which means that the offeree must unconditionally accept the term of the offer. Thus, if the offeree rejects the offer or makes a counter offer in response to the

offer, that counter offer will destroy the original offer and no contract comes into existence. This was seen in *Hyde* v *Wrench*,[7] when
the plaintiff made a counter offer to the defendant, and then tried
to accept the original offer. However, in *Stevenson* v *McClean*[8] it was
held that a mere request for further information was not a counter
offer and that such a request does not destroy the original offer.
Secondly, there must be communication of the acceptance – the
offeree must clearly communicate the acceptance to the offeror.[9]
Actual communication does not have to take place if the offeror has
waived the requirement of acceptance, as in the *Carlill* case, or where
the acceptance is made by post, in which case the acceptance is valid
once the letter is sent. However, the postal rule does not apply to
telexes or, probably, e-mails, and it cannot apply where the parties
have made it clear that they want a different method of acceptance.[10] It must also be stressed that silence cannot amount to
acceptance.[11]

In our case the acceptance does not appear to have taken place at
all. Sam telephoned in his offer and the company immediately
rejected it by saying the goods were out of stock. The company can
do this, as there was no obligation to accept this offer in the first
place. In Ella's case she made an offer by ordering the fridges but
was then told that she would have to fill in a form. This amounts to
a counter offer as it is introducing new terms into the agreement,
and before the new agreement is signed the company inform Ella
that the goods are no longer for sale as they have sold out. Although
this appears unfair and contrary to what the company said in the
advert, I think they can do this because there was no contract in
existence at that point and an offer can be revoked at any time
before acceptance.[12]

In conclusion, therefore, there appears to be no contract in existence between the company and Sam and Ella. Their offers have
been rejected by the company, and without a clear acceptance there
can be no contract. Perhaps Ben and Ella could ask the company to
sell them some fridges when it gets some more in stock. Although
they will not necessarily be on special offer then, perhaps the company can give them a discount to make up for the fact that it treated
Sam and Ella unfairly.

[1]*Currie* v *Misa* (1875) LR 10 Exch 153.
[2][1983] AC 552.
[3][1961] 1 QB 394.
[4][1953] 1 QB 401.
[5]*Partridge* v *Crittenden* [1968] 1 WLR 1204.
[6][1893] 1 QB 256.
[7](1840) 3 Beav 334.
[8](1879–80) LR 5 QBD 346.
[9]*Entores* v *Far Eastern Miles Corp* [1955] 2 QB 327.
[10]*Holwell Securities* v *Hughes* [1974] 1 WLR 155.
[11]*Felthouse* v *Bindley.*
[12]*Routledge* v *Grant.*

What was wrong with the answer?

- The student gave his conclusions right at the start of the answer without considering the law or the cases.

- The first paragraph considers possible remedies for breach of contract before deciding whether there has been a breach of contract.

- The student lists all the requirements of a legally binding contract and then admits at the end of the paragraph that only one of those requirements is relevant to the question.

- Although the next paragraph defines an offer, he gives hypothetical and case examples that do not appear to be relevant to the scenario.

- His paragraph on invitations to treat is too general and does not concentrate on advertisements, merely mentioning them as one example without explaining the rationale of the rule and the relevant case law.

- He concludes that the advert in this case was only an invitation to treat without fully considering the possibility that it might be a unilateral contract.

- He mentions *Carlill* but fails to see that that case might be relevant and then distinguishes it purely on the ground that this company did not deposit money as a sign of good faith.

- His treatment of the acceptance issue is again too general, and he does not deal with the specific issues raised by the scenario, or the relevant cases such as *Clifton* v *Palumbo*. He fails to recognise that the contract with Ella might already be in existence before the completion of the order form.

- His conclusion is very one-sided, and he finishes by giving vague and meaningless advice as to what Sam and Ella might do to ease their disappointment.

Overall, the student was on the right lines and had basically identified the relevant legal areas. However, he had failed to spot most of the specific factual and legal arguments raised by the scenario. As a result, his answer was general and largely unhelpful to the parties concerned. His use of cases was also rather poor. He mentioned many cases that were not particularly relevant to the question and failed to pick up on the importance of many other cases. He lacked the ability to analyse the law and the cases and to apply those principles to the facts before him. In particular, he made his conclusions early on in the essay and refused, or was unable, to consider other possibilities.

What is it worth?

The marker might make the following comments:

> **Marker's feedback**
>
> You were in the right area and you used some very relevant cases. However, you also included some irrelevant material and failed to apply the really relevant cases and principles to the facts in hand. Your conclusions were not based on the application of the strict contractual principles or the cases and you failed to consider a number of possible arguments. Do not conclude at the start of your essay; instead, work through the facts, considering every possible solution before coming to a firm conclusion. I think the parties would have been somewhat confused with the advice you gave and would have expected you to address further legal possibilities. In addition, your concluding advice was legally unhelpful. Look at the facts closely and try to apply the law and the cases clearly to the scenario – **35%**

The piece *might* just obtain a provisional pass if that boundary is 35%.

NOTE
- -

In both answers A (sound) and B (poor) the students used essentially the same law and cases, but the answer A receives double the marks.

- -

QUESTION 2: STATUTORY INTERPRETATION/JUDICIAL REVIEW PROBLEM

The following problem question is on judicial review and is typical of those set on many constitutional and administrative courses, requiring the student to comment on the possible unlawful or unfair use of power by someone acting under an imaginary Act of Parliament. This sort of question may also appear on legal system and skills courses, because they involve the interpretation of statutes and require the student to display interpretation skills.

This type of question has been chosen because, generally, students find them particularly difficult for a number of reasons:

- It requires the student to study the words of an imaginary Act of Parliament and then to offer a plausible interpretation of those words.

- It requires the student to apply quite abstract and complex concepts such as irrationality, abuse of discretion and proportionality to factual situations.

- This type of question is perceived by students (sometimes wrongly) as requiring an appreciation of political matters (as opposed to an awareness of constitutional concepts).

To answer the question the student must concentrate on the words of the imaginary Act of Parliament and/or any imaginary secondary legislation. The ultimate answer to the question, therefore, lies within the words of those imaginary provisions, and not the textbooks or the cases – although you will need to apply the legal principles and the case law to the factual situation. Consequently the student must examine those words very carefully and always keep them in mind when giving advice.

Pre-practice question

Before we tackle our specific problem, take this example as an illustration of the above problems.

EXAMPLE QUESTION

In June 2015 Parliament passed the Local Authority (Provision of Resources) Act 2015, section 1 of which provides as follows:

> If the Secretary of State is of the opinion that a local authority requires resources to deal with an exceptional contingency affecting the duties of any local authority, he may order that such sum as he thinks fit to meet such a contingency be given to that authority.

Acting under that provision, the Secretary of State decided to give £25,000 to assist every County Council to erect an appropriate statue outside the council buildings to commemorate the Queen's birthday. Grumpy, a resident of Coventry, claims that the Secretary of State has acted unlawfully and has applied for permission (leave) to apply for judicial review on the following grounds:

1 That the power to order payment under section 1 only applies if the contingency relates to the duties of a public authority, the erecting of memorials not being such a duty as envisaged under the Act.

2 That the words 'exceptional contingency' only apply to a situation faced by a particular local authority and not one faced by all authorities.

3 That the Secretary has abused his discretion by giving an identical sum to each local authority irrespective of their needs and resources and, specifically, by ignoring the fact that a statue of the Queen was erected in 1954 to mark her coronation.

Advise Grumpy as to the possible success of his action in judicial review.

The question requires the student to address issues that have been specifically identified in the question (in points 1–3). Thus, the format of the question has performed one essential task for the student – rather than simply saying 'Discuss', leaving the student the task of identifying the potential grounds for review, it has listed the arguments that the applicant is making. Nevertheless, many students will still find it difficult to identify what the claims are getting at and what specific grounds (and cases) are relevant in answering the question.

The student must address and answer the following questions:

- Is erecting memorials *a duty* of a local authority? (What *are* the duties of a local authority?) If that is a duty, is it the sort of duty that was envisaged by this Act? This depends on the construction of the words of the Act, and the intention and purpose of the Act. Students must look in the area of illegality and *ultra vires* and use cases such as *A-G* v *Fulham Corporation* and *Padfield* v *Ministry of Agriculture*.

- Does the Act apply to an exceptional contingency faced by *all* local authorities, or only ones faced by specific authorities? Can it be *exceptional* if faced by all? Again, the answer depends on the interpretation of the words of the Act – '*a* local authority requires resources to deal with an exceptional contingency affecting the duties of *any* local authority' – and the application of the *ultra vires* doctrine.

- Has the Home Secretary fettered his discretion by awarding the same sum, irrespective of each local authority's resources and needs? Explain the concept of fettering of discretion and include relevant case law (e.g. *Roberts* v *Hopwood*). Also, could the allocation of such funds be *Wednesbury* unreasonable?

NOTE

There can be no definite answer, the Act is imaginary, and students do not have access to Hansard and so on. However, students should be able to identify the possible arguments and apply the general principles that they have found from the relevant case law.

Main practice question

Now let us look at our specific example.

EXAMPLE QUESTION

Under s. 1 of the (imaginary) Public Order (Emergency Powers) Act 2015 the Secretary of State may pass such regulations as he thinks fit for the purpose of protecting the public from serious public disorder and for restoring stability to the community. Section 2 of the Act requires the Secretary to lay the regulation before the House of

---

Commons for its approval and s. 3 states that the Secretary shall consult with such persons as he considers appropriate before acting under any regulation approved by Parliament.

In November 2016, following a serious disturbance at a Gay Rights meeting in Bognor Regis, the Secretary laid the following regulation before the House:

> If the Secretary of State is of the opinion that there has been an instance of serious public disorder in a locality, he may order police officials and local authorities to take such action as he thinks necessary.

Two days after receiving approval, and acting under the regulation, the Secretary ordered the local authority and the local police force in Bognor Regis to prohibit and disperse any political meeting which in their opinion may lead to serious public disorder. Although he did not consult with anyone before making and laying the regulation, he did consult with the local authority and police before issuing the order; however, he refused to hear representations from several groups that had their planned meetings cancelled.

Advise the local Amnesty International Group, which has always held its rally in the town, and fears that it may be cancelled, whether and how it can challenge the Secretary of State's regulation and his order.

The question has been set in Constitutional and Administrative (Public) Law in the second term of the first year. Thus, the students are well into their legal studies, are expected to have acquired a reasonable understanding of the constitutional and legal system, and should be able to tackle a question in this specific area of public law.

The word limit is 2,000 words (with a 10 per cent leeway), excluding references and citations.

How to tackle this question

The relevant law

Students require a sound knowledge of the grounds of judicial review, and a general awareness of procedure and remedies. In addition, as seen in the sample answer, the scenario raises a variety of legal areas and issues. Accordingly, students must ensure that each point is dealt with directly and succinctly and that the answer does not include any unnecessary detail with respect to the law or particular cases.

More specifically, students must discuss the following:

- the availability of judicial review and whether the applicants are eligible to claim it;
- the doctrine of *ultra vires* and the ground of illegality with respect to the legality of the regulation and order;
- wrongful delegation and the consequent legality of the Secretary's regulation and order in granting discretion to the police and local authorities;
- abuse or non-use of discretion with respect to the Secretary's regulation and order, and in particular whether the regulation and order are *Wednesbury* unreasonable;
- the possible breach of Convention rights by the regulation and the order and the relevant powers of the court under the Human Rights Act 1998;
- the legality and proportionality of the regulation and order with respect to any breach of Convention rights;
- any possible breach of the rules of natural justice and the duty of consultation, including the effect of the Human Rights Act 1998 on such.

The relevant points

The making and passing of the regulation and the subsequent order give rise to a number of factual and legal problems, which students should identify in their plan before embarking upon the answer.

The regulation

- Does the regulation have to protect the public from serious public disorder *and* restore stability to the community?
- Does 'the public' mean the general public, or a section of the public? In other words, can the regulation be passed to deal with the situation in Bognor Regis or must it apply to the whole country?
- Can the Secretary give himself a power to deal with *an instance* of serious public disorder or does there have to be a general breakdown in public order?

- Does the regulation interfere with European Convention rights of free speech and peaceful assembly? And, if so, did the Act authorise such and is the regulation lawful and proportionate?

- Does the regulation effectively delegate public order powers to the police and the local authorities?

- Can the Secretary give himself a discretionary power to decide whether there has been an instance of serious public disorder?

- Does the fact that there was no consultation make the regulation invalid? In other words, does there have to be any consultation before the regulation is made?

The order

- Does the order attempt to protect the public from serious public disorder and to restore stability?

- Was it ever intended by the Act or the regulation that the Home Secretary would interfere with the Convention rights of expression and assembly?

- If so, does the order unlawfully or disproportionately interfere with those rights?

- Has the order delegated the public order powers to the police and the local authorities? In particular, how are the police and local authorities to decide whether to take action, and might this lead to bias?

- Was there any duty on the Secretary of State to hear representations from the groups that had their meetings cancelled?

A: sound answer

Below is a good and appropriate answer to the question, displaying relevant problem-solving skills and identifying the essential issues as outlined previously. **Note: this answer should not be used as a research tool for your assessments in this legal area; in particular there may be more recent cases that could be used to answer the question.**

Introduction

The regulation and the order can be challenged via the process of judicial review, regulated by the Supreme Court Act 1981 and the Civil Procedure Rules (CPR) 1998. Under that procedure Amnesty International would need to apply for permission to apply for review within three months of the decision[1] and must show that they have sufficient interest in the matter.[2] The court would also need to be satisfied that this was a public law matter brought against a public body[3] and that if the applicants are to raise Convention rights under the Human Rights Act 1998, they are victims or potential victims of any violation.[4] The applicants in our case have a direct interest in the regulation and the order, and the Home Secretary is clearly a public body, acting under a public law power under the 2015 Act. However, the court would need to consider whether the group has been affected by the regulation and order (or whether they are victims for the purpose of s. 7 of the Human Rights Act 1998) *before* the local authority or police have made any decision with respect to their particular rally. Given the fact that the regulation and order have a real and potential effect on the rally, and that it might be unjust for the group to have to wait for the rally to be affected, the court should consider the challenge to the regulation and order's validity at this stage.[5]

The task of the courts in the present case is to see whether the Home Secretary's regulation and order are *intra* or *ultra vires* the powers given to him via the 2015 Act and the traditional grounds for judicial review have been classified as illegality, irrationality and procedural impropriety.[6] However, as the applicant's Convention rights might be at issue in this case, we will also need to consider any claim for breach of Convention rights as well as any claim that the regulation and order is disproportionate.[7]

The Secretary's regulation

We must firstly examine the regulation to see whether it is *intra vires* the powers under the parent Act. Section 1 of the Act allows the secretary to pass regulations for the purpose of protecting the public from serious public disorder and restoring stability to the community. It would need to be established, therefore, that the regulation was passed for, and was capable of achieving, that statutory purpose, as all discretion needs to be exercised within the scope of the statutory provision.[8] One initial question is whether any regulation must seek to achieve *both* the protection of the public from serious disorder *and* the restoration of stability to the community, or whether it is sufficient that it is passed for one of those purposes. The secretary's regulation does not mention the latter purpose and might be challenged on that basis, although it could be argued that any measure intended to protect the public from serious disorder will, by its very nature, restore stability to the community, and that the Minister's regulation appears to achieve both purposes.

Further, the regulation appears to have been passed in response to trouble in one particular location (Bognor Regis), and the resultant order applies to that area only. The parent Act talks of protecting *the public* and it could be argued that any regulations and orders should apply nationally and not locally. It is possible, therefore, that the Minister did not have the jurisdiction to make the regulation in this case.[9] As the Act talks of restoring stability *to the community* it appears to envisage the Secretary dealing with local issues. However, it is doubtful that the Secretary has the power to initiate his powers, which he intends to use nationally, on the basis of disorder which has occurred in one locality only. This could make the regulation *ultra vires* on this ground. Further, Amnesty International could argue that a regulation inspired by a serious disturbance at a specific meeting, and which then provides the basis of interference with all meetings, is *ultra vires* and that Parliament did not intend such a wide power to be given on such flimsy evidence. Specifically, it could be argued that the Home Secretary has acted irrationally by passing the regulation and that no reasonable Home Secretary would have made such a wide-ranging regulation on the basis of such evidence.[10]

Turning to the wording of the actual regulation, it could be argued that the Secretary has acted *ultra vires* in a number of other respects. First, the regulation appears to give him a wide discretion to make orders *if he is of the opinion* that there has been sufficient evidence of public disorder. This is acceptable provided that discretion is exercised for the correct lawful purpose and used rationally and proportionately (see below). Further, such discretion will have been countenanced by Parliament when the laying procedure under s. 3 was carried out, and although Parliamentary approval is not determinative of the regulation's legality, the regulation should not be declared invalid on the ground that it allows the Secretary some discretion.

There is also the possibility that the Secretary of State has abused his discretion under the parent Act by wrongfully delegating his powers and discretion to bodies that have not been authorised by the Act. Under the principle of *delegatus non potest delegare* a person charged with statutory powers must not unlawfully delegate those powers to another body, and consequently an act carried out by that body will be *ultra vires*.[11] Further, if it can be shown that the Secretary has abused, or failed to exercise, his discretion by passing on his statutory power and duty to the local authorities and the police, then it could be claimed that the regulation was unlawful for that purpose.[12] In the present case it was obviously not the intention of Parliament that the Secretary deals with public disorder on his own, and any Secretary would need to employ the assistance of bodies such as the local authorities and local police to ensure that his policies were carried out lawfully and effectively. Government ministers may certainly devolve powers to officials within their own department,[13] provided such a power is exercised rationally,[14] and equally the courts would expect that the Secretary would use other bodies to effect his actions and policies. In the present case the regulation makes it clear that the actions of the police and the local authority are subject to what the Secretary regards as necessary to deal with the situation. Such delegation does not, therefore, authorise the transfer of policy-making and appears *intra vires*.[15]

The Secretary's order

For the Secretary of State's order to be valid it must be *intra vires* both the parent Act and the regulation passed under that Act, assuming that the regulation is valid. In our case, it could be argued that the order, like the regulation, was not passed in order to restore stability to the community, but simply to protect the public from serious public disorder and the success of this claim will depend on the success of the similar claim with respect to the regulation (above).

In addition, the order appears to impact on the enjoyment of Convention rights, thus bringing into play the Human Rights Act 1998.

Under that Act it is unlawful for a public authority to act in breach of Convention rights,[16] and in our case the order affects the applicant's rights under Articles 10 and 11 of the European Convention (respectively, the rights to freedom of expression and peaceful assembly). In such a case the courts have a duty under s. 3 of the 1998 Act to interpret any primary and secondary legislation in line with the Convention, if that is at all possible.[17] This does not give the courts the power to ignore the clear wording of the Act or the regulation,[18] but the Act, the regulation and the order can be interpreted with the assumption that Parliament did not intend to give the Secretary a power to violate Convention rights when acting under the Act.[18A] In particular, the court could ensure that any interference with the applicant's Convention rights of speech and peaceful assembly are prescribed by law and necessary in a democratic society for the purpose of achieving a legitimate aim,[19] which in our case would be to achieve public safety and the prevention of disorder and crime.[20] Although the order, and the regulation, was passed for the legitimate aim of protecting public safety, it could be argued that the order is so wide and discretionary that it provides an unfettered and unclear power to interfere with Convention rights. Further, because such a power was given on the basis of isolated trouble in one locality, it could be argued that the measure is disproportionate to the aim which the Secretary hoped to achieve.[21]

That claim is supported by the argument that the Secretary's order unlawfully and unreasonably bestows on the local authority and the police a power to prohibit and disperse meeting which *in their opinion* may lead to serious public disorder. This raises the question whether he has unlawfully delegated his discretionary powers to those bodies instead of exercising such discretion himself. As stated above, he would be allowed to employ the services of the local authority and the police to assist him in carrying out *his* policy and discretion. However, it would be unlawful for him to divest himself of his statutory powers and duties and allow such bodies to make decisions on which meetings to disperse. This would appear to be contrary to the main aim of the parent Act and the regulation passed under that Act, which states that he may order these bodies to take such action as *he* thinks necessary. For example, in *Vine* v *National Dock Labour Board* (above) it was held that the Board could delegate powers to a committee to gather

$\rightarrow$

evidence for subsequent dismissal proceedings, but could not allow the committee to make the actual decision. In addition, by allowing these bodies to make such decisions, the Secretary appears to be creating an arbitrary power to interfere with people's Convention rights, which would be relevant to the legality and proportionality of that order with respect to any claim under the Human Rights Act 1998.

Finally, the order may be challenged because the Secretary failed to hear representations from groups that had been affected by it. Section 3 of the 2008 Act states that the Secretary must consult with such persons as *he considers appropriate* before acting on any regulation, and although this provides him with a reasonably wide discretion to choose who he is to consult, such discretion must be exercised reasonably and within the purpose of the parent Act. Thus, in *Agricultural, Horticultural and Forestry Industry Training Board* v *Aylesbury Mushrooms*[22] it was held that the Minister had acted unlawfully in not consulting with the Mushroom Growers Association, which, in the court's view, was a group that was 'representative of a substantial number of persons employed in the industry' as defined in the parent Act. The argument for consulting with potentially affected parties may be strengthened given that the order might impact on the applicant's Convention rights, and in such a case consultation with the police and local authority might be regarded as insufficient. Although consultation with such groups might be impracticable it could be argued that the Secretary should have provided for consultation between the police and any affected group. Further, the group may claim that the Minister has acted unlawfully in not consulting anyone before laying the regulation before Parliament. However, as the parent Act does not prescribe any consultation process before laying the regulation before Parliament, and specifically prescribes a process before acting on the order, it may be difficult to imply a duty of consultation before the regulation comes into force.[23]

Conclusion

Although the Secretary appears to have the general power to pass regulations of this nature, his regulation and his order may be challenged on the grounds that it allows the Secretary to act where there has been a single instance of serious public disorder. Equally, the order could be said to unduly interfere with the Convention rights to free speech and assembly, wrongfully delegates too much discretion to the local authorities and the police with respect to policy judgments best decided by the Secretary himself, and fails to provide the applicants with a reasonable opportunity to make representations before the order affects them. Accordingly the court is likely to invalidate both the regulation and the order and the group should seek a quashing order (certiorari) to that effect.

---

[1]Section 31 Supreme Court Act 1981 and CPR 54.5.

[2]Section 31(3) Supreme Court Act 1981; see also *R v IRC, ex parte National Federation of Self-Employed and Small Businesses* [1982] AC 617.

[3]*O'Reilly v Mackman* [1983] 2 AC 286.

[4]Section 7 of the Human Rights Act 1998.

[5]It has been held that a statutory instrument that was allegedly in violation of the European Communities Act 1972 could be challenged before it came into operation: *R v HM Treasury, ex parte* Smedley [1985] 1 All ER 589.

[6]*Council of Civil Service Unions v Minister for the Civil Service* [1985] AC 374. Illegality is defined as the misinterpretation or misapplication of the legal power, irrationality refers to *Wednesbury* unreasonableness (see below) and procedural impropriety is either a breach of a statutory procedure or a breach of the rules of natural justice.

[7]Under s. 7(3) of the Human Rights Act 1998 the provisions of the Act apply to judicial review proceedings provided the applicant is a victim for the purpose of s. 7 of the Act.

[8]*Padfield v Ministry of Agriculture, Fisheries and Food* [1968] AC 997.

[9]*Anisminic v Foreign Compensation Commission* [1969] 2 AC 147.

[10]Associated *Provincial Picture House Ltd v Wednesbury Corporation* [1948] 1 KB 223.

[11]*Vine v National Dock Labour Board* [1957] AC 488.

[12]*Lavender v Minister of Housing* [1970] 3 All ER 871.

[13]*Carltona v Commissioner of Works* [1943] 2 All ER 560.

[14]*R v Home Secretary, ex parte Oladenhinde* [1991] 1 AC 254.

[15]See *Barnard v National Dock Labour Board.*

[16]Section 6 Human Rights Act 1998.

[17]*R v A* [2002] 1 AC 45.

[18]*Re S and W* [2002] 2 WLR 720.

[18A]*R v Home Secretary, ex parte Simms* [2000] 2 AC 115.

[19]*R v Home Secretary, ex parte Farrakhan* [2002] 3 WLR 481.

[20]See Articles 10(2) and 11(2) of the European Convention on Human Rights.

[21]See *R v Home Secretary, ex parte Daly* [2001] 2 AC 532, where Lord Steyn held that any interference had to meet a specific and pressing social need and had to be proportionate to the legitimate aim being pursued.

[22][1972] 1 All ER 280.

[23]*Bates v Lord Hailsham* [1972] 1 All ER 280.

What was good about this answer?

- The student concentrates on the facts in the scenario and builds the answer around those facts.
- Explanation and discussion of general principles are kept to a minimum and are linked to the actual issues arising from the facts.
- The student does not get bogged down in the general law or get too involved in the theoretical and constitutional issues surrounding judicial review.
- The introduction highlights the central issues and contains just enough information on the general legal principles.
- The student examines the wording of the imaginary Act, regulation and order very carefully and displays very good interpretation skills.
- The student displays a good knowledge and appreciation of the principles of judicial review and uses relevant case and other authority where necessary.
- The student deals with each legal issue in order and explains the relevant law and its application in a clear and structured manner.
- The answer uses useful sub-headings and considers the legality of the regulation and the order in turn.
- The answer considers a range of possible interpretations and conclusions before settling on the most likely result.
- The conclusion is clear and incisive.

What is it worth?

The marker might make the following comments.

Marker's feedback

This is a very good effort to address all the issues raised by the scenario. The structure is excellent and you deal with each aspect in a logical and constructive manner. You show a very good understanding of the relevant principles and have made a very good attempt to apply those principles to the facts. Very sound interpretative skills displayed, although some of your suggestions are a little far-fetched. Discarding some possible interpretations might have allowed you more time to consider the substantive law in more detail.

Overall, a very good, clear and interesting answer – **72%**

B: poor answer

The following answer is provided as an example of poor problem-solving skills. Try to spot where the student is going wrong and what errors he is making. Then read the commentary and points at the end of the essay.

The purpose of judicial review is to ensure that public authorities who are invested with statutory powers by Parliament carry out those powers lawfully, reasonably and fairly. Thus, the courts have an inherent jurisdiction to ensure that public bodies and inferior courts and tribunals keep within their jurisdiction.[1] This ensures that the rule of law is upheld because public authorities will need to show that they have acted within the law and the courts will be able to invalidate their actions if they have acted beyond their powers.[2] The grounds of judicial review were summarised by Lord Diplock in the famous GCHQ case,[3] where it was stated that administrative action could be challenged on grounds of illegality, irrationality or procedural impropriety.

Illegality, according to Lord Diplock, consisted of the wrongful interpretation and application of legal powers and would thus cover the situation where the public authority acts in breach of their jurisdiction,[4] takes into account an irrelevant factor (or fails to take into account a relevant one),[5] or where that body acts for an improper purpose or otherwise abuses its powers.[6] On the other hand, irrationality would cover the situation where the person has acted within his or her legal powers but has nevertheless come to a decision which defies all logic, or where it could be said that the decision-maker has taken leave of his political senses. This ground of review is more commonly referred to as *Wednesbury* unreasonableness.[7] Finally, Lord Diplock referred to 'procedural impropriety', which covers either the breach of a procedural requirement laid down in the parent Act itself, or otherwise involves a breach of the rules of natural justice. Lord Diplock also left open the possibility of the development of the ground of proportionality, which is used by both the European Court of Human Rights and the European Court of Justice in determining whether individual rights have been infringed under both the European Convention on Human Rights and EU law. This ground of review was rejected by the House of Lords in *ex parte Brind*[8] because it might involve the courts in determining the merits of the administrative decision, but the Human Rights Act 1998 now allows the domestic courts to use the doctrine of proportionality and this will subject executive decision-making to a more rigorous challenge.[9]

However, although delegated powers are subject to judicial review, the domestic courts have made it clear that judicial review is concerned with the decision-making process rather than the decision itself.[10] Accordingly, the courts are not allowed to review the merits of the decision itself, but must concern themselves with the process by which that decision was made. In other words, judicial review is concerned with the decision-making process rather than the decision itself, ensuring that the courts keep to their traditional constitutional role of declaring and applying the law, and in this way the courts will respect both the separation of powers (by showing respect to the judgment of the public authority) and the sovereignty of Parliament.[11] Thus, the courts have traditionally held that the doctrine of proportionality cannot be applied in domestic judicial review proceedings (*ex parte Brind*, above) for that would allow the courts to substitute their view for that of the original decision-maker.[12] In this case, therefore, the courts will not be able to strike down the Secretary's regulation or order simply because they do not regard it as effective or wise, for that would be encroaching on the role of the executive and would involve a merits-based review.

For a person to be able to begin judicial review proceedings, they must seek leave for permission from the High Court under the Civil Procedure Rules 1998. This will involve a two-stage process (permission to apply for leave and the actual hearing itself) and to be eligible under the Rules the applicant needs to have sufficient interest in the matter to which the application relates.[13] It has been held that representative groups can have sufficient interest if they are representing the genuine interests of their members,[14] and thus in our case Amnesty International would have sufficient interest to bring an application with respect to the cancelling of their proposed rally. If the person succeeds in their action the courts can award a number of remedies including a quashing order (formerly known as Certiorari), a mandatory order (Mandamus), or a prohibition order (Prohibition). In addition, they can award civil remedies such as a declaration, an injunction and, in appropriate cases, damages. It must be noted, however, that the private law remedies can only be awarded in judicial review proceedings if the dispute relates to public law.[15]

As stated above, an administrative act may be quashed if it is *ultra vires* the parent Act. Thus, the court must interpret the relevant primary legislation to see whether the public body has acted within its powers. For example, in *Attorney General v Fulham Corporation*[16] it was held that the power to set up baths and washhouses under the Baths and Washhouses Acts 1846–1878 did not give the local authority the power to set up a laundry service. This case illustrates that the courts will interpret statues in the light of constitutional principles to ensure that the public body in question uses its powers both lawfully and reasonably and in the public interest. In addition, the courts will assume that Parliament did not intend to approve of any act which offends certain constitutional principles, such as the denial of access to the courts,[17] or the raising of taxes by bodies other than Parliament.[18] However, local authorities have got a power under s. 111 of the Local Government Act 1972 to do such things which are incidental to their statutory powers.[19]

Turning to the present application, it is clear that the Home Secretary does have the power to make regulations for the protection of the public from serious public disorder. Thus, under s. 2 of the Act the Secretary of State may pass such regulations as he thinks fit for the purpose of protecting the public from serious public disorder and for restoring stability to the community. It is also clear that he passed the regulation in this case for that purpose, because he passed it following a serious disturbance at a Gay Rights meeting in Bognor Regis. Thus, the regulation is clearly *intra vires* the Public Order Act 2015. The regulation would also appear to be reasonable. In the case of *Associated Provincial Picture House Ltd v Wednesbury Corporation* (above) Lord Greene held that a decision could be challenged if it was so unreasonable that no reasonable person would have arrived at that decision. In this case a reasonable Home Secretary would have reacted to the trouble in Bognor Regis by passing

→

the regulation, which is not excessive and attempts to deal with serious public disorder in the locality. Further, in this case the Home Secretary has sought the assistance of the police and the local authorities in helping him carry out those powers. This appears very reasonable and prudent and will ensure that each situation is dealt with according to the circumstances that prevail in each community.

However, from the facts it is clear that he has not consulted with anyone before issuing the order under the regulation, even though he did consult with the police and the local authorities. One of the grounds of judicial review identified by Lord Diplock in the GCHQ case was procedural impropriety, which includes the duty to abide by the rules of natural justice. One principle of natural justice is *audi alterem partem* – that a person is entitled to a fair hearing and has the right to be heard before any decision is made against him. Thus, in *Ridge* v *Baldwin*[20] it was held that a person had the right to know the charge made against him and should be provided with an opportunity to refute that charge. In that case, therefore, it was held that a police officer who had been dismissed from the police force without being given an opportunity to attend a hearing could challenge that decision, and it was held that the decision was void for want of natural justice. The decision in *Ridge* was important because it applied the rules of natural justice to all decisions which affected the rights of others, whether that decision was judicial, quasi-judicial or purely administrative.

In our case, Amnesty International had not been given the opportunity to make any representations to the Secretary before he made the order. In the case of *Agricultural, Horticultural and Forestry Industry Training Board* v *Aylesbury Mushrooms*[21] it was held that the applicants should have been consulted before the Minister made a regulation which directly affected them, and that it was not sufficient that the Minister consulted generally with the National Farmers Union. In the present case, therefore, Amnesty International is affected by the order and should have been consulted, either before the regulation was made or at the very least before the order was issued. In addition, the Secretary may have offended the second rule of natural justice – *nemo judex in causa sua* – which provides protection against bias or the appearance of bias. In this case, therefore, the Secretary has passed his regulation after a disturbance at a Gay Rights meeting. Thus, the Secretary may be biased against gay people and have passed the regulation as a consequence of that prejudice.[22]

It could also be argued that the Home Secretary has violated Amnesty International's human rights. Under Article 10 of the European Convention on Human Rights, everyone has the right to freedom of expression, including the right to receive and impart information and ideas without frontiers. This right was described by the European Court in *Handyside* v *United Kingdom*[23] as one of the essential foundations of a democratic society, applying also to views which might shock and offend the reader. However, according to Article 10(2) of the Convention, this right is conditional and carries with it duties and responsibilities. Accordingly, freedom of expression can be violated provided the restriction is prescribed by law and necessary in a democratic society for achieving some legitimate aim. In this case the right to hold a demonstration is not an absolute right and can be restricted if the Home Secretary does so for the purpose of protecting the public from serious public disorder. In our case the Home Secretary had very good reasons for doing what he did and thus there does not appear to be any ground for suggesting that he has breached their Convention rights, either under Article 10, or under Article 11 which guarantees the right to peaceful assembly.

In conclusion, the Home Secretary appears to have acted lawfully, rationally and proportionately in making the regulation and ordering the local authority to interfere with Amnesty International's proposed rally. The regulation was made to protect the public from serious public disorder, and it does not appear that he has used his powers for an improper purpose or taken into consideration any irrelevant factors. The regulation is one which a reasonable Home Secretary would have made in the circumstances and constitutes a proportionate interference with the group's right to hold their meeting. However, there appears to be a breach of the rules of natural justice and Amnesty International may have been denied the right to a fair hearing under Article 6 of the European Convention on Human Rights. This is because the Secretary of State did not consult

→

with it before passing the regulation or telling the local authority and police to ban its meeting.

---

[1]See Keith Ewing and Anthony Bradley, *Constitutional and Administrative Law* (13th edition Longman, 2008), at page 695.
[2]See, for example, *Entick* v *Carrington*, where the courts held that the Secretary of State was not beyond the law.
[3]*Council of Civil Service Unions* v *Minister for the Civil Service* [1985] AC 374.
[4]*Anisminic* v *Foreign Compensation Commission* [1969] 2 AC 147.
[5]*R* v *Home Secretary, ex parte Venables and Thompson* [1998] AC 407.
[6]*Congreve* v *Home Office* [1976] 2 QB 629.
[7]From the decision in *Associated Provincial Picture House Ltd* v *Wednesbury Corporation* [1948] 1 KB 223.
[8]*R* v *Home Secretary, ex parte Brind* [1991] AC 696.
[9]*R* v *Home Secretary, ex parte Daly* [2001] 2 AC 532.
[10]See Lord Brightman in *Chief Constable of North Wales* v *Evans* [1982] 1 WLR 1155.
[11]See Paul Craig, *Administrative Law* (Sweet & Maxwell, 2003), 5th edition, at page 24.
[12]That ground of review is relevant when Convention rights are at issues under the Human Rights Act 1998.
[13]See s. 31(3) Supreme Court Act 1981 and *R* v *IRC, ex parte National Federation of Self-Employed and Small Businesses* [1982] AC 617.
[14]See *R* v *Inspector of Pollution, ex parte Greenpeace (No2)* [1992] 4 All ER 329.
[15]See *O'Reilly* v *Mackman* [1983] 2 AC 286.
[16][1921] 1 Ch 440.
[17]*Raymond* v *Honey* [1983] AC 1.
[18]*A-G* v *Wilts United Dairies* (1931) 37 TLR.
[19]*Attorney-General* v *Crayford UDC* [1962] 2 All ER 147.
[20][1964] AC 40.
[21][1972] 1 All ER 280.
[22]See *R* v *Sussex Justices, ex parte McCarthy* [1924] 1 KB 256.
[23](1976) 1 EHRR 737.

What is wrong with this answer?

- The opening paragraphs contain some fair general points on judicial review, but do not mention the actual facts of the question or the legal issues arising from those facts. Any introduction to the subject area needs to focus much more on the question and identify the specific problems evident from the facts. This can then be combined with some of the general information contained in these paragraphs.

- The student spends a lot of time explaining the purpose of judicial review and the constitutional role of the courts and then provides some history of the ground of proportionality, only to say that it is now an accepted ground of review.

- Paragraph 3 repeats some points already mentioned in paragraph 2 and does not take the reader much further.

- The general information relating to procedure and standing is relevant but could have been mentioned very briefly at the outset. The author has mis-understood the rule about representative actions; *Greenpeace* is not relevant, as our group is directly affected. Also, the student has missed the point about whether the groups can bring proceedings before the regulation actually affects their rally.

- The information on remedies will only be important *if* the applicants are successful and thus should be given only at the end of the advice. The comment about exclusivity at the end of paragraph 4 is unnecessary as the issue in this case is clearly a public law one.

- The student uses the *Fulham Corporation* case but does not explain why that case was decided in that way; then providing a list of possible general grounds of challenge without applying them to the facts or indeed explaining whether they are relevant to this case.

- When the student addresses the facts and the issues, the conclusions are inflexible and not supported by a proper examination of the words of the statute or the relevant principles. Importantly, it fails to consider the possible interpretations of the Home Secretary's powers and their use (see the good answer in the preceding section). Accordingly, his advice is very vague and subjective, and there is little reasoning to his conclusions; he fails to consider all possibilities and gives a rigid and unconvincing answer.

- The student identifies the relevant issue of consultation, but spends too much time discussing procedural impropriety in general, instead of concentrating on the statutory duty to consult.

- The student raises the relevant and important case of *Aylesbury* but does not examine the wording of the legislative provision in that case so as to explain the rationale of the decision. Neither does it examine the wording of the 2015 Act so as to consider who should be consulted, and when. Instead the author makes a bald assertion that the group should have been consulted, and ignores the fact that the police and the local authority have been consulted.

- The student makes a confusing observation about possible bias, which is not supported on the facts and which does not affect the validity of Amnesty International's claim.

- The student raises Article 10 of the European Convention, but includes too much general information about the theory and status of freedom of expression and then concludes that the Home Secretary was justified in passing and acting on the regulation without considering the necessity and proportionality of his actions.

- There is no consideration of whether the Home Secretary has wrongfully delegated his powers to the police or the local authority.

- The conclusion summarises his findings quite succinctly, but again those findings are not based on any real analysis of the facts and the principles of judicial review, but rather are a product of the student's own opinion and refusal to examine viable alternatives.

- The student introduces Article 6 of the European Convention into his conclusion without discussing it in the main body of his answer, and fails to realise that the Article is probably not relevant as there is no 'criminal charge' or 'determination of civil rights' in this case.

Overall, the student found it difficult to engage with the question and was unable to identify the real legal arguments or to resolve them by applying the relevant legal principles or cases. The student has a reasonable knowledge of the general principles but has not really appreciated the principles of judicial review or the legal problems raised by the question. The answer is reasonably well written and the structure is fair. There is also evidence of some research. However, most of the content is not particularly relevant and the student has thus wasted a great deal of effort by not addressing the issues.

What is it worth?

The answer might receive the following comments.

Marker's feedback

You do include some useful general information and, occasionally, address the question. However, you spend too long on general issues that have little or no bearing on the outcome of this particular dispute and fail to address the specific legal problems raised by the scenario. Your appreciation of the law is rather limited, and you make a number of errors based on a partial understanding of some legal principles such as irrationality, proportionality and the right to a fair trial. You also fail to show a real appreciation of the cases and how and why they were decided in that way. You fail to consider whether the Home Secretary has wrongfully delegated his powers to the police and the local authority. You need to display the necessary interpretation and analytical skills to spot the possible meaning of the statutory provision and to consider the range of possible answers. Your conclusions are unsupported by the facts and are not reasoned. Instead you make bald and often unjustified assertions. Overall, although you have identified some of the general issues, your answer fails to show an appreciation of the question and its various aspects – **45%**

NOTE

In answer B the student has undertaken very similar research to that used in the good answer (answer A). In fact, he has cited even more law, but has received a substantially lower mark because of the inability to use legal sources and employ interpretation and application skills.

TIPS FOR PROBLEM-SOLVING QUESTIONS

- Always ensure that you can identify the relevant area of law and the specific legal and factual problems that are raised by the scenario.

- Go back to your previous study in the area to ensure that you are confident with the law and the cases. If the area has not been studied before, ensure that you learn it thoroughly before planning your answer.

- Make a plan of your answer, illustrating how you are going to identify and address the issues, and placing them in the order in which you are going to address them.

- Begin your answer by briefly outlining the relevant legal issues and explaining the significance of the outcome of any claim.

- Do not get drawn into long and detailed accounts of the law or the cases.

- Keep your account of the law and the cases as succinct as possible, concentrating on their application to the facts.

- Write in a clear and structured way, dealing with each issue in turn, applying the law and cases clearly and correctly.

- Read the facts of the question or the wording of any imaginary provision very carefully and consider a number of possible interpretations.

- Do not just explain the law and then state that 'X will win his action if the above law applies.'

- Always keep relating the law to the facts and never lose sight of the main task – to advise the parties.

- Always explain the reasoning behind any findings or conclusions, including whether the advice is conditional on things such as the uncertain state of the law or the lack of factual evidence.

- Always consider every possibility or possible interpretation of the law and the facts.

- Conclude by giving a brief overall summary of your findings, along with any relevant reasoning.

- Consider all possible and reasonable answers before coming to a firm, or the most likely, conclusion.

3

Researching and writing legal essays: specific legal skills

This part of the text provides detailed guidance with respect to the researching and referencing of law assessments. It explains those skills and teaches the student how to employ them.

- Chapter 6 provides advice on researching law assignments, including where to locate necessary materials and which materials to use for specific questions, depending on the nature of the question and the level of study. It illustrates the use of legal materials, both primary and secondary, in the presentation of law assessments, including specific guidance on the use of cases and statutory provisions and of books, journals and other secondary sources.

- Chapter 7 explores the rules relating to legal referencing and citation of authority, including how to cite cases, statutes, books, journals and other sources. (Please note that if the name Foster is used, the case, article or book is fictitious and is being used to illustrate general citation and referencing skills.)

6

- - - - - - - - - - - - - -

Researching and using legal materials

RESEARCHING FOR ASSESSMENTS

Although this chapter is primarily concerned with *using* legal materials in law assessments, some space will also be dedicated to the process of researching and locating the sources that you will use in your assessment, including how to make the best of the library and other sites, and how to conduct effective research.

This advice is used in Chapter 9 on writing extended essays and dissertations, but at this stage the text will provide some general tips on researching for your assessments, followed by some advice on the process of locating those sources.

WHAT SOURCES?

TIPS FOR USING SOURCES IN YOUR ASSESSMENT

- Assessments at undergraduate level cannot be answered simply by relying on your notes and the standard textbook: you will need to go beyond them to get the sort of information required to complete, and do well in your assessments.

- You will need to make use of other sources, such as cases, statutory materials (including EU law), other texts and academic journals (to get different views or more specialist information), and, occasionally on the first stages of your course, Government reports and comparative materials.

- Begin your research with your standard text and your notes (provided they are full); this will allow you to appreciate the basic legal rules and their impact on the law and your question.

- A good text or cases and materials book will provide you with references to further reading, which you can then explore as part of your research.

- Then move on to advanced sources – articles, specialist texts, additional cases and so on. Do *not* 'jump in at the deep end' by starting your research here.

EXAMPLE QUESTION

Critically assess the impact of the Human Rights Act 1998 on the British constitution. (1,500 words)

This, question, to be found on a constitutional course in year one, will require research beyond your standard legal system and constitutional and administrative law texts (although at stage one those texts will provide a substantial part of the information).

- Begin with the relevant chapters in your set text and perhaps read similar chapters in one or two other main texts to see what views and ideas those authors have on the topic. This will identify the central issues: why the Act was passed and how it changed the law; its central provisions and leading cases, and, more specifically, the basic constitutional concerns and dilemmas that the Act has impacted on.

- Access and read the central provisions of the Act to ensure that they are consistent with your knowledge of the Act and the book's coverage.

- Now consult chapters in more specialist texts – on the Human Rights Act 1998 or constitutional reform; these will identify and discuss the specific constitutional issues surrounding the Act and its operation (and possible repeal). The standard text will have identified the general constitutional issues, but these texts will be dedicated to identifying specific concerns and discussing them in detail.

- Locate and use a number of journal articles (say two) dealing with these controversial constitutional issues, allowing you to address the question: to 'critically analyse'.

NOTE

You are now beginning to distinguish your research and your essay from the bulk of other students, who may simply be repeating basic points made in the text – '. . . the Act has raised a number of constitutional issues affecting parliamentary sovereignty and the separation of powers.'

- Access and read any necessary primary sources which are going to provide you with a *fuller* understanding of the essay title and the issues – judgments of leading cases decided under the Act; provisions of the European Convention on Human Rights (together with any relevant case law); government and other papers on reform. These primary sources can be accessed earlier in your research provided you are sufficiently confident about the basics; it is often a matter of instinct – ask yourself: *Do I need to look at the wording of the Act, or a specific judgment, to get a proper understanding and before I move on to my next source?*

LOCATING YOUR SOURCES

Your skills text (and specialist texts) will provide detailed guidance on how to use a law library and other resource sites and how best to conduct your research; you will also be given research exercises as part of your induction or skills course – they may not appear important at the time, but when you are required to research for your assessments it will be those students who have taken the exercise seriously that will be in the better position to get higher marks.

This part of the text will identify some basic search strategies and provide some tips on how best to find what you are looking for.

- Do not use general search engines to conduct serious legal research: by all means use Google to find reliable sites, and to make you aware of recent events, but your legal research must be conducted on acceptable and accepted sites.

- Ensure you know how to use sites such as LAWTEL, WESTLAW, LEXIS LIBRARY etc.; they will give you access to the type of sources that you will be expected, as a law student, to access and use – the type of source that your lecturer (and marker) uses.
- Avoid Wikipedia and other general sources – their citation and use will not create a good impression with your lecturers.
- Be aware of relevant and appropriate journals, blogs and other sites.

Let us look now at how we could research that question.

EXAMPLE QUESTION

Critically assess the impact of the Human Rights Act 1998 on the British constitution.

(1,500 words)

To answer this question you need to provide various relevant authorities. The question is basically about the Act and the British constitution, so you will obviously have to acquire knowledge of both.

You can see that you will need to (at the appropriate stage) access both secondary sources (books) about the constitution, and a primary source (the Act itself) before you attempt any critical analysis.

Then, to attempt the specific question, you will need to access and read cases decided under the Act (and indeed cases from the European Court of Human Rights), academic opinion on the passing, content, interpretation (and possible repeal) of the Act, and any government or other official documents which discuss the Act (and its possible repeal).

NOTE

- -

Always be mindful of the question whilst researching, and ensure you understand the question and its scope – otherwise your research will become random and you will waste valuable time researching and reading irrelevant material.

- -

Books

Read the relevant chapter of your set text to get a general overview of the Act and the British constitution, and use the search tool in your library to locate other general texts (use search terms such as 'constitutional law' or 'public law.' Consult your lecturer's general and further reading list.

Specialist books

Locate books on 'the Human Rights Act' and 'Human Rights and Constitutional law' through your library, as above. The reading lists of standard texts can also be useful in identifying these texts, as well as reading lists provided by staff.

Blogs

Search Google for 'law blogs' or blogs on 'human rights' or the 'Human Rights Act' – ensure they are from a sound source (universities or practitioners). Blogs can be very useful because they discuss recent and controversial issues and refer you to leading cases and other sources.

Journal articles

Use various search engines (LAWTEL etc.). Submit search terms such as 'Human Rights Act' or 'Human Rights Act and the constitution'. Read the abstract carefully to see whether the article is likely to be useful in answering the question. Ensure that the article is academically appropriate (of the right status and level). It also helps if you are familiar with the leading journals in that field, for then you can do a search of *Public Law* or *European Human Rights Law* to see what has been written in this area. Again, consult your lecturer's reading lists and recommended reading in textbooks.

Government and other papers

Visit relevant government and other sites (Parliament, Home Office, Ministry of Justice) and search for recent reports in the area. In addition, legal search engines (such as WESTLAW) will have current awareness items that you can select and input the relevant phrase into, which will then identify any recent reports or papers in that area.

Statutory materials

Rather like reports (see above) and cases (see below), it is getting rarer these days that students access hard copies of statutes and statutory instruments. Statutes, statutory instruments, EU legislation etc. can be accessed online and again legal search engines are invaluable. Inserting 'Human Rights Act' will provide you with the Act and any statutory instruments passed under the Act. These sources are also available on government sites (and indeed most non-legal sites). You can then read and run off any relevant provisions.

NOTE

Search engines such as WESTLAW have a facility which identifies whether the provision is in force or has been repealed.

Cases

Again, you can access cases on all the legal sites mentioned in this section instead of going to the library and leafing through hard copies of law reports (accessing them online has the advantage of allowing you access cases the day after the decision is made).

Your secondary sources will identify the leading cases in the area (especially at this level), so that you can then read the whole decision if need be. This is preferable to just searching for 'human rights' cases, because this will provide you with hundreds of cases with no way of determining their relevance to the question (it is different if you are researching something more specific, such as 'Human Rights Act and prisoners' rights').

For our example question, if you want to locate cases on the Act other than those in the text or journals, undertake a search on the 'cases' and recent developments/current awareness facility, but remember, you are looking for cases that raise constitutional issues so do not include new cases at random.

NOTE

Again, search engines such as WESTLAW have a facility which will identify whether the case has been overturned, or cited elsewhere; you can also locate articles and case notes about the case by scrolling down on the WESTLAW case analysis and looking under 'Journal Articles'.

USING LEGAL MATERIALS

As with the study of any academic subject, law students must give authority for their views and in their assessments. In particular, students must use a variety of legal sources, both **primary** and **secondary**, in presenting their work and any argument.

The use of these sources is governed by a number of rules, some of them specific to legal materials, and you must learn and apply these rules when submitting your assessments.

PROVIDING AUTHORITY

As with all academic subjects, you must provide authority for the things you say in their assignments. You cannot simply make a statement relating to the subject without providing the source of that statement and providing evidence that what you are saying is correct and established.

EXAMPLES

'Serious crime is on the increase these days.' Where is the evidence for that? Are the figures contained in an official document? Has someone undertaken research?

'It is unlawful for a person to commit an act of theft.' Is this the law? If so, which law, in which particular provision is this law located, and what does that provision actually say?

'There are a number of cases that show that the courts are prepared to uphold the sovereignty of Parliament.' Which cases support that proposition? Has an author assimilated those cases and analysed or criticised them?

For all these questions, some evidence exists to back up what you are saying. This will show that you have read the primary or secondary sources (see below) and are relying on those sources. It will also provide you with the opportunity to display your academic and legal skills in citing and referencing those sources (see below).

Never use lecture notes, or statements made by lecturers, as legal authority

Lecture notes are *not* authority for the law and they should not be referred to either in the main body of your work or in the bibliography. In other words, avoid 'See Lecture Notes on Offer and Acceptance' or, in your bibliography, 'Foster, Lecture Notes'. This might be acceptable on sub-degree courses but not on undergraduate courses.

So, too, lecturers are not authority unless they have published (a book or an article in an official journal or newspaper). In that case, by all means refer to their views (if relevant) and provide the reference.

If secondary sources have been distributed in class, give the proper reference for that source; do not put 'Article distributed in class'. If the source of the article is not clear, find it out.

You can, and should, however, listen to what the lecturer has to say on the law and keep those views in mind when researching your work and structuring your arguments. The lecturer will expect you to have picked up these points and to show that you have understood them. Always back those points up with proper authority.

Do not simply follow the pattern of, or copy out, lecture notes. This suggests you have not looked at proper secondary sources. You can, however, use the lecture notes for general guidance on how to approach a subject or order specific points.

NOTE

Although lecture notes are not an official source, you can be guilty of **plagiarism** (as well as poor scholarship) if you copy them in your work.

Do I always have to give authority?

As indicated in the following examples, you are not obliged to give authority for obvious statements, such as:

> 'The United Kingdom consists of Great Britain and Northern Ireland, but not the Republic of Ireland.'

Also, if you have been asked for, and are giving, your opinion you do not use authority, because it is *your* opinion. For example:

> 'It is suggested that it should not be an offence to blaspheme against established religious views because free speech should be more important than protecting religious sensibilities.'

If this is your observation then it does not need referencing. However, if your opinion is based on another source, such as a textbook or journal, you must credit that source.

EXAMPLE

'With respect to the protection of human rights, I am more convinced by the natural lawyers rather than utilitarian arguments, because the utilitarian view might lead to the suppression of minority rights.'

In this case, you need to show an awareness of those arguments and to refer to specific authors (secondary sources). If your opinion is one that is shared by an author, then you should indicate that.

You must also ensure that your opinion is consistent with the legal facts.

EXAMPLE

'It is submitted that judges should not be so reluctant to interfere with decisions made by the Home Secretary and should invalidate such decisions if they are inconsistent with human rights.'

This would be a valid point to make, provided the case law supports the statement. In this case, there are a number of cases in which the courts have interfered, and you need to refer to them.

The difference between primary and secondary sources

Many students get confused between primary and secondary sources, and this leads to further confusion with respect to the crediting and referencing of such sources.

A **primary source** is the original source of that law, where that law originates; without that source, the law would not exist. For example, an Act of Parliament, an EU Directive, a piece of delegated legislation, an international treaty and a case are all primary sources and must be treated and sourced as such.

EXAMPLE

If you say, '. . . it is offence to commit an act of theft,' you are referring to the law on theft, and there is a primary source for that law (Section 1 of the Theft Act 1968 (as amended)). Without that primary source, that law would not exist in England and Wales, and thus you must refer to that source. This is the case even if you read about that law in a textbook, a website or an article. Consequently, you cannot say, '. . . it is an offence to commit an act of theft' and then credit that statement by putting '(Steve Foster, *Criminal Law* (2nd edn, Longman 2015) 67.)'. You have referred to a secondary source (see the following example) and have indicated that this author is the primary source, which of course s/he is not: the law of theft would exist even if that book had not been written. Also, you are not guilty of plagiarism by failing to mention the book in such a case. The law does not belong to that author, and you simply must refer to the primary source; although you must refer to the book if you have taken the author's explanation or analysis of the primary source.

With cases, you must refer to the case itself, and not the book that you read the case in. You can then give the appropriate reference to that case – usually the official law report. Thus, avoid doing this:

EXAMPLE

'An advertisement can be construed as a contractual offer. (See Steve Foster, *Contract Law* (2nd edn OUP 2015)16).'

In such a case you must refer to the case itself and provide the reference (*Carlill* v *Carbolic Smoke Ball Company* [1893] 1 QB 256).

A **secondary source** is where an account of or a commentary of the law can be found. For example, a textbook, a journal article, a website and a conference paper are all secondary sources. They are not the original source of the legal rule, and if they did not exist the law would still be there (in its original source). Thus, do not refer to them as primary sources.

This rule also applies to information found on websites. If you access primary sources on websites (e.g. treaties, Acts of Parliament, cases), refer to the primary source (and its proper reference) and not the website.

EXAMPLE

Do not put: '*Smith* v *Hughes* (see www.casefind.com).'

You can, however, put a website in your bibliography to indicate that you have researched and accessed that source. It is permissible to refer the reader to a website to gain primary sources:

'The Human Rights Act 1998 can be downloaded by accessing www .statuteuk.co.uk.'

If you are using the website as a secondary source (for views or explanations of the law), refer to that website as your source.

Try not to use websites as a substitute for textbooks and articles. If you access these materials on the website, obviously refer to the book or the article, not the website.

Using secondary sources

You can use secondary sources to explain, criticise or summarise the law. An author will have read the primary source and is now explaining to the reader how that law originated, how it has been interpreted and applied, whether it is correct or just, whether it should be amended and so on.

- If you are making use of other people's academic efforts and views, you *must credit* them. This is the case even if you are not copying those views word for word.

- If you are copying word for word, use inverted commas and provide the reference.

- If you are taking the thrust of the author's work or view, make it clear that you are using another's views and credit that author.

EXAMPLE

'It has been suggested that the cases in this area lack principle and have thus caused uncertainty and injustice.'

By using the words **'it has been suggested'**, the student is obviously refer- ring to an established view on this aspect of the law. He or she must, therefore, credit that source '(**Steve Foster, 'The Human Rights Act and its application' (2004) 66 MLR 333, 346)**'. The student should also refer somewhere – either before or after the statement is made, or in a footnote – to the primary sources (the case law that is allegedly uncertain).

EXAMPLE

'The courts have consistently adopted a "hands-off" approach in this area and have refused to interfere in matters of national security.'

If this view is taken from an author, it should be credited as such, like this: **'Foster has noted that . . . '** then provide the reference or put the opinion in quotes and then provide the reference. Again, there should be some reference to the primary sources that are alluded to in the statement.

EXAMPLE

'The protection of public morality *per se* is not a reason for restricting free speech, despite such expression causing offence to the recipient. In such cases the law should only interfere where there is some evidence of an identifiable harm to society or its citizens.'

If this is a textbook author's subjective view, it must be credited as such; you cannot pass it off as your own. Thus, you must either put the words in inverted commas and then give the reference, or precede the statement by saying, **'Foster argues that . . . '** and then providing the reference. **Remember, you will be rewarded** for crediting this source because you are using appropriate authority and displaying your referencing skills.

You can then indicate whether you agree with that view (and submit your own opinion), or whether it is supported by primary or academic authority (providing that authority either in support or in opposition of the view).

EXAMPLE

'There are various examples of this trend to be found in the case law of a number of Commonwealth jurisdictions.'

The answer then can use a footnote to detail cases from various countries and to provide references to various academic opinions in articles and texts.

However, you must avoid simply copying the footnote from a text or article you have read. In this case you are relying on the author's own research and hard work to support your answer; unless you credit it, you will be passing this work off as your own – i.e. giving the impression that you have looked up and assimilated all these sources – and you will be guilty of **plagiarism**. In such a case, you must make it clear that this compilation is the work of another: **'Foster provides a number of cases from other jurisdictions which support this view'** [reference to the article or book].

Secondary sources within secondary sources

Some textbooks, articles, websites and so on refer to other secondary sources, either to support their arguments or to assist in the explanation of the law. This is particularly true of cases and materials books, where a book will provide a number of (secondary) sources.

You must refer to the original secondary source and not the text or article that referred to such a source.

EXAMPLE

'Dicey always maintained that there should be no separate public law and that the government should be bound by the ordinary private law (Steve Foster, *Constitutional Law* (3rd edn Longman 2015) 23).'

This reference is wrong; you should refer to the original source of Dicey's views:

'(A.V. Dicey, *Introduction to the Study of the Law of the Constitution*, 13th edn Macmillan 1885, at page 22).'

You should read the original source if possible or practicable. If the original secondary source is not available, then it is permissible to rely on the later source. In such a case indicate that you have not accessed the original source.

> EXAMPLE
>
> 'John Locke, *The Second Treatise of Government* (1689), as cited in Steve Foster, *Constitutional Law* (3rd edn Longman 2015, 32).'

Do I always have to credit secondary sources?

To be on the safe side, or because they are not sure about the rules on crediting, some students credit the author with everything they put in the assessment. This is not always necessary and gives the impression that they have no understanding of the subject beyond what they are taking from the textbook.

As mentioned previously, do not credit the author for primary sources, even if you learned about that source from the textbook or other secondary source.

- You can cite both the primary source and the author if you are not only saying what the law is, but what an author's views are of it (**'s.1 of the Theft Act 1968, as criticized by Steve Foster, *Criminal Law*, 2nd edn, Longman 2015, at page 6'**).

- You do not have to credit the author with the simple facts and decisions of cases (as opposed to the author's analysis of that case or his or her views on it). They do not belong to the author, and you can take the facts and decision from the textbook (or casebook, or, where appropriate, the law report). Very often, students get into difficulties by trying to give their own version of the facts and the decision – if you find a simple and appropriate account of the facts and the decision, you can use it. You should, however, practise explaining facts and decisions of cases in your own words, so that you can use them in examinations.

- Avoid using one author for all the statements you make – this will indicate that you have only read that source, or that you have no ideas of your own.

- You do not have to credit the author for trite law (obvious and accepted legal statements) such as **'the British Constitution is unwritten'** and **'England and Wales have a common law system'**.

- You do not need to credit an author if you make a general legal comment and use different words than those employed by the author. For example, if an author says, **'In all but exceptional cases, a contract is based on the agreement of the offeror and the offeree,'** you can say, **'In most cases a contract will be based on agreement between the parties.'**

Can I use the author's style of writing and format?

Generally, it is acceptable to employ the same sort of **style and format** adopted by an author; indeed, students will be encouraged to employ a similar style. However, it is important that you begin to develop your own style, based on the style you witness in textbooks etc.

Adopt the legal style used by authors and employ appropriate phrases such as these:

EXAMPLES

'The claimant brought an action for breach of contract.'

Not: 'The innocent party sued the other in court.'

'His Lordship referred to a number of authorities.'

Not: 'The judge looked at a lot of cases before making his decision.'

Adopt authors' methods of explaining legal principles, cases, statutory provisions and so on, including the order in which points are made and the structure of the explanation. Thus, if a number of authors deal with a legal issue (e.g. contract formation) in a particular manner (e.g. offer and acceptance, consideration, intention, capacity), it is acceptable for you to follow that order. If one author adopts an unusual approach, then you may credit that author for such.

EXAMPLE

'On the other hand, Foster believes that the following approach should be used in determining whether a contract exists (Steve Foster, *Contract Law*, 2nd edn, Longman 2015, at page 6).'

In particular, follow an author's *style* (not the exact words) in how he or she uses legal materials to explain and illustrate the law – how to cite and refer to a case or Act of Parliament, how to explain the significance of a case, how to introduce a case into the discussion and so on.

Do not use the style adopted in sub-degree texts – lists, bullet points, questions and so on. That style is inappropriate for undergraduate work.

USING CASES

Case law is central to answering many (though not all) legal questions – essays or problem based – and it is essential that you are comfortable with using this source. A large number of students struggle when using cases in their written work. They are not sure why the case must be used, how to use it, what the case is saying and so on. Because of this confusion, a student's answer is often made worse by the inclusion of case law.

- Learn how to use cases and become familiar with how they are written and structured.
- Read as many cases as possible and become familiar with law reports.
- Note how authors in good textbooks and articles use cases and acquire that style and those skills.
- Do not rely on lecture notes when providing an account of the case; read the law report, a casebook or, at the very least, a good account of a case in a textbook.

Reading cases

As seen above, you have to become familiar with cases and case reports if you are going to succeed in your law studies and your assessments. The following tips should be followed when reading cases.

TIPS FOR READING CASE LAW

- Always remember *why* you are looking at and reading a case. Generally, looking at and learning the case will assist you in understanding a particular area of law and allow you to apply the relevant legal principle.
- If you have covered the case or the legal area in lectures, refresh yourself of the basic legal rules so that the case makes sense from the start.
- Remind yourself what you want to take from this case, which is basically an account of the facts and the decision in that case and, *more importantly,* how that case impacts on and informs that area of law.
- Thus it is the *ratio* (the reasoning) of the case that is the most important element of the case as that element will help you apply the law to a particular set of facts. The facts and decision are important in helping you understand the

context of the case, and in identifying similar (or dissimilar) factual situations, but they are of secondary importance to the principle that the case stands for.

- Whether you access the case from a full law report or not, always ensure that the source provides you with sufficient detail: a clear account of the facts, the decision, the *ratio* and the impact of the case. Taking cases from revision aids or other insubstantial texts can often provide the reader with an incomplete and misleading account of the case.

- If you are accessing the case via an official law report, and you feel daunted by the size of that report, begin by reading the head note to the case (at the start of the report). This will allow you to get a basic grasp of the facts, decision and ratio; and it will refer you to specific aspects of the judgment which will enable you to fully appreciate the case – for example, the head note might state.

  'There is no common law rule which precludes the courts from enforcing unreasonably wide exclusion clauses (see Foster LJ, at paragraph 23).'

- The head note is thus providing an overall picture and pointing you to relevant extracts and this is often preferable to simply launching into the judgment and trying to read it from start to finish.

- Read the full judgment to get information beyond the head note and a textbook account of the case: to see how the decision was arrived at; to identify the legal arguments that have been raised by counsel; to see what previous cases have been considered by the judge(s) and how the case impacts on those cases and the general legal area.

- Take your time over reading the case. Allocate yourself sufficient time to read it thoroughly and make notes as you go along; if you have photocopied the case, highlight relevant and important sections of the case.

Building your own case notes

To assist you in learning cases, and in complementing your reading of law reports, it is often helpful to build your own case notes. Students often find it helpful to write down information about such cases – it assists them in remembering the necessary details – and this practice can also assist you during revision.

- Build up a list of important (and subsidiary) cases for each module.
- Divide the cases up into separate categories or headings, such as offer and acceptance, defences in negligence, crimes of strict liability.

- Cross-reference cases if they are relevant to more than one category:

Consideration – *Carlill* v *Carbolic Smoke Ball Co.* – see also offer and acceptance.

- Include enough information to allow you to identify the central facts and decision and, most importantly, the impact of that case on the relevant area of law and on your study of the subject:

Offer and acceptance – *Carlill* v *Carbolic Smoke Ball Co.*

A company placed an advert promising to pay £100 to any person who contracted influenza after using its product, depositing £1,000 in the bank as a mark of its sincerity. C claimed the reward and it was held that the advert was clearly worded and showed an intention on behalf of the company to be bound. C had accepted the offer by complying with the conditions and did not have to notify her acceptance of the offer formally.

The case is authority for the principle that an advertisement aimed at the public at large is capable of being construed as a contractual offer, which can then be accepted by those to whom it was directed, and is an exception to the general rule on advertisements and circulars (*Partridge/Spencer*). The advert forms the basis of a unilateral contract, whereby the person placing the advert agrees to be bound if the other party performs an act that has been specified in the advert. The case also lays down rules with respect to unilateral contracts and their acceptance.

See also Consideration and Intention to create legal relations, below.

- Do not simply put down the name of the case with bare information as to its category. This is simply building up largely unhelpful data for the sake of it:

Carlill v *Carbolic Smoke Ball Co.* – advert held to be an offer, not an invitation to treat, £100 reward granted.

- For cases which are simply further examples of the same point made by major cases, write a shorter account of the case and relate it to the main example:

Esso Petroleum v *Commissioner of Custom and Excise* – promotion involving collection of World Cup coins, available when purchasing petrol – held to be legally enforceable as a collateral contract – see *Carlill*, above.

A sound collection of personal case notes will allow you to learn the cases and their impact as you study the subject and will enable you to apply the case clearly in seminar questions and formal assessments. It will also be useful during revision.

Why use cases and when do I use them?

Cases can be used to provide legal authority or to explain and illustrate a legal principle or argument. Students should use cases to *enhance* their work, by displaying legal skills in respect to citation and referencing or by using cases to better explain particular rules or views. They are not to be used simply to show that you know a case; they should be relevant and fulfil some purpose in the presentation of your work.

Cases as simple authority

Cases can be used as simple authority for a legal proposition and can be cited as such.

> **EXAMPLE**
>
> 'Generally, for an acceptance to be valid, it must be communicated to the offeror.'
>
> There is case authority for that proposition *(Entores* v *Far Eastern Miles Corporation)* and you can use that case, along with its reference, to provide such authority. This follows the principle that you always provide authority for any statement made in assessments. In addition, you can also display your skills in citing and referring to cases properly.

To illustrate a legal principle

A case can be used to explain the law and to provide an illustration of how a legal principle is applied in practice. In this way, you are not merely providing authority but using the case to enhance your work and your explanation or analysis of the law.

EXAMPLE

'Case law is a major source of the British Constitution, and some cases have established fundamental constitutional principles, such as the rule of law and the accountability of government. Thus, in *Entick* v *Carrington* [reference], it was held that government officials had to show legal authority in order to enter an individual's land, and could not rely on the arbitrary principle of state necessity.'

Here, the case is being used to explain what would otherwise be a rather dry and abstract principle. It shows that you understand that principle and you have brought the law to life by providing a real case example.

To support an analysis or criticism of the law

You can use a case to support an academic argument.

EXAMPLE

'Foster argues that there is no need for a written constitution, because the courts will protect individuals from arbitrary and unreasonable interference with their liberty via the common law [refer to Foster's text]. This can be illustrated by cases such as *Entick* v *Carrington* [case reference], where the individual's rights were upheld within the traditional common law principles of trespass.'

Alternatively, it can show your analytical or critical skills.

EXAMPLE

'Although the quote in the question (that "human rights are best protected by the general law") can be supported by cases such as *Entick* v *Carrington* [reference], it should not be forgotten that the courts have on occasions failed to recognise certain fundamental rights. Thus, in *Malone* v *MPC* [reference] the domestic courts failed to recognise a general right of privacy.'

To assist you in answering problem questions

Specifically, cases can be used to help you answer problem questions and to give advice on the likely outcome of a dispute.

> EXAMPLE
>
> 'It is to be noted that in this case Jack, by offering to pay only half of the original debt, appears not to have provided any fresh considera-tion for Bill's acceptance of that offer. In this respect, one could refer to the principle in *Pinel's Case* [reference] and conclude that in the absence of any fresh promise by Jack, Bill will not be bound by that acceptance.'

So too, you can use the facts and decision of a previous case and apply it to (or distinguish it from) the present facts.

> EXAMPLE
>
> 'In our case the advertisement states quite clearly that the customer merely needs to "take the voucher to the store to receive a discount on those goods". This is similar to the situation in *Carlill v Carbolic Smoke Ball Company* [reference], where it was held that a contract was concluded when Mrs Carlill followed the company's instructions and used the smoke ball without success to claim a reward that had been promised in a newspaper advertisement.'

Do I have to give (all) the facts and details of the decision?

This will depend on whether an account of the facts and the decision will assist you in answering the question. As indicated previously, you can use cases for a number of purposes, and sometimes the facts of and decision in the case are not relevant to the point that you are trying to make.

It will be rare for the lecturer to expect you to give the full facts of a case and/or a full account of the decision in that case. However, you may need this information if the question is principally concerned with one or a limited number of cases, or where you are asked to write a case note on a specific case.

Giving the facts of the case might help readers (and students) understand a legal issue (and why it was in dispute), and help them explain the decision and its rationale. If you are explaining something theoretical or legally com-plex, the facts of a case might help readers engage with the area and the spe-cific issues.

> **EXAMPLE**
>
> 'The rule of law demands that government is equal before the law and should not rule via arbitrary discretion.'
>
> Giving the facts of (and decision) in *Entick v Carrington* might help the reader understand the significance of that case and the principles it upholds.

In problem questions, only give the facts of a case if they are similar to the ones in the scenario, or if they allow you to draw a distinction between the case and your facts.

Generally, it is more important to explain the principle behind the case (or its rationale or significance) than to tell the lecturer what happened and what was decided in that case.

Often it is better to give an extract from the judgment rather than the facts and the decision.

> **EXAMPLE**
>
> 'Recent case law suggests that the courts are prepared to interfere with executive discretion where fundamental human rights are under threat. Thus in *A v Secretary of State for the Home Department* [reference] Lord Bingham stated that "Even in a terrorist situation, the courts were not precluded by any doctrine of deference from scrutinising the issues raised" [provide reference to page or paragraph number in the law report].'

If the facts and decision are relevant to answering the question, and if you have time and space to give the facts and decision of the case, ensure that you do so as briefly as possible. Learn how to digest the facts and decision of the case in one or two sentences.

> **EXAMPLE**
>
> 'In *Carlill* it was held that an advertisement which clearly stated that any person who used the company's product and still caught

influenza could claim a reward of £100 constituted a contractual offer, which was accepted by the claimant when she followed the relevant instructions.'

That would be sufficient to inform the reader of the basic facts and decision and to make some accompanying comment such as **'Thus, an advert can be an offer if it is couched in sufficiently clear terms,'** or **'Thus, in such cases the acceptance is valid on performance of the act.'** If the case is being used in a problem question as an analogy (or otherwise), then you could give more detailed facts (perhaps mentioning that the company deposited £1,000 as a mark of its sincerity).

Is it sufficient to give the case name and reference?

If you are using the case simply to provide authority for a general legal principle then it is sufficient to give the name of the case (either in the main body of the work or by creating a footnote, along with the reference).

EXAMPLE

If you are answering a problem question on judicial review, and the scenario raises a specific ground of review such as natural justice, you might want to make a general point about the general grounds of review:

'Lord Diplock has identified the general grounds of judicial review as illegality, irrationality and procedural impropriety.'

You can then refer to the case (*Council of Civil Service Unions v Minister of State for the Civil Service*) and then give the reference ([1985] AC 374), either in a footnote, or by putting:

'In *Council of Civil Service Unions v Minister of State for the Civil Service* [create footnote for the case reference], Lord Diplock identified . . . '

There is no need to give the facts or the decision in that case, or even to analyse the significance of the case. You are using the case simply to provide authority for a general point, and it is acceptable to give just the case name and reference.

Do I need to read the (whole) law report?

You will be encouraged by your lecturers to get into the habit of accessing law reports and reading a case in its entirety. Most lecture notes and reading lists for seminars and coursework will refer you to the official law report.

- By reading the law report, you will get a fuller picture of what the case was about, what legal and factual issues were raised and how the case was decided. You will also become familiar with the style of language used by judges, which will help you in explaining, distinguishing and analysing cases.

- If you are going to use the law report, you might not have to read the whole judgment(s). If you read the head note to the case, you will be referred to relevant and the most important parts of the judgment. Practise locating the most important sections and getting the essential gist of what the judge said.

- If you have read the law report, make sure you receive the benefit of that research. Indicate to the lecturer that you have taken the trouble of accessing the law report by, for example, quoting from the judgment(s).

- Remember, many law reports (and other sources) can be accessed via websites; you do not always need to go the library to read a case. Make sure the site provides proper references to pages or paragraph numbers.

- However, it is not practicable for you to access the law reports for every case that you are referred to. In many cases you can rely on a good casebook to give you an account of the case and its decision. The advantages are that the casebook will digest the facts and the judgment and provide you with a relevant analysis of the case and its impact on the general law (in which case, if you use that information you should credit it – beware of **plagiarism**).

- Do not use casebooks that provide the barest detail – one or two lines on the facts and then the same on the decision. They will not provide sufficient depth or analysis for assessment purposes.

- Sometimes your textbook might provide a sufficient account of the case, and you can use it in your work. This can be done if you are using the case as simple authority or giving a very basic account of the case.

- You can often find suitable accounts of cases in journal articles. Sometimes the author will examine a case in detail, and you can get the facts and decision from this source. Ensure that you distinguish the account of the facts and the decision from the academic commentary provided by the author. You will need to credit the latter; otherwise you will be guilty of **plagiarism**.

- Beware that some authors will not refer to the facts (or decision) of the case, but will simply analyse or criticise the decision. In that case, find out the facts and decision yourself (if they are relevant).

EXAMPLE

Do not make vague statements such as '. . . the case of *Foster* v *Foster* shows the courts' reluctance to interfere with domestic arrangements.'

- When you get the facts and decision of a case from a textbook, casebook or article, do not refer to that secondary source, but use the primary source.

EXAMPLE

Do not say: 'This was decided in *Foster* v *Jones* (See Steve Foster, *Contract Law* (3rd edn, Longman 2015) 6; or Steve Foster, 'Analysing offers' (2004) OJLS 213, 216).'

Newspaper and journal reports

You should be regularly scanning the respectable newspapers (*The Times, The Daily Telegraph, The Guardian* and *The Independent*) and reading their daily law reports. Cases are normally reported within days of the judgment, and reading these reports is a useful way of keeping up to date with new cases.

- Most of these reports will be fairly brief and thus provide only a superficial account of the case; you will normally need to research to find a fuller report of the case.

- Some such reports are more comprehensive and provide a useful account of the case; unless the case is particularly important for your studies, this report may suffice.

- Always check to see whether the case has been reported in the official law reports, and cite that later reference if possible (the full text of judgments are generally available on line the day after the judgment).

- In addition, journals such as the *New Law Journal, Legal Action, Criminal Law Review, Solicitors Journal, European Human Rights Law Review* and so on have their own law reports; in the absence of something more official, you can use that reference:

'*Foster* v *United Kingdom* [2005] EHRLR 236.'

Many journals and legal blogs have case commentaries by academics, in which the case is analysed and criticised. These are not reports of the case and should not be used as such. You can, however, refer to them as a secondary source after referring to the official report.

EXAMPLE

'This was confirmed in the recent House of Lords' decision in *Foster* v *Smith* [2005] 2 AC 333. For an analysis of the case see Steve Foster, 'What was wrong with the decision in *Foster* v *Smith*?' (2005) 68 MLR 298.'

Unreported cases

Some cases are not reported in the official law reports or elsewhere. In such a case follow these rules:

• Cases are now given a neutral citation, separate from any particular law report. Different abbreviations are given, which depends on where the case was heard – the House of Lords (UKHL) or now the Supreme Court (UKSC), Court of Appeal (EWCA Civ or EWCA Crim) or the High Court (EWHC). If the case has not yet been reported in a law report, use the neutral citation:

'*Foster* v *Worthington* [2011] UKSC 57.'

• If it is not reported in the official law reports, or subject-specific reports, but has been reported in a reputable newspaper law report (see the preceding section), it is acceptable to use that reference:

'*Foster* v *Jones, The Times,* 1 April 2005.'

• If it has not been reported in official, specific or newspaper law reports, you may use a reference from a legal journal (see the preceding point).
• In the previously mentioned situations, check whether the case has subsequently been reported in the law reports or a newspaper law report. You can do this by accessing websites such as LAWTEL or WESTLAW.

- Check whether the case has subsequently been reported elsewhere.

- For cases without any reference at all, refer to the name of the court and the date of the decision:

  '*Foster* v *Home Office,* unreported, decision of Manchester County Court, 14 April 1987.'

- Unreported decisions of the European Court or Commission of Human Rights can be referred to via the application number:

  '*Foster* v *United Kingdom* (Application No 23456/04).'

Multiple references

A case may have been reported in a number of law reports and thus have a number of references. For example, an important case may be reported in the Appeal Cases (AC), the Weekly Law Reports (WLR), the All England Law Reports (All ER) and various sections of the law reports (Queen's Bench Reports (QB), Chancery Reports (Ch) and Administrative Law Reports (Admin LR)). In addition, it might be reported in specialist law reports such as the Industrial Relations Law Reports (IRLR), Human Rights Law Reports (HRLR) or the Criminal Appeals Cases (Cr. App R).

- If the case has multiple references, generally refer to just one established report; you do not have to use all the references – 'WLR, All ER, AC' and so on. It is, however, quite common for texts or journals to refer to both a newspaper report and an official report, and it is common now for both a law report and a neutral citation (see above) to be used.

- Some journals tend to use one particular report (e.g. the WLR), but unless your lecturer specifies which report should be used you can use any of the established ones. Having chosen one, try to use that one consistently (unless the case has not been reported there; in which case, use another).

- If it has been reported in the official reports, ensure that you use that reference and not one from a newspaper or journal.

- Check with your lecturer and any departmental guidance as to what is acceptable, including which official law reports should be used.

Footnotes and cases

Check whether you are required to use footnotes in your coursework. You can then follow these basic rules:

- You can use footnotes to locate the case reference.

EXAMPLE

'This was established in *Jones* v *Foster*[1] ...

[1][1876] AC 23.

- Note that you do not have to give the case name in the footnote, as you have already supplied it in the text.
- You can also use footnotes to place the whole case reference.

EXAMPLE

The Court of Appeal has established that a Minister's decision in this area can be subject to judicial review.[2]

[2]*Foster v Secretary of State for the Home Department* [2004] WLR 234.

- Some texts cite the year of the case and then create a footnote.

EXAMPLE

This was decided in *Foster* v *Brown* (1998).[3]

[3][1998] 2 WLR 67.

- Check with your lecturer whether this is acceptable.
- You can also place additional cases in footnotes.

EXAMPLE

This was decided in *Jones* v *Foster*.[4]

[4][2003] 2 AC 345. See also *Foster* v *Holmes* [2004] 2 WLR 567.

- You can use a footnote to refer to a part of the judgment.

EXAMPLE

In *Foster* v *Singh*[5] it was held that an exclusion clause was not unreasonable simply because there was an inequality of bargaining power between the parties. Thus, Lord Foster held that the question of whether the clause was reasonable had to be decided on more specific factors.[6]

---

[5][1990] 2 AC 236.
[6]At para 44 [or ibid. at para 44, or [1990] AC 236, at page 240].

How many cases should I use?

Students often ask this question, and the answer can be very frustrating: 'It depends; how long is a piece of string?'

Of course it does depend, and all we can do here is highlight relevant factors to decide how many (and what type of) cases you should use.

TIPS ON CHOOSING WHICH CASES TO USE

- It will depend on the nature of the question. Some questions deal with institutions and procedure rather than substantive law, so you will not be expected to use any (or many) cases to illustrate your answer. For example, '*Outline the court structure in the English legal system and suggest proposals for reform.*' If the question is on theory – '*What is justice?*' – the answer should concentrate on conceptual and theoretical arguments, and does not require much case law in illustration. What case law you use in such questions must illustrate the theoretical principle (e.g. the fairness and justice of the case), rather than the substantive legal issues (e.g. whether a duty of care existed and was broken on the facts).

- Questions that deal with substantive legal areas (the substantive areas of contract, tort, employment or property law and so on) will require you to be familiar with the leading case law in that area. You should include, or refer to, the leading case authorities, either to illustrate your answer or to provide authority.

- Your textbook will give you a fairly good indication of the leading cases in that area, but make sure they are relevant to the question you have been set, and always ensure that you include recent cases not included in your text: check on legal websites such as WESTLAW to discover recent cases.

- For more advanced work, you will be expected to be conversant with all significant decisions in that area. Even if you cannot comment on them all, ensure that you indicate your awareness of them in footnotes and so on.

- Some substantive legal areas are governed primarily by statutory provisions and, thus, there may be little case law. In this situation, concentrate on the wording and interpretation of the statutory provisions to make up for the lack of case law.

- Use case law whenever it helps you answer the question. Do not cite cases just to show that you know that case or to show off your knowledge of a range of cases.

- If you use a case as authority or to illustrate a point, do not use other cases unless that enhances your answer – if it shows how the case was distinguished, applied to different circumstances and so on.

- You can refer to similar cases in footnotes:

'This principle was also applied in the subsequent House of Lords decision in *Foster* v *Harrison* [reference].'

- For problem questions, only use cases that are relevant to addressing and answering the specific issues raised by the scenario (**see Chapter 5**). If you do refer to a case as authority for a basic point, merely give the case name and reference.

- You may have to use cases from different jurisdictions, or European or international cases; in that case ensure that you cite and reference them properly and indicate whether they are authority (binding or persuasive).

Hence, there are no strict rules on how many cases you should use. If you look at the 'good' answers in Chapters 4 and 5 of this text, you will see that the student uses between ten and fifteen cases to answer the question. However, it is more important to bear in mind the rules set out here, rather than saying, '*I must use X number of cases.*'

Make cases work for you

Remember, you use cases to *enhance* your answer. Ensure that the case has made your answer more authoritative and more convincing. Do not make your answer less impressive by the use of cases, by a muddled account of the facts and decision or by a confused explanation of its ratio or importance.

EXAMPLE

'The courts have always upheld individual liberty and have safe-guarded such liberty from arbitrary governmental interference. In *Entick* v *Carrington* [reference] the court upheld the individual's right to privacy when they held that the police had no right to seize the plaintiff's property, even though the Secretary of State said they could do it. This case shows that freedom of expression has always been important.'

The initial point is well made, but when the case is introduced, the author makes some mistakes on the facts, the relevant law and the ratio of the case, and the reader is thus confused about what happened in the case and its importance. The case could be explained thus:

EXAMPLE

'The courts have always upheld individual liberty and have safe-guarded such liberty from arbitrary governmental interference. In *Entick* v *Carrington* [reference] it was held that in the absence of legal authority a trespass on the claimant's property in the name of state necessity was actionable in the ordinary courts. The case illustrates the principle that the government is bound by the law and must provide formal legal authority for its actions.'

Introduce the case in the context of the question or the point that you are trying to make

Some students just drop cases into their answer without explaining their relevance or what purpose the case is serving.

EXAMPLE

'The grounds of judicial review include substantive as well as procedural wrongdoing. In *Congreve v Home Office* the Minister had recalled validly granted television licences and Congreve claimed that this was not allowed. It was held that the Minister had no right to revoke the licence.'

This account of the case does not tell the reader why this case, as opposed to others, has been chosen in illustration. Neither does the student use the case to illustrate the previous statement: it does not tell the reader whether there was substantive or procedural wrongdoing, what the difference is between the two, or why the court thought it was beyond the Minister's powers to do what he did.

Instead, after the initial statement the student could say the following.

EXAMPLE

'A public authority might have gone beyond its substantive powers by exercising them for an improper or unlawful purpose. Thus, in *Congreve v Home Office* [reference] it was held that a Minister could not exercise his statutory right to revoke television licences [refer to the relevant Act of Parliament and its section] in order to raise extra revenue for the government. The Minister's substantive powers were restricted to cases where the individual had broken the terms of the licence or had failed to pay the fee.'

This account of the case provides a good, clear example of the point that the student made originally and explains the court's reasoning.

Explain the ratio and the rationale of the case

You can use a case to give an example of how the law operates or to illustrate the law's fairness (or otherwise).

Do not spend too much time explaining the facts and decision of the case – instead concentrate on the legal ratio and the general reasoning of the case. For example, in the preceding *Congreve* example, although the facts and the decision are quite interesting, and might be useful in helping you to illustrate a point, it is the ratio and rationale of the case that must be stressed.

Thus, you should indicate why the court came to this decision, the ratio (that public authorities must not act for an improper purpose) and its rationale and significance (that courts will ensure that public authorities do not abuse their public powers).

Explain the significance of the case, not just the decision

The decision in a case only affects the parties to that dispute. It is the ratio of the case and the principles it upholds that are significant.

Do not just give the facts and decision of the case, without explaining why this case is significant in answering the question.

EXAMPLE

'An offer has to be distinguished from an invitation to treat. In Fisher v Bell a flick-knife was placed in a shop window and the shopkeeper was charged with offering for sale an offensive weapon. It was held that the display was an invitation to treat.'

Here, the student has used the case of *Fisher* v *Bell* without telling us why the court decided the case as it did – *why* was the display not an offer? Also, why has the student used *Fisher* v *Bell* to distinguish offers from invitations to treat, or a case on shop window displays?

Let's try again.

EXAMPLE

'An offer can be contrasted with an invitation to treat, where the person making the proposition does not intend to be bound at that stage and is merely inviting others to make an offer. For example, in Fisher v Bell [reference] it was held that the display of an item in a

---

> shop window was not an offer for sale and that such a display merely invited the potential customer to make an offer. Thus, the presumption is that the shopkeeper does not intend to make a binding offer and that in such cases he or she can refuse to sell the item to a customer.'

The student has left out the facts and has given a brief account of the decision, so that he can concentrate on the important point – that shop window displays are normally invitations – and explain the rationale and effect of such a rule.

The two/three/four/five-step approach

As mentioned previously, you should introduce the case properly into your work and within the context of the question, making it clear why you have used that case.

- If you are going to use the case as simple authority then ensure that it is relevant and appropriate.

EXAMPLE

Step 1 Make the legal statement. ('Not all adverts are necessarily invitations to treat.')

Step 2 Cite the relevant authority ('*Carlill v Carbolic Smoke Ball Co.*', plus the appropriate reference).

- If you are going to use the case to explain a point then ensure that you not only refer to it but also explain its significance.

EXAMPLE

Step 1 As in the previous example.

Step 2 As in the previous example.

Step 3 'Thus, an advert can be construed as an offer if (as in *Carlill*) the terms are sufficiently certain.'

- If you are going to explain the facts and decision of the case (because of its importance and/or relevance), ensure that you introduce the case properly, that the facts and decision are explained clearly and that you explain the ratio and significance of the case.

EXAMPLE

Step 1 As in the previous example.

Step 2 As in the previous example (in other words, 'Thus, in *Carlill* v *Carbolic Smoke Ball Co.. . .* ').

Step 3 Give brief but clear facts.

Step 4 Explain the decision clearly and simply (with perhaps a quote from the judge).

Step 5 Provide some analysis of the case and summarise its significance: 'The decision in *Carlill* shows us that although most advertisements lack the certainty required of a contractual offer, it would be wrong to conclude that all advertisements are mere invitations to treat. In *Carlill*, therefore, the advertisement was clearly worded and the court was satisfied that the company intended to be bound by the promise it made. In such a case, the courts will not apply rigid rules, and will look at the particular wording and actions of the parties.'

- If you are going to explain the decision of the case but you are not going to give the facts (because of lack of space or because they are not particularly relevant, then follow the five-step approach, but leave out Step 3 in the above example.

Read cases properly

It is essential that you read the case as carefully and as fully as possible, and that you understand the case before you include it in your work.

- Do not rely on your notes for the facts, decision and ratio of the case. At the very least, take the facts and decision form a suitable textbook or a casebook.
- You may need to read the full report to get appropriate detail or to use quotations from the judgment(s).

- Ensure that your account of the facts and of the decision is correct.
- Do not use a case in illustration unless you understand the facts and decision and the significance of the case.

Explain the facts and the decision clearly

If you are going to provide the facts and the decision of the case, ensure that you do so clearly and simply. A muddled account of the case will detract from the quality of your answer and confuse the reader.

EXAMPLE

'In *A* v *Home Secretary* the Home Secretary was detaining foreigners suspected of terrorism in a detention centre. The Home Secretary had permission to do this under the Terrorism Act and the detainees claimed that this detention was unlawful. Article 15 of the European Convention allows a state to derogate from Article 5 of the Convention and the Home Secretary claimed that this detention was necessary in times of emergency. The House of Lords held that the Act of Parliament was incompatible with Article 5 of the Convention and that the courts should not be reluctant to interfere simply because there was a state of emergency. Lord Hoffmann held that there was no state of emergency, but the House of Lords held that the detention of the foreign suspects was disproportionate, even though they were detained to prevent them being tortured. Lord Walker held that the detentions were lawful and that there was a state of emergency.'

This account of the case shows that the student is confused on the facts, the background of the case, the relevant statutory provisions and the decision (and which of the Lordships were dissenting). There is no logical sequence to this account of the facts and decision, and the author jumps from one point to another. Consequently, the reader is confused as to what was held and the significance of the case.

Let's try again.

EXAMPLE

'In A v *Secretary of State for the Home Department* [reference] the House of Lords held that the detention without trial of foreigners suspected of terrorism, under s. 26 of the Anti-Terrorism, Crime and Security Act 2001, was contrary to Article 5 of the European Convention, which guarantees the right to be brought before a judicial authority. The provision had been introduced in order to detain individuals who could not be deported to another country because of the risk of them facing torture (thus complying with the European Court's decision in *Chahal* v *United Kingdom* [reference]). The government had lodged a derogation order with respect to Article 5, claiming that there was a public emergency threatening the life of the nation and that it was necessary to derogate from Article 5. The majority of the House of Lords accepted that there was such an emergency (Lord Hoffmann dissenting), but held that the provisions were discriminatory and disproportionate and thus incompatible with the government's right (under Article 15 of the Convention and s. 14 of the Human Rights Act 1998) to derogate from its Convention obligations. In reaching that decision, their Lordships (Lord Walker dissenting) stressed that the courts would not show deference to Parliament in cases of national security where fundamental human rights were endangered.'

This account clearly sets out the facts of and the background to the case and summarises the main thrust of the decision. It also highlights (albeit briefly) the impact of the case on the constitutional role of the courts.

This student has only used fifty more words than the other account, but the difference in quality and clarity is marked, and the lecturer will appreciate this and will reflect this in the marking of the script: it would not be surprising if there was a difference of two grades in the script – first one 45%, second one 65% – clarity and displaying understanding is *that* important.

Using extracts from the judgment

You can quote from the judgment in the case to highlight any specific aspect of the decision or the judge's reasoning. This will also indicate to the lecturer that you have accessed the full law report and have read the case fully.

- Ensure that the extract is relevant and that it supports the point you are trying to make.
- Ensure that it is properly cited and referenced and that you highlight the extract appropriately.
- Try not to use too long an extract.
- You should refer to the case name and reference, and provide a separate reference for the relevant extract.
- You might wish to highlight particular words in the judgment to stress a particular point. If the judge did not highlight the words, but you want to stress them, then put 'italics added'.

EXAMPLE

'In *Smith* v *Foster*[1] it was held that an acceptance does not have to be recorded in writing and that it could be made orally. Explaining that decision Harrison LJ held that:

'although for evidential purposes it is obviously preferable for the acceptance to be communicated in writing – so that both parties have an official record of such acceptance – *a written acceptance is not a formal requirement of a legally binding contract* [italics added]. An oral acceptance is in law just as effective, despite the evidential difficulties such a method might cause.'[2]

---
[1] [1990] 2 AC 236.
[2] [1990] 2 AC 236, at 40, or page 240 [or Ibid., at 40, or page 240].

Here the student has made the general point and has then illustrated it by the extract, highlighting the most pertinent words. The student has also referenced both the case and the extract, and can then comment on the extract and refer to subsequent authority in a footnote.

EXAMPLE

'Thus, in that case his Lordship drew a distinction between legal and practical difficulties and this approach has been followed in subsequent cases.[3]

---

[3]See *Holmes* v *Foster* [1998] 1 AC 333, and *Foster* v *Jones* [2000] 2 AC 444.

Use relevant cases

This may seem an obvious point, but a common complaint of lecturers is that many students use irrelevant cases in their answers.

- Do not use cases just because you know them and they are in the right general legal area. Many students will do this (particularly in examinations) when they do not understand, or cannot answer, the question, in the hope that the lecturer will be impressed by their general knowledge and their ability to remember lots of cases.

- You are more likely to use relevant cases if you have a sound knowledge of the legal area and you have attended classes and contributed in seminars. This is because you will already have engaged in that subject and subject area, and will recognise what the question is about and what cases are needed to address the question.

- Look at the question carefully and compile a list of relevant cases to use in the answer.

- Always ask yourself whether that case is assisting you in answering the question or addressing the issue.

Cases with more than one ratio

Many cases deal with more than one legal issue and have a number of ratios. For example, a case might raise the following issues: *Did the defendant make a valid offer? If so, did the claimant accept that offer? If so, did both parties provide consideration?* In such a case students must ensure that they use the relevant part or ratio of that case, and that the question concerns that part of the case.

For example, *Carlill* deals with a number of issues: Was the advert an offer? Was it accepted? Was there any intention to create legal relations? Did Mrs Carlill provide any consideration? In such a case it is relatively easy to use the wrong ratio to explain the point you are supposed to be making.

EXAMPLE

'Not all advertisements are invitations to treat. Thus in *Carlill* it was held that Mrs Carlill had provided consideration for the reward by simply using the product. In addition, it was not necessary for her to communicate her acceptance by indicating that she was going to use the smoke ball.'

What the student has written is correct, but it is not relevant to the point they were trying to make. They deal with two legal issues that were raised in the case, but neither is relevant to the question of whether the advert was an offer.

The student knows the case is relevant to the question (because it is on the reading list or on the lecture handout), but they fail to recognise that the case raises several points and that he or she should be talking about the issue of offers and invitations to treat.

The student has gone to the case in the book (or his or her notes) and has not checked whether this is the relevant point to make in the assessment.

You are unlikely to make this mistake if you are conversant with the relevant legal principles and have attended all sessions, because in such a case you will have spotted that the case has come up on several occasions and deals with different issues.

Use up-to-date cases

As a law student, you will be expected to keep up to date with new cases and to conduct the necessary research in order to locate them.

- Although 'old' cases are still valid, particularly in subjects such as contract and property law, you should ensure that you are aware of new case law in the relevant legal area.

- This is particularly so where the case deals with a traditional legal principle in the context of modern technology (e.g. the application of the postal rules to emails or faxed communications) or if it reflects a modern political or other problem (e.g. a challenge to recent government policy).

- You can access these cases by reading newspaper law reports, journal articles (particularly the weekly journals such as the *New Law Journal*).

- You can search for new case law (and other legal developments) on legal websites, such as WESTLAW or LAWTEL: they have current awareness and daily update sections that allow you access such developments.

- Check your lecture and seminar materials to see if there is any reference to new cases and other legal or political developments. Don't just rely on your textbook in this respect; the text will be at least six months out of touch with new cases.

- Always ensure that the case that you use is consistent with recent authority and that it has not been overturned or qualified by more recent cases.

USING STATUTORY MATERIALS

The rules in the preceding section relating to the use of case law also apply to the use of statutory materials.

Statutory materials are primary law, the law's original source, and include Acts of Parliament and their sections, Parliamentary Bills and their clauses, and delegated legislation such as statutory instruments. It also includes legislative provisions of the European Union such as treaty articles, regulations and directives.

You may also have to refer to provisions (articles) contained in international treaties such as the European Convention on Human Rights and Fundamental Freedoms (1950) or the Universal Declaration of Human Rights (1948).

Quote the relevant section or sub-section and the year of the Act or regulation

When you are using an Act of Parliament as authority, you should refer to the specific section of the Act as well as its short title (the Human Rights Act) and the year it was passed (1998), rather than the year it came into force.

EXAMPLE

'Section 3 of the Human Rights Act 1998 provides that . . . '

Or: ' . . . the courts are now empowered, so far as is possible, to read and give effect to *primary* and subordinate legislation in a way that is compatible with Convention rights.'[15]

---

[15]Human Rights Act 1998, s.3

If the section has sub-sections, then you should cite that as well:

EXAMPLE

'Section 4(2) of the Human Rights Act 1998 provides . . . '

Or: '. . . sub-section (2) of section 4 provides . . . '

When you are using the word 'section' in the middle of a sentence, you should abbreviate it to 's.'; likewise, the word 'sections' should be abbreviated to 'ss.'.

EXAMPLE

'This is contained in s. 4 of the Human Rights Act 1998 and ss. 6–8 of that Act provide for the granting of remedies for human rights violations committed by public authorities.'

Learn to extract the relevant words of the statute, rather than copying out the whole section

If the statutory provision is particularly central to the question then you may quote the whole section as long as it is of manageable size.

For example, if the question is about the courts' new interpretative powers under the Human Rights Act 1998, then it would be appropriate to quote at least sub-section 1 of section 3 in full early on in the assessment so that you can refer to the wording as you answer each aspect of the question.

EXAMPLE

'The courts' new interpretative powers are contained in s. 3(1) of the Human Rights Act 1998, which provides that "so far as it is possible to do so, primary legislation and subordinate legislation must be read and given effect in a way which is compatible with Convention rights".'

If, however, s. 3 is just one of a number of sections that you are referring to, then you can paraphrase the wording, provided you get the gist of the provision.

> **EXAMPLE**
>
> 'The courts now have a duty (under s. 3) to interpret both primary and secondary legislation compatibly with Convention rights, at least in so far as it is possible to do so.'

If the provision is long, or technical, then try to paraphrase it, rather than copying it out in full. For example, s. 3(2) of the Human Rights Act provides as follows:

(2) This section –

a. applies to primary legislation and subordinate legislation whenever enacted;

b. does not affect the validity, continuing operation or enforcement of any incompatible primary legislation; and

c. does not affect the validity, continuing operation or enforcement of any incompatible subordinate legislation if (disregarding any possibility of revocation) primary legislation prevents removal of the incompatibility.[7]

It would not really be appropriate to copy out the whole of s. 3(2), particularly in an essay with a word limit. Instead, you should paraphrase the sub-section and contain the gist of that provision in your answer.

> **EXAMPLE**
>
> 'Sub-section 2 states that this new power can be used in respect of both primary and secondary legislation, whenever enacted. However, s. 3(1) does not affect the validity of incompatible primary legislation, or of secondary legislation where the primary legislation would prevent the removal of the incompatibility.'

Paraphrase the technical words of a statutory provision and allow time and space to explain or analyse the provision.

The use of a statutory provision will not necessarily assist you in explaining the law. You will need to add comments and analysis to show that you understand the provision and its relevance to the question.

EXAMPLE

'Sub-section 2 states that this new power can be used in respect of both primary and secondary legislation, whenever enacted; in other words, either before or after the coming into effect of the Human Rights Act. However, s. 3(1) does not affect the validity of incompatible primary legislation, or of secondary legislation where the primary legislation would prevent the removal of the incompatibility. Thus the sovereignty of Acts of Parliament is preserved and the courts have no power to strike down legislative provisions which have been clearly sanctioned by Parliament.'

If you are paraphrasing the provision, ensure that you convey the correct gist of the provision

Some students rely on a general textbook, or their lecture notes or handouts, to explain what a statutory provision says. As a result, readers may be left with an incomplete picture of the provision and its content and scope.

EXAMPLE

'Section 3 of the Human Rights Act allows the courts greater powers to interpret legislation in line with the Convention, and s. 4 allows certain courts to issue declarations of incompatibility.'

This statement is perfectly true, but if a question asks you to explain and analyse the provisions of the Human Rights Act, this answer fails to explain what the section says. The lecturer will note on your essay that you are being vague and ask, 'What is meant by 'greater powers?' *Which* courts have powers under s. 4? What *is* a declaration of incompatibility?'

Make sure that the statutory provision is not out of date and has not been repealed or amended

If you include out-of-date provisions, or fail to include new provisions, you are exposing your lack of knowledge and your inability to keep up with new law. In particular, you run the risk of making a clear error on the law.

EXAMPLE

'Under s. 14 of the Sale of Goods Act 1979 all goods sold in the course of a business must be of merchantable quality.'

As the 1979 Act has been amended and the term is now satisfactory quality, the student has quoted the law incorrectly. In addition, as the amendment was made in 1996, the student is showing that he or she is relying on a hopelessly out-of-date textbook!

In the vast majority of cases this type of mistake can be avoided by relying on the most recent edition of the recommended textbook and by consulting the lecturer's handouts; lecturers often make students aware of recent developments in this way.

The easiest way to check whether the provision is still in force is to use websites such as WESTLAW or LAWTEL. You can simply punch in the provision and it will tell you its status – whether it is in force, if it has been repealed, amended, and so on.

In addition, you should make a regular search of such websites and their current updates service to see whether any new statutory provisions have been passed or proposed.

If a statutory provision has been amended by a later Act of Parliament, but is still in force, then you should use the original provision as amended and should not quote the amending provision as the primary source. For example, s. 14A of the Public Order Act 1986 now covers the offence of 'trespassory assembly', and this was introduced via s. 70 of the Criminal Justice and Public Order Act 1994. In this case, you would cite s. 14A of the 1986 Act and not s. 70 of the 1994 Act (although you can mention that s. 14 was amended by s. 70).

Use these materials to help you answer the question, to get a point across, to come to a conclusion and so on

Do not just quote or use a statutory provision for the sake of it. Ensure that it serves a purpose and enhances your answer.

You can use a statutory provision to provide simple authority.

EXAMPLE

'Section 2 of the Unfair Contract Terms Act 1977 states that exclusion clauses that seek to exclude business liability for death and personal injury caused by negligence are void.'

Or: 'Clauses that seek to exclude business liability for death and personal injury caused by negligence are void.'[16]

---
[16]Unfair Contract Terms Act 1977, s.2.

EXAMPLE

'The criminal law often reflects the view that certain conduct is morally wrong. Thus, s. 1 of the Theft Act 1968 (as amended) reflects society's disapproval of stealing by providing that it is an offence to commit an act of theft.'

EXAMPLE

'Most criminal offences require a specific mens rea, and are not committed unless the defendant has a guilty mind. For example, s. 1 of the Theft Act 1968 (as amended) provides that a person is guilty of theft if he *dishonestly* (italics added) appropriates property belonging to another.'

Note here that the student has stressed the word dishonestly to show that they appreciate which word in the section is relevant to the point they are making.

EXAMPLE

'It is fundamental that the law is prospective and not retrospective. Thus, s. 1 of the War Damage Act 1965, which retrospectively over-ruled the decision in *Burmah Oil* v *Lord Advocate* [reference], thus depriving individuals of the right to compensation, is regarded as morally wrong and unconstitutional.'

USING LAW JOURNALS

There are dozens of English legal journals and periodicals (and hundreds of international journals) that can assist you with your law study and the research and presentation of your work. Get used to reading these journals and using them as a secondary source for your work. You can use these journals for a number of purposes:

- Some journals, particularly the weekly and monthly trade journals, can be used to keep up to date with recent cases, statutory developments, and current legal and political debates. They also contain short articles on legal issues, which are of interest to both the practitioner and the law student. Get into the habit of reading these regularly, even if it is only to skim though them to check for relevant information. For example, consult the *New Law Journal*, *Solicitors Journal*, *Legal Action*, *Law Society Gazette*, *Legal Counsel* and *Legal Executive*.

- Academic legal journals contain articles, commentaries and analysis on recent cases and statutory developments. These articles explain a specific aspect of the law and its significance and can be used by the student in their work as a secondary source to address the question and back up any arguments.

- Soundly researched legal articles will contain references to a variety of primary and other secondary sources and can thus be useful in your general research of a legal area.

Use your research skills to find appropriate journal articles

You will need to use relevant journal articles in your work and you need to know how to research and locate them (see the beginning of this chapter – **researching for assessments**. You will need to employ the basic research skills that you have been taught in your Legal Method or Legal Skills course, but you may wish to follow this advice:

TIPS FOR FINDING THE RIGHT RESOURCES

- Consult the lecture and seminar handouts to see if the lecturer has listed any journal articles in the area covered in the assessment.
- Consult your recommended textbooks and cases and materials books to see if they refer to any relevant articles.
- Conduct a search on the library facilities to see what journals they house and whether there are any articles in this area.
- Conduct a search on websites such as LAWTEL or WESTLAW to locate articles in the area.
- Ensure that your search is not too wide. If you are doing an essay on freedom of expression and the Human Rights Act, for example, don't just put in 'freedom of expression' or 'free speech' because you will get an unmanageable number of results. Instead, put in both terms together (or 'Section 12 of the Human Rights Act 1998').
- Read the abstract of the article before you download it or photocopy it and see whether it is relevant to your research.
- If the journal is in the library, look at the relevant issue and skim through the contents to check its relevance.
- Ensure that the journal is of an appropriate academic standard (see the next point).
- If your assessment is in a specialist legal area, you will need to research and use journals in that specific area (e.g. *Public Law* for constitutional and administrative law, *Criminal Law Review* for crime).

The quality and status of law journals

Some journals may not be appropriate to your level of study; they may be too low or high level. Some journals are regarded as more authoritative than others.

Leading academic journals, such as *Modern Law Review, Oxford Journal of Legal Studies, Law Quarterly Review, Legal Studies, Journal of Law and Society, Cambridge Law Review* – often referred to as 'weighty' journals, or the 'academic heavyweights' – are examples. Others are often aimed at a wider audience, including practitioners, and are referred to as trade journals (see the preceding section). There is also a wide range of journals in between, which cover either general legal issues or specific legal areas, such as employment, criminal law, property and so on.

Trade journals serve a very useful purpose (see the preceding paragraph), but it is not always appropriate to use them in academic assessments. Articles and case notes in these journals can be used to keep up to date with the law and can be used in your work to draw attention to a new development. However, they should not be cited as leading academic authority, and you should use articles and case notes from weightier journals for this purpose.

Articles and case notes in trade journals might not provide sufficient detail or academic analysis, and you might have to refer to weightier journals for this purpose.

You will find more detailed case and statute commentaries in the weightier journals, such as *Modern Law Review, Cambridge Law Review* and *Law Quarterly Review*, and some specialist journals, such as *Public Law* or *European Human Rights Law Review*.

Try to maintain a balance and include articles and case notes from both types of journal. This will show a wide research of the subject and an appreciation of a variety of sources.

EXAMPLE

'See Steve Foster, 'Human Rights and Prisons' (2004) 67 MLR 66. For a useful account of the recent case of *Foster* v *Home Office*, *The Times*, 12 April 2005, see Steve Foster, "Prisons and Legal Correspondence" NLJ (2005) 152 (7050) 1480.'

Do not cite or refer to journals that you have not read

If you have not accessed and read a particular journal article, do not cite it in your bibliography; otherwise, your bibliography is misleading. Neither should you indicate in the text that you have read and used an article when you haven't.

EXAMPLE

'This point is neatly summarised by Steve Foster, "Human Rights and Prison Life" ([2004] EHRLR 69, 70).'

Many students employ this technique because they have seen the article cited in a book or a journal in that way, but it is usually quite clear that they have not read the article themselves. The lecturer will then comment on the script, 'What did Foster actually say in this article?'

Do not use articles that you do not understand

Avoid using journal articles that contain views or language that you do not understand. Try to avoid using articles that are beyond the level that you are studying at and do not use an author's view if you can't comprehend what he or she is getting at. It will usually be very clear that you do not really know what you are talking about.

EXAMPLE

'Judges are sometimes afraid to interfere with government decisions and it would not be very fair if they did this. Indeed, Foster notes that this judicial deference is most acute in cases involving sensitive policy decisions where the judicial decision-making is ill-equipped to second guess executive expertise. In such cases the court's interference lacks democratic legitimacy (Steve Foster, "Making Human Rights Complicated" (1995) OJLS 23).'

It is clear from the language used in the first sentence that the student is simply quoting the author and does not really appreciate what the author is getting at. If they did, they would probably simplify the author's words and provide a brief illustration.

Again, the lecturer is likely to comment, 'What is Foster *actually* getting at here? Give a simple example.' The student should read the article again and see if they can simplify and illustrate the argument or avoid this source and use a plainer one that they do understand. This is where the adoption of your own writing style pays dividends.

Always explain the meaning and significance of views in journals

When you have found and used journal articles in your work, your task is not complete. You must introduce the source at the relevant point in the work and ensure that the article assists you in making that point or supporting an argument. You can then comment on that view and see whether it is backed up by case or other authority, and whether you agree with it.

In the following example, the student is answering a question on the court's role in protecting human rights.

EXAMPLE

'If human rights are to be protected it is essential that the courts do not show too much respect to the administrative authorities, for Foster argues that this deference will "compromise the court's constitutional role in protecting individual liberty."[66] In particular, the courts might be reluctant to interfere where national security is an issue [provide reference to a case].'

---

[66]Steve Foster, 'Judicial Deference and the Protection of Human Rights' [2003] PL 348, 357.

This is quite a simple use of an author's view. The view is introduced at the relevant stage of the discussion, it is referenced and the student puts the statement in some sort of context.

Students answering the question at a higher level might adopt a more sophisticated style and show greater knowledge of various sources.

EXAMPLE

'If human rights are to be protected it is essential that the courts do not show too much respect or deference to the administrative authorities. In this respect, Foster argues that judicial deference will lead to a compromise of the courts' constitutional role and inadequate protection of individual liberty.[43] This is supported by a number of cases on national security, where the courts have refused to interfere with decisions which impacted on liberty and security of the person

---

[refer to those cases in a footnote]. **However, as the recent case of A v** *Secretary of State for the Home Department* [reference] **suggests, the courts will not always decline to interfere, and Foster's views should be examined in the light of the approach taken in that case.'**[44]

---

[43]Steve Foster, 'Judicial Deference and the Protection of Human Rights' [2003] PL 348, 357. See also Steve Foster, 'The Constitutional Role of the Courts' (2002) OJLS 1, and Steve Foster, 'Human Rights and the Separation of Powers' [2002] PL 98.

[44]For an analysis of that case, see Steve Foster, 'The House of Lords, Terrorism and the Human Rights Act 1998' (2005) 64 MLR 111.

Here the student is aware of relevant cases to support the author's views. (If the author has used them, then the student should say so: **'Foster cites a number of cases to support his contention.'**) The student has also used a more recent case to qualify the author's views and has provided a reference to an academic analysis of that new case, which could then be used to explore new views on the topic. There is also a reference to other articles on the same area, showing off the student's research.

Do not use journals and views expressed in them as primary sources

Students often use articles as a source of cases, statutes and other primary sources. They do this because they read about the source in the article and think it is acceptable to cite the journal article rather than the primary source.

EXAMPLE

- Do *not* say: **'The leading authority is** *Smith* v *Jones* **(See Steve Foster, "Contract Terms" [2003] CLJ 20, 34)'**; instead, put the reference to the case.

- Do *not* say: **'There are a number of cases to illustrate this point (see Steve Foster, "Contract Terms" . . .)'**; instead, refer to the cases and provide the reference.

- Do *not* say: **'The Human Rights Act 1998 gives a power to the courts to interpret statutes in line with the Convention if at all possible (Steve Foster, "The Human Rights Act 1998" [2000] PL 678, 687)'**; instead, refer to the statutory provision (s. 3 of the Act).

- Do *not* say: 'The International Covenant on Civil and Political Rights 1966 protects freedom of expression. (Steve Foster, "The ICCPR and Democratic Rights" [2004] EHRLR 370, 380)'; instead, refer to the article in the Covenant (Art. 17).

In all these examples, the student has made a statement about the actual law; it is not his or her view on the law. In such a case do not credit the author as the source.

USING WEBSITES

Access and use a variety of legal and other websites during your studies. The modern student relies very heavily on this source of information; however, it is essential that you cite them and use them appropriately.

- Use law websites to carry out searches for both primary and secondary sources. These websites (e.g. LAWTEL, WESTLAW) will have a search engine for cases, statutory provisions and articles. You can put in a keyword, and it will provide you with all the relevant cases and so on that it stores on that topic.

- Don't make your search too wide – put in 'statutory interpretation and the Human Rights Act 1998,' rather than 'statutory interpretation' or 'Human Rights Act 1998'.

- Look at the abstract of the case, article and so on to check for its relevance to your work before you download or print.

- Some cases, statutes and journal articles can be accessed in full, and you can use this facility to download or print off primary sources, particularly if your library doesn't have these resources.

- If you access a primary source on this website, cite the primary source and not the website. (You can indicate that you have visited the website in a footnote or in your bibliography.)

- Some websites are very useful in accessing primary sources and specific information not available elsewhere. Websites such as those attached to government departments or non-governmental organisations (e.g. Amnesty International) are particularly useful for accessing information and statistics relating to that organisation or its work. In this sense, the website is more useful than texts or articles, and you are advised to make full use of them.

- Some websites provide general textbook-style information on legal topics. They should be treated with great caution and should not be used as a substitute for standard textbooks. Some of these websites are aimed at sub-degree students and are not suitable for undergraduate courses. They can be useful for grasping the basics but might be too superficial or simplistic to use for your assessments. Be careful not to cite them as academic authority unless they are written by experts in the area and are intended for academic analysis.

- Some textbooks and publishers provide regular updates on the law and can be used to keep up to date in the specific legal areas covered in the text.

- You can access these websites by visiting the publisher's website or visiting an address in the book. Some update facilities are better than others, and they are obviously limited to the content of the book. You should not rely solely on this source to keep up to date with recent developments. Similar information is available through academic and practitioner blogs.

- Use websites to check for new cases and statutory developments and for new secondary sources such as articles, books and newspaper items.

- As mentioned previously, some websites give you access to primary and secondary sources. This also allows you to check the website for recent cases and other developments and thus keep up to date with the law. This is much easier than looking through recent journals, law reports and so on in the library; however, note that a website might only let you search or access specific journals and law reports.

7

Legal referencing and citation

There is a proper way of citing and referring to cases, statutory materials, books and journals, and as a law student you must get used to employing it.

NOTE

The **citation** is how the source should be stated – for example, *Foster v Jones*.

The **reference** is where the source can be found (the law report: [1998] 2 AC125).

As an undergraduate you will be expected to acquire and employ referencing and citation skills, and your marks will suffer if you fail to do so; you will also be rewarded for appropriate referencing. *Do not* leave your referencing until the end: do it as you go along; otherwise you will hurry it and risk losing marks, or facing a charge of plagiarism.

On an undergraduate course you will be required to employ either the Oxford method (OSCOLA) or the Harvard method of citation and referencing. Check with your lecturers which one you should use. Students from non-law courses undertaking law modules may be given a choice.

NOTE

The Oxford method (OSCOLA – The Oxford University Standard for Citation of Legal Authorities) is commonly employed in law books and legal journals in Great Britain. The system is available on the following website: http://www.law.ox.ac.uk/publications/oscola.php

This text will adopt the OSCOLA system to any example citations and references, but access the website to get detailed information on citation and referencing, including how to cite and reference government papers parliamentary reports and overseas legislation and cases.

LEARN HOW TO CITE CASES

You must employ the correct method of citing cases and providing the proper reference.

The Oxford (OSCOLA) method

The Oxford method is used at most institutions; check with your lecturer, but you will normally be expected to use this method, which is adopted in most texts and journal articles.

- The names of the parties to the action should come first (in italics preferably, but you can underline the names in exams). This should be followed by the year of the law report in brackets (check whether the law report uses square brackets or parentheses) and then the volume of the report for that year. You should then refer to the relevant abbreviation of the law report, rather than the full name (e.g. WLR for Weekly Law Reports; All ER for All England Reports; AC for Appeal Cases). Finally, include the page reference – the page on which the report begins.

NOTE

It is common now to include the neutral citation of the case before the law report reference, so become familiar with the abbreviations, for example:

UKSC = (United Kingdom) Supreme Court

EWCA Crim. = (England and Wales) Court of Appeal Criminal Division

EWCA Civ. = Court of Appeal Civil Division

EWHC (QB) = High Court, Queen's Bench Division

EXAMPLE

'*Foster* v *Jones* [2010] EWCA Civ 330; [2010] 2 All ER 555'

If there is no neutral citation, just provide the law report reference, followed by the court in brackets:

' *Foster* v *Jones* [2010] 2 All ER 555 (CA)

Do not put: '**FOSTER ~v~ JONES (1999) All England Law Reports, July 5 1999'.** Here the student is using the information appearing on the front of the specific issue, which is there as part of the packaging. That information is not the correct reference.

• If you have already provided the full citation in your work, you can just refer to the case name subsequently.

EXAMPLE

'This was decided in *Foster* v *Home Office*[72] . . . Thus, in *Foster* v *Home Office* it was held that a prisoner who . . . '

It is also acceptable to refer to just the claimant's name: '. . . **Thus, in Foster . . .** '

---

[72][1990] 3 All ER 444 (CA)

• Some cases are more commonly known by a name other than the full case name. You can refer to this name instead of giving the full name, but ensure that you provide the full citation and reference somewhere.

EXAMPLE

'This was decided in the GCHQ case[91] . . . '

---

[91]*Council of Civil Service Unions v Minister of State for the Civil Service* [1985] AC 374.

- If you are using a particular part of the judgment, use paragraph numbers [-] or page numbers to identify the specific extract:

> EXAMPLE
>
> *Foster* v *Jones* [2010] EWCA Civ 330 [66]; [2010] 2 All ER 555, 560-1

You may identify the judge thus:

> EXAMPLE
>
> *Foster* v *Jones* [2010] EWCA Civ 330 [66] (Foster LJ)

- For EU cases

  Case C-176/03 *Commission* v *Council* [2005] ECR 1-7879

  Case C-176/03 *Commission* v *Council* [2005] ECR 1-7879, paras 47–48

- For European Court of Human Rights cases

  Foster v *United Kingdom* (or UK) (1998) 26 EHRR 10, or

  Foster v *United Kingdom* 1988-VIII 3123

- For Grand Chamber cases

  Foster v *United Kingdom* (1998) 26 EHRR 10 (GC)

- For unreported cases

Application No. 3456/94, judgment of the European Court of Human Rights, 12 September 1998

NOTE

OSCOLA provides detailed guidance on citing and referencing EU cases and European Court and Commission decisions: http://www.law.ox.ac.uk/publications/oscola.php (at pages 31–32)

The Harvard method

The Harvard method is employed in a number of social science journals. In this case you give the full citation (as is done in the Oxford method) in the bibliography or your references, but not in the main text of your work. Instead you simply put the case name and then the date (in parentheses). Thus:

> EXAMPLE
>
> *Smith* v *Foster* (1999)

CITING STATUTORY MATERIALS

Acts of Parliament and their sections

- It is sufficient to refer to the short title of the Act and the year that it was passed by Parliament.

> EXAMPLE
>
> 'The Human Rights Act 1998 gives further effect to . . . '

- If the Act is mentioned in the middle of a sentence use lowercase for 'the'.

> EXAMPLE
>
> 'The rights contained in the European Convention are given further effect by the Human Rights Act 1998.'

- If you are referring to a specific section of the Act, cite that section (s. for section, ss. for sections) and not just the Act itself.

EXAMPLE

'This duty is contained in s. 3 of the Human Rights Act 1998.'

- If using a footnote, put the Act first followed by the section:

EXAMPLE

'Human Rights Act 1998, s.2.'

- If you are referring to a sub-section of the act, you should put either sub-section 2 of section 3, or, preferably, s. 3(2).
- If an Act of Parliament is split into parts, then cite the part of the Act and the relevant sections.

EXAMPLE

'The offences concerned with racial hatred are contained in Part III of the Public Order Act 1986, in ss. 18–23.'

- If you are referring to a Schedule of an Act of Parliament, use the abbreviation Sch. and refer to the paragraph number of the schedule:

EXAMPLE

'Human Rights Act 1998, Sch. 2, paragraph 1.'

- If the schedule has Parts, then include that information:

EXAMPLE

'Human Rights Act 1998, Sch. 1, Part II.'

- If you have already referred to the title and year of the Act, you can abbreviate the Act, or shorten its title, in subsequent references. After you have given the full title, state in parentheses how you are going to identify the Act during the remainder of the work.

EXAMPLE

'The Human Rights Act 1998 (hereafter the 1998 Act or the Act or HRA) provides . . . 'This is contained in s. 4 of the Act/the 1998 Act/ HRA . . . '

Statutory instruments

Statutory instruments are the commonest form of delegated legislation, passed by virtue of a parent Act of Parliament. For example, under s. 47 of the Prison Act 1952 the Home Secretary can make regulations for the control of prisoners, and those regulations (the Prison Rules 1999) are delegated legislation, added to by specific statutory instruments.

- You must identify whether the provision you are referring to is primary or secondary legislation.

EXAMPLE

Do not put: **'Section 47 of the Prison Rules 1999.'**

Rather, put: **'This is contained in Rule 23 of the Prison Rules 1999** [reference, see below]**, passed under s. 47 of the Prison Act 1952.'**

Note, the Prison Rules 1999 have a specific reference (SI 1999/728). Refer to the specific number of the (Prison) Rules:

EXAMPLE

'This is contained in Rule 23 of the Prison Rules 1999 (SI 1999/728).'

- If you are referring to a specific statutory instrument then cite that instrument by its title and its year, and then provide the reference (year passed followed by its number).

EXAMPLE

'These changes were introduced by the Prison (Amendment) Rules 2003,[57] which amend rules 35 and 43 of the Prison Rules 1999 (reference if required).'

[57]SI 2003/3301

International treaties

- If you are referring to an international treaty you should put the title of the treaty, and the year in parentheses: The International Covenant on Civil and Political Rights (1966).
- Use the full title of the treaty: the European Convention for the Protection of Human Rights and Fundamental Freedoms (1950), not just the popular title: the European Convention.
- Once you have used the full title, you can then use an abridged form (the European Convention, the Convention or, commonly, the ECHR).
- Treaty provisions are known as articles, and you can use 'Article', 'article' or 'Art'.
- If the treaty has been incorporated into domestic law, do not confuse the treaty article with the statutory section.

EXAMPLE

'The right to a fair trial is guaranteed by section 6 of the Human Rights Act 1998.'

The student has confused s. 6 of the Act (liability of public authorities under the Act) with Article 6 of the European Convention. They should write:

'. . . guaranteed by Article 6 of the European Convention (as contained in s. 1 and Sched. 1 of the Human Rights Act 1998).'

- For European Community (or Union) Law, you should refer to the name of the treaty and the article; for example:

> **EXAMPLE**
>
> 'Article 25 of the EC Treaty', or 'EC Treaty, Art 25'.

- Note that some article numbers have changed following the passing of the Amsterdam Treaty 1997. In that case put:

> **EXAMPLE**
>
> **'Article 25 of the EC Treaty (formerly Article 12).'**
>
> Or, if referring to the old number:
>
> **'Article 189 (now article 239).'**

- For Directives, refer to the number and year of that provision:

> **EXAMPLE**
>
> **'This was contained in EC Directive 64/221/EEC.'**

- For Council Regulations:

> **EXAMPLE**
>
> **'Council Regulation (EC) 139/2004.'**

NOTE

OSCOLA provides detailed guidance on citing and referencing EU legislation (at pages 28–29: http://www.law.ox.ac.uk/publications/oscola.php

CITING JOURNALS

Under the Oxford system – the one preferred on most law courses and adopted by most English law journals – you put the author's first name followed by surname, the title of the article, year of publication, volume number (if used), journal abbreviation, page number on which the article begins and the page number of the specific view (if you are highlighting or quoting a specific passage).

EXAMPLE

If you are referring to an author's views you can write:

'See in particular Steve Foster "How to Write a Lousy Essay" (1999) 62 MLR, 123, 140.'

Do not write: **'Read Foster's article on lousy essays, summer edition of the *Modern Law Review* for 1999.'**

Here the student is referring us to the information on the front cover of the relevant issue of the journal and thus fails to give us the proper citation and reference.

In the bibliography, as with books, use the surname followed by the initials: Foster, S.

Alternatively, you can use the Harvard method of citation and referencing for journals. This is often employed in social science journals, including some law journals. Check with your lecturer as to which system you should use, but for the Harvard system, put the author's surname and initial(s), the year of publication, the title of the article, the name of the journal (underlined), the issue number and the date of that issue (if given) and the page numbers from the start to the end of the article.

EXAMPLE

'Foster, S. (2001) "Human Rights and the Judges", *Modern Law Review*, 64, Issue No 4, September, pp. 567–590.'

You can put this reference in your bibliography (or references) at the end of the work, and then during the work you can refer to the article by referring to the specific page number, like this:

> **EXAMPLE**
>
> 'Foster, S., 582.'

If you are referring to more than one article by that author, you can indicate which article you are referring to by including the date:

> **EXAMPLE**
>
> 'Foster, S. (2004).'

When using this method, ensure that you list this author's work chronologically in your bibliography. If there are two articles by that author from the same year, you can put this:

> **EXAMPLE**
>
> 'Foster, S. (2004) (2).'

That will refer to the order in which you referred to the author's work in your bibliography.

Citing specific law journals

You should learn how specific journals are cited and use that citation and referencing system. Articles in journals must be cited and referred to properly, especially if you are submitting work in the second and third year of your study, and for project work and on postgraduate courses. In particular you will be expected to get acquainted with and use accepted abbreviations.

Abbreviation	Title of journal	Example citation
BLR	*Business Law Review*	(2003) BLR 66
Crim LR	*Criminal Law Review*	[2004] Crim LR 33
CLJ	*Cambridge Law Journal*	[2004] CLJ 1
ILJ	*Industrial Law Journal*	[2002] ILJ 33
JBL	*Journal of Business Law*	[2005] JBL 66
J Crim Law	*Journal of Criminal Law*	[2005] J Crim Law 33
JLS	*Journal of Law and Society*	[2006] 27 JLS 234
JP	*Justice of the Peace*	JP (2005) 169(23) 428
LS	*Legal Studies*	(2004) LS 330
LQR	*Law Quarterly Review*	[2000] 116 LQR 212
MLR	*Modern Law Review*	(2002) 65 MLR 360
NLJ	*New Law Journal*	NLJ (2002) 152 (7050) 1480 (or (2001) NLJ 1480)
NILQ	*Northern Ireland Legal Quarterly*	[2002] 53 NILQ 34
OJLS	*Oxford Journal of Legal Studies*	(2004) OJLS 11
PL	*Public Law*	[2005] PL 44
SJ	*Solicitors Journal*	SJ 2004 148(41) 1226

In addition, you may need to become familiar with some international journals, such as the following:

Abbreviation	Title of journal	Example citation
CMLR	*Common Market Law Review*	[2000] CMLR 33
ICLQ	*International and Comparative Law Quarterly*	[2004] ICLQ 222
EHRLR	*European Human Rights Law Review*	[2005] EHRLR 56
ELR	*European Law Review*	[2002] ELR 118

You will notice that some journals use square brackets and others use parentheses.

Some journals use the volume number; for example, LQR: the reference '[2000] 116 LQR 212' refers to the year of publication, the volume number, the appropriate abbreviation for the journal and then the page number where the article starts.

Some also use the issue number; for example, JP: the reference '(2005) 169(23) 428' refers to the year of the journal, the volume number and the issue number and then the page that the article starts on.

You will soon acquire this information and if you are in doubt about how you cite these journals, see how they are cited in textbooks, journals and reading lists and so on. You can also look inside the journal itself – they will tell you how they should be cited.

CITING BOOKS

The Oxford method

The Oxford method is most commonly used for English law books and most commonly used on law courses in England and Wales. You should refer to the author's first name and surname, followed by the title of the book (in italics), then the edition (if more than one edition), publisher, year of publication.

EXAMPLE

'Steve Foster, *The Law Relating to Football* (14th edition, Sweet & Maxwell, 1998).'

If you are referring to a specific page number, then use the preceding reference style, followed by ', at page(s) or p(p). 33(–37)'.

The Harvard method

The Harvard method is used on many social science courses and is very often an acceptable way of citing law texts. Check with the lecturer to see which method is preferable. In this method, you give the author's surname and initial(s), the year of publication, the title of the book (in italics or underlined), and then the place of publication, the publisher and the edition. For example:

EXAMPLE

'Foster, S.H. (1998) *The Law Relating to Football*, London: Sweet & Maxwell, 14th edition.'

CITING WEBSITES

NOTE

- -

OSCOLA provides detailed guidance on citing and referencing websites and on line journals: http://www.law.ox.ac.uk/publications/oscola.php

- -

If you have accessed a website to find primary and secondary sources that are reported elsewhere (e.g. WESTLAW), then cite those sources and not the website.

However, you should indicate that you have visited that website in your bibliography by putting the web address (URL) and the date you visited the site.

EXAMPLE

'http://www.westlaw.com (last accessed 24.4.2008).'

You can also refer to the website if a case or statute and so on can be accessed on that site. For example:

EXAMPLE

'See *Foster* v *Jones* [2004] AC 333. The case can be accessed on www.casesrus.com.'

If the website provides you with an authoritative source or statistics, then cite that website as the source.

EXAMPLE

'Department of Trade and Industry (2004) UK Energy Sector Indicators, http://dti.gov.uk.'

followed by the address of the specific page of the website.

BIBLIOGRAPHIES

Your bibliography should contain a list of references to any sources that you have used in the research and preparation of your work.

- Put the bibliography at the end of your work and on a separate page if it runs to more than one page.

- Note, no page numbers for books at this stage and no specific page numbers for articles.

- If you have read other sources, but not used them in the essay, cite the source in your bibliography; you do not have to use all the sources you read but ensure that there is not a great discrepancy between the two.

- Do not just list all relevant sources in that area; the list should be relevant to the question and you must have accessed them.

- Only cite websites if you used them to access information that is not available in official texts, journals, law reports, Acts of Parliament etc – cite the official source instead.

- You may categorise your entries under 'primary sources' and secondary sources' or create further categories such as' books', 'journal articles', 'websites', 'cases', Acts of Parliament (NB you may include a list of cases and statutes if that is required by the module leader, check first).

Examples of entries are given below, but see the bibliographies to the various essays used in this text for fuller guidance (note the different system for citing an author in bibliographies – surname, followed by initials).

Textbooks

- Ryan, M. *Unlocking Constitutional and Administrative Law* (2nd edn, Hodder 2010)
- Foster, S. *Human Rights and Civil Liberties* (2nd edn, Longman 2008)
- Fenwick H. *Civil Liberties and Human Rights* (4th edn, Routledge 2007)

Journal articles

- Foster, S 'Protecting privacy from press intrusion' (2009) Cov. Law J. 1

Cases

- *Douglas* v *Hello!* [2001] 2 WLR 992

Statutes

- Human Rights Act 1998 (do not put specific sections here)

References and Latin words and phrases

You can use a number of Latin words and phrases when referencing your work. It is not so essential that you do this in your first year, but you should use some for extended essays, projects and postgraduate work.

Many texts and journals are now abandoning the use of these terms, apart from *ibid.* (described next), so this text will refer to the more modern approach as well.

- ***Ibid.*:** If you have cited a reference in your previous footnote then, instead of giving the whole reference again, you can use *ibid.* and just refer to the actual page number.

> **EXAMPLE**
>
> 'The principle of proportionality was established in *Foster* v *United Kingdom*[45] and in that case the European Court stressed that any measure that interfered with political free speech had to be strictly proportionate.'[46]
>
> ---
> [45](1993) 27 EHRR 236.
> [46]ibid. at para 45.

You can use this equally for books, journals and statutory materials that have been cited in the previous footnote.

- *Supra*: Rather like *ibid.*, *supra* is used when you have already made reference to a particular source in your work, but not in the immediately preceding footnote.

EXAMPLE

'The courts have adopted the doctrine of proportionality with respect to human rights violations.'[90]

Or: 'In *Foster v Home Office*[91] it was decided that . . .'

---
[90]*Foster v Home Office, supra note 4, or* note 4, above.
[91]*supra*, note 4, or note 4, above.

- *Op. cit.*: Used to refer to a textbook or article that has already been referred to in your work and where you have already provided the full reference (e.g. Foster, *Human Rights* (Hughes & Hughes, 1998)). It can be used instead of citing the whole reference again, leaving you the task of referring to the previous reference (the footnote in which the reference first appeared) and then adding the page number of the already cited text.

EXAMPLE

'The Human Rights Act 1998 has been criticised on the grounds of its limited scope and the ambiguity of its central provisions.[99] Foster has argued that this provision is ambiguous.[100]

---
[99]Steve Foster, *The Human Rights Act 1998* (2nd edn OUP, 2004), 12.
[100]op. cit., note 1, at page 40, or note 1, above, at page 40.'

If you are referring the reader to a footnote at a later stage of the work, then use the expression 'see note x below.'

EXAMPLE

As we shall see later, the courts have also shown deference to Parliament with respect to the regulation of obscene and indecent expression.[29]

---
[29]*Ante*, note 46 and the cases cited therein, or note 46, below.

NOTE

The use of referencing and citation skills, as with all the other skills, is acquired *gradually* and via regular *practice*. You can usually find out how to cite and refer by consulting your textbooks and good law journals. The more journals, books, law reports, Acts of Parliament and so on that you read, the quicker you will pick up these skills.

TIPS FOR REFERENCING AND CITATION

- Always provide authority for any legal statement or academic opinion given in your answer.
- Make sure you appreciate the difference between primary and secondary sources and know the rules on crediting such sources.
- Use your library and research skills to locate relevant legal materials.
- Use primary and secondary sources to illustrate your answer and to enhance your work.
- Ensure that the source is properly incorporated into your work and that the reader understands its significance.
- Read the source properly and ensure that you understand it and its relevance before using it in your work.
- Ensure that the source is up to date and relevant to your answer.
- Make proper use of legal and other websites.
- Always apply legal reasoning in your answers, and think and adopt critical thinking and writing in all your assessments.
- Cite primary and secondary sources correctly and provide the correct and accepted references in your work.

4

Tackling exams and extended essays and projects

This part of the text addresses first the skills you will need to tackle law assessments in exam conditions, and, finally, those skills needed for enhanced and extended law assessments, including long essays, case notes and dissertations.

Chapter 8 examines the skills required of a law student when answering questions in exam conditions. In particular, the chapter includes guidance on the following:

- The expectations of the examiner and the skills that are tested in law exams.
- The difference in technique when answering questions in exam conditions.
- Preparation and revision for examinations.
- Question spotting.
- Identifying the legal areas and the scope of the question.
- Planning answers to exam questions.
- Using authority in exam conditions.
- Answering questions in open-book and seen exams.
- Time management in exams.

The purpose of Chapter 9 is to help you to acquire and practise the skills necessary to research and present written work on the advanced stages (years two, three and four) of a law programme. Earlier chapters concentrated on basic essay writing and legal skills, and whilst these skills must be practised beyond year one of your undergraduate studies, coursework and project work in these later stages of your law study will impose further demands on your research and writing skills. In particular, Chapter 9 gives guidance on:

- writing extended and advanced essays on your undergraduate programme, including case notes;
- researching and presenting undergraduate dissertations.

This section does not provide detailed information on how to research and present these assessments, but the skills highlighted in Chapter 6 on researching and using the law library, and in Chapter 3 on legal reasoning and critical analysis, can be used in conjunction with this chapter. Instead it will provide some basic advice on matters such as style, depth of research and employment of academic writing skills. **Please note** that the substantive law in these examples may well be out of date, and in any case students should not use such for the purpose of submitting work on their courses.

8

Preparing for and answering exam questions

GENERAL EXAM SKILLS

What skills do law exams test?

A law examination will test your knowledge of a particular subject area, together with your ability to apply that knowledge to different essay or problem questions. In that sense it is little different from coursework assessments, which test other academic skills (see the following sections).

Equally importantly, it will test your ability to use that knowledge in exam conditions, where you are expected to identify the scope and meaning of the question and to write the answers in a limited space of time, often without the aid of materials. Thus, to succeed in examinations you must display:

- a sound overall knowledge of the general subject area and the specific legal areas tested on the examination paper;
- an ability to quickly identify the scope and legal areas covered by the question;
- an ability to quickly identify the specific issues raised by the essay question or the problem scenario and to place those issues in the order in which you are to address them;

- an ability to write clearly and legibly and to provide a structured answer under examination conditions;
- an ability to keep calm in the face of time and other pressures and to manage your limited time in completing the paper.

How do exam answers differ from coursework answers?

Many of the general assessment skills discussed in the preceding chapters with respect to coursework assessment apply to answering examination questions. In particular, you should, as far as possible:

- employ clear and appropriate writing and grammatical skills;
- ensure that you are addressing the question, and use case and other legal authority constructively and appropriately.

In many respects, therefore, your answers in examinations should be smaller versions of answers provided in coursework assessment. However, given the time constraints and other pressures imposed in examinations, some of the rules applicable for coursework assessments will have to be adjusted.

- You will not be expected to employ the same level of professional style of presentation in an examination. For example, you will not be expected to employ footnotes or to provide full legal citations and references for legal authority. It is perfectly acceptable to cite a case by using an abbreviated citation and omitting the full reference:

EXAMPLE

'This was decided in *Carlill v Carbolic Smoke Ball* (1893),' or even 'This was decided in *Carlill*.'

- If you forget the case name, it is permissible to identify it by its facts, but do not make a habit of this. If you continually use the phrase 'there was a case where . . . ' you will create a poor impression.
- In most cases you will not be expected to quote a statutory provision verbatim (unless it is a central provision, such as s. 3 of the Human Rights Act 1998). Try to remember section numbers of the Act, but if you cannot remember them, at least identify the relevant Act.

- You are generally not expected to support your answers by formal citation of academic authority. Reference to secondary sources should be fully credited and referenced in coursework assessment, but this is not generally required in an examination. For example, in an exam you can write:

EXAMPLE

'This has been supported by various academic opinions, and Professor Foster believes that the above case law recognises a wide area of judicial discretion in this area.'

NOTE

It may be different in an open-book examination, where students *may* be required to use some referencing and citation skills; if you are in doubt, consult the module leader on this matter.

- In the vast majority of cases you will be required to write out your answers and will not be allowed to use a word-processor. Thus, you must write in a clear and *legible* fashion, whilst employing the writing skills expected in law assessments.

- There will be *some* allowance made for spelling and grammatical errors, and you should not have marks deducted for scrappy presentation, for example, crossings out. However, scrappy presentation can be a product of confusion and lack of time management, which will affect your marks.

- You will include your question plans and rough work in the examination script. Ensure that such work is distinct from the formal answer and that the marker can see the difference.

Why do students find law examinations more difficult?

Students often say that they are fine with coursework but that they cannot perform in examinations, but in fact they perform *better* in examinations. This might be because they lack the enhanced academic and writing skills required for coursework at undergraduate level but nevertheless possesses the basic legal knowledge, and ability, to apply that knowledge to succeed in examination conditions. Students can benefit from a marker's more liberal approach to grammar, spelling and citation and referencing of legal materials; equally, some students can provide a good concise answer to a question in 1,000 words but then find it difficult to elaborate on that answer so as to complete a 2,000-word essay.

Despite this, students may not be suited to examinations for a number of reasons.

They lack a sound overall knowledge of the subject area

To tackle most exams, the student needs a sound and broad knowledge of the subject area – for example, the law of contract. Although the student can have relative success in question spotting (see the next section), they are going to require a good grasp of most of the general principles in that area.

For example, a student studying contract law will need a good appreciation of contract formation, terms, breach of contract and remedies for breach of contract, in addition to some knowledge of a number of specialist areas such as mistake, misrepresentation, undue influence and restraint of trade.

If students lack this foundation knowledge, they will find it difficult to spot the scope and sense of the question (see the next section). Equally, they may be left floundering after answering one or two of the compulsory three, four (or five) questions, having exhausted their limited knowledge of specific subject areas. This limited knowledge is all too often caused by the following factors.

They concentrate too heavily on coursework assessment instead of engaging with the whole subject and obtaining a broad knowledge of that subject

Some students put all their effort into the research and preparation of coursework rather than attending lectures and seminars and fitting the coursework around the teaching programme.

This strategy may succeed in the short term because the student may receive a high(er) mark, but inevitably the student fails to acquire an overall understanding of the subject.

Thus, in examinations they may struggle to identify and tackle enough exam questions, having acquired a very specific knowledge of the area covered in the coursework (which might not even appear in the exam).

They do not engage with the subject area

This may not be the fault of the student, but those who do not attend lectures and seminars on a regular basis, and who do not undertake regular and consistent study of their texts and other sources, will find it much more difficult to tackle the examination at the end of the term or year.

In contrast, students who attend and study regularly will acquire confidence and competence in the area, which should serve them well in the examination.

Poor management of the revision process

If you start your revision programme too late, or fail to get the right balance between each subject area, you may be left with an inadequate or incomplete knowledge of the legal area for the examination.

This problem is often combined with non- or late engagement with the subject area (see the preceding sections), because students may find that some subject areas are more difficult than they imagined when they start researching and studying them. Consequently, students can find themselves with knowledge in too few areas.

This can be a particular problem with re-sit examinations, where the student discovers that they are missing basic knowledge when trying to revise for the exam.

Inability to think and write quickly enough

This is a genuine concern and problem for some students, even those who are intellectually prepared for the examination. Students can often be galled by the fact that they must write three, four or five answers in an examination, particularly if the examiner expects those answers to be in the region of four to six sides. In addition, some students find it difficult to identify and articulate the relevant legal points in time.

TIPS FOR EXAM PRACTICE

- Practise writing exam answers in longhand, particularly if you have not done this before and you are used to using the word processor. If you are a slow writer, do this to a greater extent.

- In addition, try to adopt a crisper, more concise writing style that addresses and deals with the relevant issues as quickly and precisely as possible. For example, do not give yourself the luxury of giving a long account of the facts and decision of cases and concentrate instead on the underlying principles and ratios. This is sound advice for all students, but particularly so if you are a slow writer.

- Practise answering questions in examination conditions so that you find it easier to identify and tackle legal issues in the exam. Again, practising these skills in seminars and throughout your study of the subject will help you in the exam.

Exam nerves

In general, you will feel *less* nervous if you have thoroughly prepared for the examination and are confident with that legal subject. Again, regular and consistent engagement with the subject area in lectures and seminars will help you feel more prepared and less anxious.

All students will experience exam nerves, and to a certain extent this is natural and can even enhance your performance. It also helps to share these nerves with your friends on the course; you will see that you are not alone in your anxiety.

For those who suffer genuine examination nerves, and where this substantially impacts on your performance in the examination, you should seek to undertake your exams under special 'sheltered' conditions.

TIPS FOR DEALING WITH EXAM NERVES

- If you *are* overtaken by nerves during the examination, try to take time to calm yourself, and notify the invigilator if necessary.
- One reason for anxiety in exams is when you cannot identify the meaning and scope of the question, and this is less likely to happen where you are conversant with the subject area and have practised such answers during the academic session.
- If you panic when finding out that the question on an area that you have revised is obscure, start off by writing some descriptive information; you can then blend that information with your analysis once the panic is gone.

EXAMPLE

In answering the question *'The nature of the British constitution shows that we do not really have a constitution or follow constitutionalism'* start off by listing the features of the British constitution, before thinking about the more complex issues in the question.

Exams as a continuation of the learning and assessment programme

Examinations are the culmination of the knowledge and skills that you have acquired on the course during the whole academic session (or semester). Although they test different skills, they should not be seen as a separate entity of your law studies. Many students who get into difficulty with examinations experience these problems because they only begin to engage with the subject at revision and exam time.

The knowledge required to tackle exam questions is generally based on what you have been taught in lectures and/or what you have been directed to study as part of the subject area.

Exam questions will often be based on similar essay and problem questions studied in seminars. The general skills necessary to answer exam questions will already have been practised in coursework and/or seminars.

NOTE

Universities now very often inform students of the content and form of the exam, so ensure you attend the relevant sessions and access relevant sites for this information.

THE REVISION PROCESS

Preparing for examinations

At the outset it should be stressed that 'examinations' now take a variety of forms; previously the examination came at the end of the academic year and tested the students' knowledge of the whole subject area via four or five questions to be answered in three hours. Such examinations still exist, but there are also in-term tests; exams where the questions, or at least the subject area, is seen beforehand; and exams with short questions and multiple choice questions. Your revision programme will vary depending on what type of examination you are subjected to.

You should begin your preparation for the examination at the *beginning* of the academic term. This text stresses that the exam is the culmination of the learning process (see the preceding section).

Always be on the lookout for hints and begin storing information for the examination (and for the rest of the course) at the earliest opportunity – for example, the module leader's favourite topic, topical legal subject areas and recent developments.

Thus, the final revision process, as described here, should be the final stage of your preparation for the examination, not the first. The whole examination and revision process will be much easier if you are confident with the subject area and the necessary legal skills *before* the revision begins.

Revising for examinations

NOTE

The information below, especially the example revision programme, is most relevant to unseen examinations which are taken at the end of the year, or semester, and which test the students' overall knowledge of the subject.

Whether you have been able to engage fully with the subject area or not, you will still need to adopt a revision programme in preparation for the examination. Remember, this should be a *revision* programme, and not an opportunity to learn the law for the first time.

- Ensure that you know everything about the format, length and scope of the examination; whether it is unseen, or seen, closed or open book, essay or problem questions (or both), contains multiple choice questions etc. **Find out this information from the relevant staff or module site, *not* other students (they will not be responsible if you get misinformation).**

- Multiple choice or short questions do not require an in-depth knowledge of the law but do require a broad knowledge of everything that you have covered so far, so ensure you have engaged with the whole module: **these tests can attract very high marks for those who have a sound overall knowledge of the subject.**

- Ensure that you have all the necessary information and sources to undertake your revision, particularly if you are going to be away from the university until the examinations.

- Make sure there are no gaps in your lecture and seminar notes, that you have the required texts and updates and that you continue to keep up to date with recent developments, at the very least by reading the newspapers and accessing relevant websites.

- Focus on relevant areas and likely sources of questions rather than trying to revise the whole subject area (see the section 'Question spotting'), but do not expect to answer a specific question, unless that question is given to you in advance.

- If you are reasonably confident with the subject at the start of your revision, then you may be ready to proceed to revision of specific subject areas, but make sure your notes and so on are complete and that there are no major gaps in your knowledge.

- If you have not been able to engage with the subject throughout the year, give yourself a day or so, at least, to acquaint yourself with the subject, and do not attempt intense revision of any areas until you are reasonably confident with the general subject.

- If you have a number of examinations, consult the timetable at an early stage and devise a revision programme that fits that timetable; for example, ensure that you allocate yourself an appropriate number of days for each subject.

EXAMPLE

I have got Contract on 20 May, Legal System on 24 May, Constitutional on 28 May and Crime on 4 June.

I will start my revision programme on 29 April, two days after lectures and seminars finish (you can start earlier if you want to). I will go over Crime for about three days to make sure I have all the notes and so on and that I understand it all, because that's my last exam and I won't be looking at it in detail until 29 May. I will also get all my notes in order for Legal System and Constitutional and do some revision for those subjects because I am going to concentrate on Contract first. I will begin my Contract revision on 12 May, leaving myself eight days, which should be ample. I will then have four days to do ELS and another four days for Constitutional. I will then have six days to revise for Crime.

- You do not have to allocate your time as in the example. Some students prefer to mix the subjects – one or two days per subject, then change – rather than concentrate on one subject for a fixed number of days.

- If you have a number of examinations over a short period of time – in other words there is not a convenient gap between each examination – accommodate for that and start your revision programme a little earlier and ensure that you are prepared for those clashes. Using the preceding example, 'As I have got Constitutional on 2 June and Crime on 4 June, I need to adjust my revision programme and I will need to do more, earlier revision for those subjects, so that I am in the last stages of revision for them by the time I finish Legal System.'

- Start your revision programme in plenty of time so that you do not have to cram information in a short space of time or spend too much of the day and night revising.

- Devise a timetable and try to stick to it, but build in time for rest and to accommodate some interruptions. Below is a typical revision programme for a student who will take a number of examinations (three, four or five) at the end of the year or semester. You do not have to, or might not be able to, use this exact programme, but it is quite flexible. In particular, if you do not have seven clear days to revise one module, then spread the programme shown in the example over a wider period. However, keep in mind that the programme in the example contains a good mixture of regime and discipline, rest and relaxation, and a variety of revision exercises.

Monday: 9.00–12.00 – Offer and acceptance (for a three-hour session perhaps have two hours revision and attempt a practice question); 12.00–14.00 – Lunch and break; 14.00–17.00 – Consideration; 17.00–19.00 – Eat and rest; 19.00–21.00 – Intention (as above); 21.00–23.00 – TV.

Tuesday: 9.00–12.00 – Terms; 12.00–14.00 – Lunch; 14.00–17.00 – Exclusion clauses; 17.00–20.00 – Play tennis and eat; 20.00–22.30 – Finish off exclusion clauses; 22.30–24.00 – TV.

Wednesday: 9.00–12.00 – Misrepresentation; 12.00–13.00 – Lunch; 13.00–16.00 – Mistake; 16.00 – Rest of the day off.

Thursday: 9.00–12.00 – Undue influence; 12.00–14.00 – Lunch; 14.00–17.00 – Breach of contract and performance; 17.00–19.00 – Eat and rest; 19.00–21.00 – Frustration; 21.00–24.00 – TV.

Friday: 9.00–12.00 – Practise breach and frustration questions; 12.00–14.00 – Lunch; 14.00–17.00 – Remedies; 17.00 – Eat and night out.

Saturday: 11.00–13.30 – Go over formation of contract and do some more practice questions; 13.30–14.30 – Lunch and go for a walk;

14.30–17.00 – Go over terms and exclusion clauses and do some more practice questions; 17.00–18.00 – Eat and rest; 18.00–23.00 – Go over misrepresentation, mistake and undue influence, doing the same; 23.00–24.00 – Some TV.

Sunday: 8.00–11.00 – Go over breach and frustration, practising questions; 11.00–12.00 – Break; 12.00–14.00 – Go over remedies, practising questions; 14.00–16.00 – Eat and rest; 16.00–18.00 – Go through an old exam paper and try a couple of questions under exam conditions; 18.00–19.00 – Eat and rest; 19.00–22.00 – Go through notes and make sure there is nothing you are unsure about; 22.00–23.00 TV.

Monday: Contract exam at 9.30.

- Try not to work too late into the night, ensure you get a good night's sleep and if you drink alcohol, cut down your normal intake and just drink occasionally and in moderation – otherwise it will make you lethargic. Always try to start early in the morning after a decent breakfast.

- On the day of the exam get up at 7.30 and get to the university half an hour before the exam starts. Try not to do any revision in the morning, but have your notes handy to avoid any panic.

Using past papers and seminar questions

The university or the module leader should be able to provide you with past examination papers in the subject area. In addition, many seminar questions, and coursework questions, are often actual, or similar, past exam questions.

- Do not expect the questions on your examination paper to be exactly the same as in previous years. Search for likely subject areas rather than the exact question.

- In many cases, some legal areas will not be examined every year. Check your notes and handouts to see what you have covered in the academic session. This will give you some indication as to which topics are likely to appear, or to be omitted from the examination.

- In addition, some subject areas that regularly appear on examination papers – offer and acceptance, damages, separation of powers, rule of law, juries and access to justice – might appear in a variety of forms; for example, they can sometimes be essays and sometimes problem questions or case studies.

- Practise writing past examination papers under exam conditions, and if the module leader holds a session to go through a past paper, ensure that you attend it.

- Practise answering discussion and problem questions in seminars. Regular attendance and constructive participation in these sessions will provide you with good experience for the examination and will ease the tension of the examination experience.

Using question-and-answer books

Some staff do not favour question-and-answer books because they lead the student to believe that there is a perfect answer to the question or students use them as a substitute for texts and overall revision.

Used properly, however, such texts can be of immense help to students preparing for examinations (and coursework – see Chapter 1). In general, they are much more likely to enhance your performance in examinations than basic revision texts, which serve their purpose in consolidating your knowledge, but which can often dilute legal knowledge and expertise:

- Such texts provide guideline answers to, and advice on the construction of, the sort of questions that *might* appear in examinations. (Do not assume that you can use the same answers for the question given to you in the exam.)

- They provide you with an overall impression of the way in which you should express yourself in exam answers, how you should plan answers, and how you should incorporate legal materials into your answers. They also offer a general guide as to the required length and detail of the answer.

- They provide an opportunity to see how your knowledge and appreciation of the law should be employed in exam conditions.

- They offer a *limited* benefit to revision, as they cover a broad range of legal areas that might appear in the examination. However, they should not be treated as a substitute for textbooks or for thorough revision.

- They presuppose that you have a good knowledge of the subject *before* you read or use them. Use them alongside your texts and other secondary and primary sources to hone your skills in addressing and answering exam questions.

Making use of advanced research in examinations

It is often a good idea, particularly in years two and three of your degree or in postgraduate examinations, for you to include information gained from extra research, such as academic articles or on recent law reform etc. Your revision programme can incorporate sources which you have been referred to during the course, or which you have found on your own initiative. This provides the marker with evidence that you have looked beyond your notes and the standard texts to revise for and write your answers and this can often make the difference between a good mark and a very good one.

- Include views from journal articles which support points raised in the question and your answer; ensure that they are relevant to the question – do not include them for the sake of it.

- Include information from government papers or Law Commission reports on recent proposals for reform.

- Include recent articles from quality newspapers or weekly or monthly journals in order to incorporate relevant and topical issues into your answer.

- Use legal websites – such as WESTLAW or LAWTEL – to keep up to date with these developments.

- Be realistic when using these sources: do not risk not addressing the issues in the question by trying to include detailed research and data.

Question spotting

It is unrealistic for you to cover the whole legal subject area in detail in your revision programme.

TIPS FOR QUESTION SPOTTING

- First ascertain what has been taught on the module over the academic year and then obviously exclude those areas included in the text but not covered on your course, unless it has been made clear that a question will be appearing in one of those areas.

- In addition, you should be able to get a reasonable indication of what is likely to come up in the examination by considering factors such as the content of past papers, hints dropped in lectures, seminars and revision sessions and the topicality of the issue (e.g. reform of the Human Rights Act 1998 is a 'good banker' on most civil liberties exams for the foreseeable future, as is the effect of the reduction in legal aid in most legal system papers). You may want to reduce the scope of your revision by predicting certain questions (or rather subject areas) and concentrating on those areas whilst excluding others.

- Do not exclude from your revision an area that is fundamental to the understanding of the whole subject and that might infiltrate other areas of study. For example, the exclusion of the Human Rights Act 1998 from a civil liberties course, or the whole of formation of a contract from a contract course.

- Do not exclude so many areas so that you are left with inadequate knowledge to tackle a whole exam paper. For example, for a constitutional exam, do not exclude the whole of administrative law, civil liberties, and Parliament and sovereignty, leaving only constitutions, the nature and sources of the British Constitution, the rule of law and the separation of powers: even if these four topics have been announced in advance, you will need information from other topics to supplement your answer (see below).

- Ensure that you have one, or a number of, fall-back positions just in case your favourite areas do not appear on the paper. For an exam requiring four answers, you should have at least two other areas in which you could provide a reasonably full answer.

- Even where you exclude a subject area, ensure that you have at least a basic understanding of that area because it will help you understand and answer other questions. For example, if you are going to exclude judicial review in your constitutional exam ensure you have some knowledge of its rationale because this will help you answer questions on the control of executive government, the rule of law, parliamentary sovereignty, the separation of powers etc.

- Your revision plan should thus identify three subject categories: (1) those that you hope will appear on the paper and which you will revise thoroughly (including your back-ups); (2) those for which you need a general knowledge because they may appear in questions under item 1 or you might have to do as a last resort; (3) those that you feel are safe to exclude.

- It is only safe to exclude a specific subject area when it is a distinct and separate topic. Thus, for example, it would normally be safe to exclude areas such as restraint of trade in contract, parliamentary privilege in constitutional law or defamation in tort law.

- Be aware that many examiners like to ask mixed questions. For example, a question in a contract law exam could cover offer and acceptance, exemption clauses and damages for breach of contract, and in a tort paper a question could cover negligence, occupiers' liability and/or nuisance, and damages.

In summary, ensure that you have a sound overall knowledge of the subject, acquired from regular attendance and engagement with the course, and exclude from your overall revision programme only those areas that you feel will not impact on the questions you will answer.

THE EXAMINATION

Identifying the legal areas and the scope of the question

When you first look at the paper, identify the legal areas tested by each question and decide as quickly as possible which questions you are going to tackle. The broader your knowledge, the more likely you are to spot that some questions cover two or more legal areas. Exam questions can be fairly similar to seminar and coursework questions, so again the scope of the question should be relatively easy to spot.

- If you have been given the subject area in advance, read the question even more carefully. You may be tempted simply to write everything in that area that you have revised in anticipation of the question, but ensure you identify which specific aspects are being tested. If the actual questions are released in advance, ensure you read them thoroughly and base your revision on supplying a model answer.

- If you are given extra reading time in the exam, use that time to look over the whole paper, excluding some questions, identifying your preferences and making a list of relevant legal points covered by each question. This should settle your nerves and prepare you for the start of the examination proper.

- If you spot a favourite topic but think that the question is obscure, do not discard that question. Move on to your other choices and then go back to that question to see whether you could really tackle it. Often the question is not as obscure as you originally thought, and the answer still requires a lot of the information that you have revised. (See the section below: 'Question 2: The constitutional law essay'.)

Understanding the question

As with coursework assessment, you must answer the exam question and cannot simply write all you know on that area or rewrite the question.

Examine the question very carefully, identifying whether it is a descriptive or analytical question, or both, and what its central features are.

EXAMPLE QUESTION

'The role of the courts is to interpret and apply the law. No more and no less.'
Do you agree with this statement?

This question is about the role of the courts in a constitutional and legal system, and you need to know how courts resolve disputes and, specifically, how they interpret statutes and develop the common law. However, the question is really about whether in practice they simply carry out that role, and whether they should or should not go further and actually make the law.

A student who simply talks about the rules of statutory interpretation, the development of the common law and the doctrine of precedent will not be addressing the central thrust of the question.

Planning the answer to exam questions

Use the reading time and then an extra minute or so to draw a plan of your proposed answer. List the points in order, according to the structure of the question, and include any relevant case or other authority. Thus the plan to the question above could look something like this.

EXAMPLE

- Explanation of the general and traditional role of the courts in a legal and constitutional system, including the courts' relationship with Parliament and the executive.
- Examples of the traditional approach, using hypothetical and case examples in illustration.
- Examination of alternative approaches and views, using specific examples to illustrate how the courts have departed from their traditional role.
- Consideration of academic and personal views on the appropriate role of the courts.
- Conclusion.

Structuring your answers

As with coursework assessment, adopt a structured approach: deal with each point in order and explain the law and the relevant cases and other authority clearly.

Begin by identifying the legal and factual issues raised by the question, and then deal with those issues in turn, adding any necessary analysis and authority. You can then include a (brief) conclusion summarising the points that you have made.

In exam conditions you will obviously make some errors in this respect and may need to revisit some of the issues if you suddenly remember a point that you have omitted. Leave a small gap between each paragraph and at the end of your answer so that you can insert additional information at a later time.

EXAMPLE

'A contract is a legally binding agreement and must contain an offer and acceptance (the basics of any agreement or consensus ad idem), consideration and an intention to create legal relations. If one of those essential elements is missing, then the agreement will not be legally binding and cannot be enforced in a court of law.

Every contract must have a definite offer . . . '

If you now remember that you should have mentioned the requirements of legality and legal capacity, you can include that information at the end of the relevant paragraph, instead of including it at the end of the answer marked by an asterisk and giving a (or a number of) complicated instruction(s) to the examiner on where to find the additional information and where it should be placed.

Writing clearly, simply and legibly

Examiners will make some allowance for grammatical and other writing errors in the examination, and you will not be expected to write with the same degree of fluency and professionalism that you displayed in coursework (for which you have had weeks to prepare and check your answer). However, in general, you should follow the basic rules relating to grammar, style and clarity that you employed for coursework assessment.

In particular, write legibly and keep crossings-out and amendments to a minimum. Always leave time at the end to check your work for grammar and sense, as well as for completeness.

Tackling problem questions in exam conditions

Adopt the guidance given in Chapter 7 of this text when answering problem questions. The difference is that you must identify the relevant issues, and plan and structure your answer to such questions, in a short space of time. Practise the general skill in seminars and throughout the course and, in particular, practise doing it under exam conditions during your revision programme.

As time is of the essence, keep your introduction and comments on the general state of the law to a minimum and proceed directly to the relevant legal point and its application to the facts. Avoid the following style.

EXAMPLE

'This problem question is concerned with the law of mistake and whether a party who has ostensibly entered into a contract can claim that the agreement is void because of such a mistake. As all contracts are based on a consensus ad idem – a meeting of the minds – the common law may refuse to enforce a contract which is based on a fundamental mistake of one or both parties to the apparent contract. According to Professor Foster, the basis of the court's intervention in this type of case is that the parties negotiate on the implied assumption that . . . '

Instead, get straight to the legal point raised by the scenario and begin addressing and answering that point.

EXAMPLE

'The first issue is whether X can claim that his contract with Y is void for unilateral mistake when he was unaware that the painting was not a Picasso, and Y was aware of his misunderstanding. A unilateral mistake is . . . '

Answering skills exercises in exams

Many Legal System, Legal Method and Legal Skills exams test your ability to interpret legal materials (imaginary and real) to see if you can apply the basic rules of statutory interpretation or case analysis in a specific setting. Below is a typical example of such an exercise. The examiner wants you to identify any potential ambiguities and to apply your knowledge and understanding of statutory interpretation to identify which words of the statute are engaged and then to provide a logical solution to that ambiguity. You will not get any or many marks if you simply say, for example, **'In this case there are three rules of interpretation and it depends which one the court favours'** (even if you give general authority for the rules).

EXAMPLE QUESTION

In 2016 Grandchester County Council made the following (imaginary) bylaw:

> 'It is an offence for any person to place an advertisement on council property without the consent of the council.'

The word 'advertisement' is defined in the bylaw as 'any written material publicising any event or cause'.

Using your knowledge of the established rules of statutory interpretation, explain whether an offence has been committed in the following cases:

A   Billy, a local councillor, places an advertisement on the doors of the council's town hall, inviting people to attend a forthcoming council meeting on housing issues.

B   Karl, the chairman of the local communist party, drapes a banner on the steps of the town hall, lamenting the fall of communism in Eastern Europe in the past 20 years.

C   Sally, a childminder registered with the local authority, attaches a number of leaflets publicising Children's Week, having received permission to do so from two local councillors.

You should proceed directly to situation A and identify the relevant words of the bylaw in dispute and what the potential ambiguities are. In other words, is a councillor 'any person' and has this advert been placed 'on council property without the consent of the local council' if it has in fact been placed there by a councillor, and to publicise council business? You should now use the relevant principles and case law to consider a number of possible interpretations.

You then do the same for situation B: is the banner an advert ('written material'), and does the bylaw apply to political and public interest speech (taking into account the Human Rights Act 1998 and applying s. 3 of that Act, along with any relevant case law)? Finally, consider situation C and whether Sally is 'any person' (as she is registered with the council), and whether she has the 'consent of the council' because she received permission from two councillors.

Open-book exams

Although many students like open-book examinations, if you are allowed to bring in your books or notes to an examination you must adjust your examination technique from that adopted in the closed-book exam.

- The purpose of this concession is to avoid the exam being a pure memory test and to put the student at ease in this respect. All you need to do now is apply the law you have before you to the questions that have been asked.

- Expect the questions to be more challenging and for you to be required to show much more analysis and application. You cannot expect questions such as 'Explain the main requirements of a legally binding contract' if you have the textbook in front of you, because you can then simply copy out the answer from the book. The questions will, therefore, be in the form of problem questions, or essay questions requiring an analysis of that legal area; for example, '*Critically analyse the extent to which the separation of powers is adhered to in the British Constitution. Are any exceptions truly breaches of the doctrine?*'

- Do not use this concession as an excuse not to do any revision for the examination. You must be ready to apply the information before you see the question. If you have not revised you will not be able to identify the question and will simply end up writing chunks out of the textbook in the hope that it is relevant.

- Thus, do not simply write out of the book or your notes, ignoring the question and failing to use those analytical and application skills. Use the text to get the basic principles, but concentrate on how that information can be used to answer the question. Unlike the closed-book exam, you will get very little, if any, credit for supplying general information from the text because you have not even used your knowledge and memory to provide that information.

- It is best to use the text as a safety net, just in case you get stuck, and to rely on it for definitions, case names, quotes and so on.

- If you are permitted to bring in a variety of sources, think about what you might bring in: index and organise those sources appropriately so that you are fully prepared to employ those sources to your answers – your time is limited, so don't waste it.

- You must not copy from texts and journal articles and pass this off as your answer: **this is plagiarism!**

Seen examinations

Some examination questions are seen by the students in advance, and students simply turn up on the day to provide the answer. In such a case, you will probably not be allowed to take in notes and texts, but this type of exam can put students at their ease and will allow them to research thoroughly and to rehearse a prepared answer to the question.

Some such examinations are not totally seen, and the student may be simply informed that the exam question(s) will be on a particular topic, without revealing the specific question. Another method employed by some universities is to provide a case study and to tell the students that they must expect a series of questions on that case in the examination.

- If you are given the question, or the area of law, in advance of the examination, ensure that you get hold of that question and any information at the first available opportunity.

- When you discover the question and/or the legal areas that are being tested ensure that you are already familiar with them, that you have attended the relevant classes and undertaken the necessary reading in those areas; if not, go back to those areas and learn them.

- If the question is entirely seen, examine the scope and meaning of the question very closely and ensure that your rehearsed answer is relevant and as comprehensive as possible within the time limit.

- Practise writing out the answer in exam-type conditions to see that your answer is feasible with respect to the allocated time.

- Revise the specific relevant areas thoroughly, but don't go into a test without **any** basic knowledge of the fundamentals of the module. For example if direct effect of EU law is being tested ensure you have at least a basic knowledge of EU institutions and principles; in constitutional law if the question is on, for example, the rule of law ensure you know at least the basics about the nature of the British Constitution, parliamentary sovereignty, separation of powers etc.

- If you are simply given the topic area, research that area thoroughly and expect a variety of questions, essays or problems. Because you have been allowed this concession, expect the question to be demanding and for you to display strong analytical skills. Check on questions asked in previous exams, but do not expect the same question.

- If the seen exam is in the form of a case study, study the case and the relevant legal areas very closely and be prepared to answer all manner of questions on it.

Time management in exams

This is a common problem with students. Always try to manage your time effectively so that you do not run out of time. Try to be strict with yourself and give yourself an allocated time in which to answer each question.

EXAMPLE

If you start a three-hour, four-question exam at 14.00, plan to have question 1 done by 14.50 (you will spend more time on the first question because it will take a while for you to get going, the first question is usually your favourite, and you will have spent time looking at the paper, choosing questions and making plans). You can then plan to finish question 2 by 15.35, and question 3 by 16.20, leaving you about 40 minutes to tackle the final question and to check all your answers at the end.

- Do not rely on one or two very full and good answers at the expense of providing four sound answers. In most cases, the marks awarded for the first two answers will not compensate for the other poor and incomplete answers.

- Avoid the temptation to spend much more time on the first answer, even though you feel confident and competent in this area.

- It is easier to acquire the first 40 or 50 marks for an answer than it is to get the next 20 or 30 marks, so try to ensure that each answer is of reasonable length and depth.

Running out of time

If you fail to follow the time management rules laid out in the preceding section, and you do run out of time, you must have a strategy to obtain the maximum marks for a short or incomplete answer. Examiners can very often distribute quite respectable marks for short or incomplete answers, and they are usually more generous towards these answers if you have already provided sound answers to the previous questions.

The guidance on this issue is based on the answer to the following question on misrepresentation.

EXAMPLE QUESTION

On 14 July 2015, Barry was discussing the possible sale of his record shop in Heavington to Harry. During the negotiations, Harry asked Barry what sort of turnover the shop had, to which Barry replied, 'Since I have been manager we have never fallen short of £200,000 a year.' Harry also asked about local competition, and Barry replied that 'apart from the megastores in Boventry (10 miles away), we are the only record shop in the area.' As Harry was leaving, Barry told Harry that Heavington was the trendiest place within 50 miles and that the local youth would always spend their money on records and clothes.

After that meeting Harry agreed to buy the business and placed the matter into the hands of his solicitor. A contract was drawn up, which made no mention of the matters stated in the previous conversation, and when Harry's solicitor asked Harry whether he wanted him to investigate the takings of the shop, Harry replied, 'No, I don't think I can go wrong in Heavington.'

Harry concluded the contract for the sale of the shop for £120,000 in October 2015 and after seven months he has recorded a turnover of just £40,000 with a projected turnover of £75,000. He has also discovered that the shop's previous turnovers were all below £90,000, that Barry was the manager (as opposed to just the owner) for only one year, and that the year in which the turnover was £200,000 coincided with a month-long national music festival held in Heavington. Finally, he has just discovered that a competing shop will open next week, having received permission to open in September 2016.

Advise Harry as to whether he can sue for misrepresentation and any remedy he may receive if he is successful.

If, for example, you are left with 15 minutes to complete your final answer, follow these rules:

- Do *not* waste time by explaining to the examiner that you are running out of time!

EXAMPLE

'Please accept my apologies, but I have run out of time and cannot complete this question. As a result I have made a brief list of issues which I believe are relevant to the question. I know this is my fault, but I hope you can take this into consideration when marking my paper.'

- Do *not* waste time providing an academic introduction to the question or talking generally about the question.

EXAMPLE

'This (problem) question is concerned with misrepresentation, where one party has been induced to enter into a contract because of a false statement of fact. Professor Foster has defined a misrepresentation as . . . and notes that the law is currently in a state of flux, particularly with respect to the award of damages for misrepresentation. In this question I will examine the facts to see whether X made a false statement of fact and whether Y was induced to enter into the contract because of that statement. I will then consider whether Y will have any remedy in misrepresentation.'

- As you only have 15 minutes, you need to proceed *immediately* to the factual and legal issues. By providing a general introduction you are not displaying much general legal knowledge, and you are failing to show whether you can or could answer the question.
- Do *not* simply make a general list of points, covering basic ground. You will get some, limited, marks for this (provided they are basically relevant) but the following list does not display any real awareness of the actual question and its scope. Only adopt this approach if you genuinely have no more time (in other words, you only have 30 seconds!); even then make sure the points are directly relevant to the problem.

EXAMPLE

- Definition of misrepresentation
- Statement of fact, not of intention (*Edgington*) or opinion (*Bisset*)
- Inducement (*Heilbut Symons, Redgrave* v *Hurd*)
- Remedies – rescission, damages, Misrepresentation Act 1967

- Do *not* spend all your time dealing with one point in detail, leaving the other points untouched.

EXAMPLE

'The first issue to consider is whether the statement about the turnover of the shop was a statement of fact and, most importantly, whether it was untrue. For a misrepresentation to be actionable the statement must be untrue and the general rule is that the representor is under no liability to provide the representee with factual information, in other words silence will not normally amount to misrepresentation. This was established in the case of *Smith* v *Hughes*. In that case . . . and it was held that there had been no misrepresentation simply because the defendant had remained silent, Blackburn J commenting that '. . .' Thus, on the facts the representation made by Barry does not appear to be untrue as the year he was manager the shop did in fact have a turnover of £200,000, even though Harry may have been misled by the way that information was presented to him.

However, silence may amount a misrepresentation in a number of circumstances. One such situation is where the representation constitutes a half-truth and thus misleads the representee. In this situation there may be a duty on the representor to break his silence and to provide fuller information to the other party. For example, if when applying for a job I tell my employer that I studied law at Oxford, I would have a duty to qualify that statement by stressing that I failed my first year and never completed the degree programme. Otherwise I am misleading the employer by this half-truth. Thus, in *Nottingham Patent Brick Co Ltd* v *Butler* it was held that there had been a misrepresentation when the defendants stated, truthfully, that they knew of no covenant on the land, neglecting to say that they had failed to make appropriate investigations into the matter. In our case, therefore, there appears to be an actionable misrepresentation because

---

> Barry neglects to provide Harry with the full facts, viz that he has not always been manager and the large turnover was exceptional because of the holding of the musical festival.
>
> Sorry, ran out of time . . .

- This answer is really quite good, but only as far as it goes. The writing style is good and the point is dealt with fully and clearly, displaying good logical skills. But the student only deals with one of the many issues raised by the problem. There is a limit to how many marks an examiner can give in this case, and the student is better advised to deal with this and other issues in less detail, thus showing a greater appreciation of the whole question.

- Try to provide a mini-answer, outlining all the relevant issues and omitting detail on cases and your full arguments. The following answer would only take up a page or so of the exam book, but it covers the essential issues and displays some understanding of those issues and their potential application to the facts.

EXAMPLE

'The first issue concerns Barry's statement about the previous profits. Although it appears literally true, and his silence does not normally amount to misrepresentation (*Smith* v *Hughes*), it may constitute a half-truth (*Notts Patent Brick*) and thus impose on Barry a duty to clarify the original statement by giving Harry information about the music festival and to clarify his position as manager.

Secondly, although the statement about the competitors was true at the time, again Barry may have a duty to notify Harry of the change of circumstances regarding the competitor, applying the principle in *With* v *O'Flannagan*.

Thirdly, although Barry's statement about the youth of Heavington appears at first sight to be a statement of opinion (*Bisset* v *Wilkinson*), it may be argued that the statement suggested that he had the expertise to back that statement up with facts (*Esso* v *Mardon*), in which case it could amount to a misrep or a negligent misstatement at common law if it was clearly not a true assessment of the spending power of the youth in that area.

Next, was Harry induced by any of the statements, and were any of them material factors in making him sign the contract? The factors do not have to be the only reason for concluding the contract (*Edgington v Fitzmaurice*), and he is not under a duty to investigate the truth of the statements (*Redgrave v Hurd*). However, if he relied on his own investigations and judgment ('can't go wrong in Heavington'), he will not be able to sue (*Attwood v Small* and *Heilbut Symons v Buckleton*).

It appears he has been induced by Barry's statements and should seek rescission, either as of right in the tort of deceit or at the court's discretion under s. 2(2) Misrep Act if it was not fraudulent – in this case it would not appear to be inequitable to deny rescission and award damages in lieu. Finally, on the question of damages, he can either sue in the tort of deceit for all actual loss (*Derry v Peek*) flowing from the representation, or under s. 2(1) if it was non-fraudulent.

The examiner may award a low pass mark, or more, as this answer provides a basic answer to the question and indicates understanding and thought from the student.

- If you haven't got time to provide even a mini-answer in prose style (as in the preceding example), make a list of relevant points, ensuring that the examiner gets the gist of the arguments that you would have presented.

EXAMPLE

- Was Barry's statement about the previous profits true, and has he a duty to break his silence (*Smith v Hughes*)?

- Did it constitute a half-truth (*Notts Patent Brick*) and thus did Barry have a duty to clarify the original statement by giving Harry information about the music festival and to clarify his position as manager?

- Did Barry have a duty to notify Harry of the change of circumstances regarding the competitor? (*With v O'Flannagan*)

- Was Barry's statement about the youth of Heavington a statement of opinion (*Bisset v Wilkinson*) or a mere advertising puff, or did it suggest that he has the expertise to back that statement up with facts? (*Esso v Mardon*)

- Was Barry induced by any of the statements – were any of them material factors in making him sign the contract? (*Edgington* v *Fitzmaurice*)

- Is he under a duty to investigate the truth of the statements? (*Redgrave* v *Hurd*)

- Did he rely on his own investigations and judgment? (*Attwood* v *Small* and *Heilbut Symons* v *Buckleton*)

- Can he rescind the contract in this case? (Depends on whether it is fraudulent or falls under s. 2(2) Misrep Act)

- What damages would he receive? – depends on whether it is fraudulent (*Derry* v *Peek*) or non-fraudulent (s. 2 Misrep Act – would it be inequitable to allow rescission – no!)

This list of points should earn you some marks. The points are all relevant to the factual scenario (not just to the area of misrepresentation). They also deal with the issues raised in the scenario in a logical order. Furthermore, the student has provided appropriate legal authority of all the points. Most importantly, the list suggests that the student has understood the factual and legal issues arising from the scenario and would have been in a position to give a full and intelligent answer to these questions.

Re-sit examinations

If you have failed the initial examination, or could not sit if for a valid reason, you may be eligible for a re-sit in that examination. This re-sit will normally take place at the end of the summer vacation and will normally be similar to the initial examination. However, re-sit students should note the following:

- As you will normally revise for this exam in the vacation, you will not have the luxury of regular contact with either the module leader or your fellow students.

- If you are re-sitting an exam at the same time as studying and revising for new exams (for example if you failed an exam in the first semester and need to re-sit alongside second semester exams), ensure you make extra room for the re-sit in your revision programme.

- Try to contact the module leader, preferably before the summer vacation begins, to discuss the re-sit paper and its likely content and format. In addition, try to keep in contact with fellow students so as to discuss the subject and the forthcoming examination.

- Ensure that you retain or get a copy of the first examination, either to work through the answers again or to see what sort of questions you missed first time round.

- If you have failed the first paper, try to find out, if you can, why you failed. Often the university will not discuss specific papers, but try to discover what was basically wrong with your paper.

- If you have failed because you did not engage with the module during the year (by reason of illness or otherwise), your revision (or learning) programme will be more intensive, and you must begin that programme in good time so that you can become familiar with the subject area. Do not expect to digest and understand that subject easily simply by looking at the texts and other materials.

- In such a case, you must go back to your basic texts and notes and familiarise yourself with the subject. In addition, you should go through the seminar and other exercises that you missed during the academic session.

- Do not expect the re-sit paper to be exactly the same as the first paper. It may contain questions on different areas, or different types of questions on the same areas. Many students fail the re-sit because they think that they will pass provided they prepare for it, but often they do not realise that, in the absence of support, they are failing to understand the subject.

EXAMPLES OF EXAM ANSWERS

We will now look at some typical examination questions to provide guidance on examination technique and to provide appropriate answers to those questions.

NOTE

The answers in this section are not intended to be perfect or model—and you must not use them as a perfect research tool for your revision – but nevertheless they employ sound legal and writing skills, address the issues raised by the question and use case and other materials in an appropriate way.

QUESTION 1: THE CONTRACT PROBLEM

This problem question tests the student's knowledge in a number of areas of contract law – intention to create legal relations, consideration, implied terms, classification of terms, breach of contract and damages. An examiner will often make such a question compulsory, in an effort to see that the student has learnt a number of basic contractual principles during the course. To answer it, students need a good overall grasp of contractual principles and the law of contract. In addition, in an exam environment, they will need to be able to quickly identify those various areas and deal with them speedily and effectively.

EXAMPLE QUESTION

George intended to celebrate his 30th birthday party at his home on 20 December 2015. He contacts his friend, Harold, who plays in a group, and asks whether the group could play at his party. Harold agrees that the group will play two two-hour sets for a fee of £500, some £250 below their normal fee. Two days later, George telephones Harold and reminds him that the band will be playing at a family party and that they must play a range of music that will keep everyone happy. Harold replies, 'Don't worry, we won't play anything too heavy.' George also contacted Barry, a professional children's entertainer, and asked whether he could perform for the children between 8 and 9 o'clock. Barry agreed and after George stated that Barry must be finished by 9 o'clock, because the children are due to leave the party at that time, a price of £120 was agreed upon.

On the night Harold and his band played two sets, but George received constant complaints from the older guests that the music was too loud. Harold and the band refused to turn the volume down, saying that some younger guests had asked for the volume to be turned up. Harold also received some complaints after the party had finished that the band had played too many Take That records and had refused to play several requests.

Barry turned up at 8.45 but stated that he could go straight on and be finished by 9.45. George was annoyed at this stage and despite the children's and parents' pleas to allow Barry to perform, George said that it was now too late and sent Barry away without payment.

> Advise George, who believes that the whole night was a disaster, whether he can sue Harold for breach of contract, and, if so, what remedy he would claim. Also, advise Barry whether he can sue Harold for breach of contract for non-payment of his fee.

Your plan of the answer should look something like this:

- Did George and Harold have the intention to create legal relations in order to enter into a legally binding contract?
- What terms have been agreed between the parties?
- Specifically, was the request to play a range of music a term of the contract?
- Did Harold and the band breach any contractual duties?
- If so, can George sue for damages and what loss can he recover?
- Was the term that Barry is finished by 9.00 a condition of the contract? Or rather was it an 'inominate' term?
- If it was inominate, was George deprived of the contract's substantial benefit?
- Can Barry sue for the contract sum?

The answer

The dispute between George and Harold

The first issue to consider is whether there was a legally binding contract between George and Harold. Although both parties appear to provide consideration, and there has been an exchange of promises, it could be argued that given the relationship between George and Harold, neither party intended the agreement to be legally binding. The parties to a legally binding contract must have an intention to create legal relations from that agreement, and in the case of a social or domestic agreement (*Balfour v Balfour*) there will be a presumption that the parties did not intend such relations. Thus, in *Jones v Padvatton* it was held that a promise made by a mother to her daughter to pay her maintenance for returning to the country was not legally enforceable. This presumption can be rebutted on the facts and in *Simpkins* v *Pays* it was held that an arrangement between friends to share a competition prize was enforceable because of the prospective sum involved as well as the continuity of the arrangement.

In our case, although George and Harold are friends, and the band are to play at a social occasion for the benefit of George, Harold and his band appear to be a professional outfit and have charged George a reasonably substantial amount of money for the performance. Thus, it could be argued that the arrangement constitutes a business arrangement, where the legal presumption is that parties do intend to be legally bound (*Rose and Frank Co Ltd* v *Crompton and Bros Ltd*). This is despite Harold making a concession on the normal charge, as the fixed terms of the agreement suggest an intention to enter into a clear and binding agreement. It is submitted, therefore, that both parties did contemplate legal relations, however remote the possibility of legal action may have been at the outset.

The next question is what terms were contractually agreed between George and Harold. It is clear that at the initial meeting the parties agreed the essential terms relating to the fee and the length of performance. However, it is not clear whether George's insistence that they play a range of music and the assurance that 'we will not play anything too heavy' are of any contractual significance. This discussion and Harold's assurance appear to come after the conclusion of the contract and thus it could be argued that George's consideration for any such assurance had already been spent on the original concluded contract and thus amounts to past consideration (*Re McCardle*).

On the other hand, George might argue that the negotiations taking place two days after the contract was concluded merely reaffirmed Harold's obligations under that contract. Hence, it could be argued that the band's duties to play a range of music and not to play anything 'too heavy' were already implied into the contract.

A term may be implied in fact if it is so obvious that both parties would have agreed to such a term had it been mentioned expressly (*Shirlaw* v *Southern Foundries*). Alternatively, the courts may imply a term if it is necessary to give that contract business efficacy, as must have been intended by both parties to the contract (*The Moorcock*). In our case, as Harold knows that he was playing at a birthday party, and should have suspected that there would be a range of family members and friends at the party, we could imply a term that he plays at least a reasonable range of music which would satisfy the broad tastes of those who would be present. In addition, if Harold has entered into the contract in the course of a business, statute will imply that he performs his undertakings with reasonable care and skill (Section 13 of the Supply of Goods and Services Act 1982).

If such a term could be implied into the contract, the next issue is whether that term has been broken. We are told that George received constant complaints that the music was too loud and that the band refused to accede to several requests to turn the sound down. Although any duty to play a reasonable range of music, and perhaps a duty to control the noise so as not to disturb specific sectors at the party, would be a flexible one, it could be argued that by deliberately ignoring the requests of the older members, Harold and the group have broken the implied term to ensure, as far as is reasonably practicable, that they play a range and type of music that would be to the general satisfaction of the people in attendance at the party.

However, as other sections of the party had asked for the music to be turned up, it would be difficult to prove that Harold and the band had broken this very general term. In addition, the complaint that the band played too many Take That songs would appear to be too specific and subjective to indicate that they were in breach of the duty to play a range of music. Finally, the refusal to play several requests would not amount to a breach of contract unless the band were capable of playing those numbers and, for example, deliberately refused to play them so as to annoy the guests. In the absence of any clear intention to depart from this duty, it is submitted that the band would not be in breach of contract and that George would not be able to sue for damages.

However, *if* the court was satisfied that the term had been broken and Harold and the band are in breach of contract, we must consider George's remedies. We are not told whether George has paid the band in advance, but if he hasn't he would be able to refuse to pay that contractual sum if Harold and the band had failed to provide substantial performance of the contract (*Bolton v Mahadeva*). That would depend on whether the broken term was a condition, or, if it was inominate, whether the breach deprived George of the substantial benefit of the contract, and in this case, despite the complaints, the band appeared to have provided the essential purpose of the contract.

If Harold was in breach, George would be able to sue Harold for damages for failing to perform their obligations. Under general rules an innocent party can sue for all loss that was in the reasonable contemplation of the parties when the contract was concluded, or which arises naturally from that breach (*Hadley v Baxendale*). This may include damages representing the disappointment suffered by George because of the complaints received about the band's performance. In *Jarvis v Swan Tours* it was held that damages to reflect the disappointment resulting from the contractual breach could be recovered where the express or implied terms of the contract promised enjoyment; in other words, where the purpose of the contract or a specific term is to provide enjoyment and/or freedom from distress. Thus, in that case, the claimant could sue for damages reflecting his disappointment and distress when the holiday fell short of the quality and facilities he was promised in the contractual brochure. In our case, a contract for entertainment would fall squarely into that type of contract, and George would be able to recover damages to compensate him for the contemplated loss of enjoyment and the anxiety caused by any breach. These damages can also reflect the loss of enjoyment suffered by the guests because of any breach by Harold and the band (*Jackson v Horizon Holidays*), particularly as that loss exacerbated George's personal distress and disappointment.

The dispute between George and Barry

Whether Barry can sue for the contract price depends initially on whether the agreed term that Barry finish by 9 o'clock was a condition of the contract. Traditionally, contract terms were divided into either conditions – important terms which allowed the innocent party to terminate the contract on its breach – or warranties – less important terms which merely entitled the innocent party to claim for damages, whilst not allowing termination. In the absence of statutory classification (see, for example, the Sale of Goods Act 1979, ss. 13–15), whether a term is a condition or not can be determined by looking at the intention of the parties when the contract was formed

(*Schuler* v *Wickman Tools*). In our case the requirement to finish by 9 o'clock appears to be a condition of the contract and thus a condition subsequent of Barry's entitlement to the contract sum. This is because George specifically stresses the finishing time to Barry and states the reason for such timing (the children leaving the party). In addition, the contract and the contract sum were not agreed until after that term was agreed. If that is the case, then the term would be a condition of Barry's entitlement to payment, even though on the night Barry's lateness does not appear fatal to the contract's performance.

Alternatively, the courts might regard the term as neither a condition nor a warranty, but instead an 'inominate' (intermediary) term (*Hong Kong Fir Shipping* v *Kaishen Kaisha*). In such a case the court will wait and see if the breach of such a term deprives the innocent party of substantially the whole benefit of the agreement, which it was the intention of both parties they should receive under the contract. In this case it could be argued that Barry was still able to deliver the essential aim of the contract despite arriving late, as the parents and children were willing to stay and watch the performance. Had the agreement been a purely commercial one, the courts would almost certainly classify the term as a condition, but given the relative informality of the arrangement in our case the courts *may* be willing to treat the term as inominate, perhaps by implying a term to the effect that the term would cease to be important if the circumstances originally envisaged changed, as they did in this case. In that case Barry would be entitled to his payment as he was ready and willing to perform the essential element under the contract, less any damages George could prove for late or defective performance, which on the facts would be very nominal.

Despite this argument, however, it is submitted that the term relating to the starting and finishing of Barry's performance was a strict condition of the contract when it was concluded. Barry is, presumably, a seasoned performer, and should have known that the starting and ending time of the act was of the essence. He should thus fail in his action for the contract price. Although in this case George is not suing for damages, any such claim *might* be reduced because claimants must take reasonable steps to reduce their loss, in this case by accepting a reasonable alternative performance (*Payzu* v *Saunders*).

What is it worth?

The answer is very competent and deals with all the salient issues raised in the question. It does not contain a detailed examination of the law and the cases, but covers the whole range of issues and is a sound attempt to apply those principles to the facts. Most importantly, it displays a sound knowledge of the basic rules on contract and of the variety of issues tested in this 'mixed' question. Perhaps falling between a first-class and high upper-second answer, it would receive the following comments on the student's script.

> **Marker's feedback**
>
> This was a very good effort to answer all the legal issues and some interesting application of those principles to the facts. You display excellent skills re the structure of your answer. You omit some detail on some of the cases, but overall a very good and clear effort – **68/72%**

QUESTION 2: THE CONSTITUTIONAL LAW ESSAY

The following essay question might appear daunting to the student at first sight because it does not allow students to write everything they know about the British Constitution, but instead asks them to consider the British Constitution in the context of the rather abstract concept of constitutionalism. This is a common problem faced by students in exams, because questions rarely say 'write all you know about.'

> **EXAMPLE QUESTION**
>
> *To what extent are the features of the British Constitution consistent with constitutionalism?*

Some students will shy away from answering this question because they feel it will not allow them to employ their general knowledge of the British Constitution and its sources and characteristics and because the question is too theoretical to be attempted. Others will press on regardless, and tell the examiner everything they know about the British Constitution, failing to address the concept of constitutionalism and thus not answering the question. As shown in the answer, below, provided students appreciate the general meaning of constitutionalism, and provided they keep referring to the central feature of the question, this question can be successfully attempted by most students.

A competent law student with no special interest or expertise in constitutional theory wrote the following answer. Despite the lack of expertise, the student appreciates the basic principles of that concept and is able to use his basic knowledge of the sources of the British Constitution to answer the question.

Your plan of the answer should look something like this:

- Definition of constitutionalism and the importance of that doctrine in constitutional theory.
- Examination of the nature and features of the British Constitution as they impact on the concept of constitutionalism, including the unwritten nature of the Constitution, a lack of entrenched constitutional rules, parliamentary sovereignty, the flexible approach to the separation of powers and the rule of law, and the protection of fundamental rights.
- Conclusions on the compatibility of the British Constitution with the doctrine of constitutionalism.

The answer

One of the essential purposes of a constitution is that it maintains an effective control over government. This involves ensuring that those who operate government do so within the boundaries of the law and the limits of the constitution. This should also ensure that there is a reasonable balance of power between the government and the citizen and that the organs of government do not exercise excessive or arbitrary power. The doctrine of constitutionalism demands that government act within the remit and rules of the constitution; the government derives its power from the constitution and must act in accordance with its provisions and remit. In addition, as constitutions should control arbitrary power, every constitution, and the doctrine of constitutionalism, insists that the rules of the constitution must adhere to basic principles of constitutional fair play, such as the separation of powers, the rule of law and the protection of individual liberty. A constitution that does not uphold these values, therefore, could be said to be inconsistent with constitutionalism.

→

One of the essential features of the British Constitution is that it is unwritten. This means that, unlike the majority of constitutions throughout the world, there is no written document containing the essential rules of the constitution. Instead, as Bolingbroke stated, the constitution consists of an assemblage of laws and customs by which the community has agreed that the country is governed. This fact in itself should not be used to deny the existence of the British Constitution, or its compatibility with constitutionalism. Written constitutions do not *guarantee* constitutional behaviour on behalf of government and may expressly provide for the use of arbitrary power. However, the fact that the British Constitution is flexible and lacks, in theory at least, any entrenched constitutional rules, does call into question its ability to effectively control governmental power. As most constitutions entrench certain constitutional values, making it impossible for them to be changed, or requiring their amendment via a special constitutional procedure, the lack of any such entrenchment in the British Constitution suggests that the government is not restricted in its power to change or depart from fundamental constitutional principles. Thus the domestic courts do not accept any restriction on the manner in which constitutional legislation can be created by parliament (*Manuel* v *Attorney General*), and accept that such legislation can depart from established constitutional conventions (*Madzimbamuto* v *Lardner Burke*), leaving the court no choice but to recognise and uphold such legislation.

This flexibility illustrates that the British Constitution lacks the fundamental and supreme status of most constitutions. Thus, in most jurisdictions, the constitution, and the state's constitutional law, is the fundamental law of the land, constituting a basic law, and possessing its own constitutional status and method of creation and amendment. In the United Kingdom, on the other hand, we have no such basic law, and there is no separate legal source of the constitution; all laws, including the majority of constitutional rules, derive from traditional sources such as Acts of Parliament and case law, which are created by a normal legal procedure and which are not subject to special amendment (*Manuel*, above). So too, unlike other constitutions, the constitution cannot be regarded as a supreme or higher law, restricting the government's power to pass legislation or to otherwise act incompatibly with the constitution. The domestic courts are thus powerless to strike down an Act of Parliament (*Cheney* v *Conn*), or executive or other acts which are clearly authorised by Parliament (R v *Home Secretary, ex parte Brind*), and this contrasts with the US Supreme Court's powers to invalidate unconstitutional legislation (*Roe* v *Wade*). It is this, the lack of entrenched constitutional rules, and a legal constitutional power on behalf of the courts to overrule the legislative edicts of Parliament, that casts doubt on the effectiveness of the British Constitution, rather than its unwritten status.

In the absence of a rigid, formal and entrenched constitution, parliamentary sovereignty and parliamentary supremacy lie at the heart of the British Constitution. Under the former principle, an Act of Parliament passed by parliament is regarded as legally sovereign, and no court of law can strike down an act that has been passed by parliament and which has received the royal assent (*Cheney* v *Conn* and *Pickin British Rail Board*). Thus, Parliament, at least in theory, can legislate on any matter it chooses, whether such legislation is regarded as unconstitutional or not. For example, the War Damages Act 1965 retrospectively overturned a constitutional pronouncement of the courts with respect to government liability to pay compensation (*Burmah Oil* v *Lord Advocate*) and the courts were powerless to strike down the Southern Rhodesia Act 1965, which overturned the constitutional convention that parliament would not legislate for its dominions (*Madzimbamuto,* above). In addition, each parliament is sovereign and one parliament cannot bind its successors (*Vauxhall Estates*), even to the extent of insisting that fundamental constitutional principles are not abrogated. This doctrine has been limited by the passing of the European Communities Act 1972, which gives EU law supremacy over domestic law in that area, and by the passing of the Human Rights Act 1998, which allows (in s.4) the courts to declare legislation incompatible with the European Convention on Human Rights. However, both acts could, in theory, be repealed, and under the Human Rights Act parliament could refuse to amend legislation that has been declared incompatible under the Act. Parliamentary sovereignty exists side by side with the notion of parliamentary supremacy, whereby parliament is regarded as supreme over executive government and, by convention, the Crown. As parliament is

→

elected democratically and regularly, this should ensure that parliamentary sovereignty becomes in reality the sovereignty of the people, although executive dominance in parliament is said to undermine such a notion (Lord Hailsham, 'The Elective Dictatorship').

Despite the absence of a rigid and formal mechanism for ensuring constitutionalism, the British Constitution does adhere to the basic principles of both the rule of law and the separation of powers. These concepts, which insist, respectively, that government acts by and within the law, and that power is not concentrated in one organ of government, are recognised as fundamental to the British Constitution and good government, and have received judicial recognition (see, for example, Lord Donaldson in M v *Home Office*, where his Lordship held that it would be divisive of the rule of law if a government minister could ignore a judicial ruling, and Lord Diplock in *Duport Steels* v *Sirs*, where it was stated that the courts' role was to interpret the law made by Parliament and not to create justice outside the law). Thus, the courts have always insisted that government act with the support of formal law (*Entick* v *Carrington*), and remedies such as judicial review ensure that executive government acts lawfully, rationally and in accordance with the principles of procedural propriety (the '*GCHQ*' case). Equally, the domestic courts have declared executive sentencing as incompatible with human right law (*R* v *Home Secretary, ex parte Anderson and Taylor*). The constitution is also founded on the basis that each government power is separated, insisting, in theory, that no one organ carries out more than one governmental power. However, the flexibility of the constitution and the sovereignty of parliament allow both doctrines to be violated. Thus various breaches of the separation of powers are evidenced within the constitution: the role of the Lord Chancellor (rectified by the Constitutional Reform Act 2005), and the sovereign parliament can sanction the passing of delegated legislation by executive government (albeit under parliamentary and judicial control). More significantly, the existence of a parliamentary executive, whereby the majority of executive government reside within a sovereign parliament, means that the courts' power to control the government is limited.

Every modern constitution should have some machinery to protect the human rights of its citizens from arbitrary interference from government. This assists constitutionalism as it ensures that fundamental rights are beyond the reach of legislative and executive interference, thus placing a limit on government power. The British Constitution has lacked, and still does lack, a formal bill of rights, which protects those rights and allows the domestic courts to overrule legislative and executive acts that are inconsistent with their enjoyment. Nevertheless, such rights have always enjoyed the protection of the domestic courts, which have controlled arbitrary interference with legal rights (*Entick*, above) and have presumed that Parliament did not intend to interfere with fundamental rights such as access to the courts (*Chester* v *Bateson*) and the presumption of innocence (*Khaawaja* v *Home Secretary*). Such protection has been re-enforced by the passing of the Human Rights Act 1998, which gives effect to the rights in the European Convention on Human Rights, and which gives the courts greater powers to interpret legislation in line with human rights (s. 3) and provides the higher courts with the power to declare primary and secondary legislation incompatible with Convention rights (s. 4). For example, in *A* v *Home Secretary*, concerning the detention of foreign terrorist suspects, the House of Lords found that such detention was incompatible with the right to liberty of the person, and declared that it was their constitutional and, since the passing of the Human Rights Act, statutory duty to safeguard such rights in a rights-based democracy. However, it must be stressed that the courts have no power to strike down such inconsistent legislation, and thus parliamentary sovereignty is preserved, even to the extent of allowing parliament to repeal, or derogate from, the 1998 Act.

In conclusion, the British Constitution lacks the *formal* qualities and features of many other constitutions and, in theory at least, the basic means to secure constitutionalism. Parliamentary sovereignty, the lack of any basic or supreme constitutional law and the limited role of the courts in declaring unconstitutional actions unlawful appear to offer little or no protection against the will of Parliament and the actions of arbitrary government. However, a general adherence to the notions of the rule of law and limited government, including a basic, although limited, respect for the separation of

➔

powers, provides some evidence of the constitution's consistency with the principles of constitutionalism. In addition, the democratic features of the constitution, including the supremacy of parliament and the holding of free and regular elections, offer some support for the doctrine in the absence of more formal and entrenched constitutional arrangements.

What is it worth?

This answer displays confidence and competence in the area, without showing any specialist knowledge and appreciation of complex constitutional theory. Many examiners would have expected the student to give more detail on the theories of constitutionalism and to examine some individual theorists in this area. Nevertheless, the answer combined the student's sound knowledge of the features of the British Constitution with the broad principles of the concept. Importantly, the student has not been fazed by the question and has been able to weave his general knowledge in the area into this apparently obscure and difficult question. In addition, it was written clearly and was well structured. It would attract the following type of comment from the examiner.

Marker's feedback

Well written and structured and including some interesting examples. You could have explored the definition, scope and theory of constitutionalism in greater depth, but overall, a very sound effort – **68/72**

The final mark may depend on what approach the module leader took to the subject – theoretical or substantive law based. If a theoretical approach has been taken, the answer may lack the quality of a first.

SUMMARY OF EXAMINATION SKILLS

At the end of this chapter you should be able to:

- Appreciate the benefits of consistent engagement with the subject and the course, and in particular of regular practise in identifying the scope and meaning of law assessments.

- Devise and carry out a suitable revision programme, balancing constructive and consistent revision with relaxation.
- Make use of a variety of sources during the revision process, including past papers, question-and-answer books and academic papers.
- Bring out the best of their knowledge and other legal skills under examination conditions.
- Identify the scope and meaning of examination questions and to apply their existing knowledge and skills to those questions.
- Adjust your skills in order to answer open-book and seen examinations.
- Make effective and simple plans before answering exam questions.
- Write in a clear, crisp and effective style under exam conditions.
- Manage your time effectively under exam conditions, including when you are running out of time.
- Prepare for re-sit or deferred examinations.

9

Researching and writing advanced essays

EXTENDED AND ADVANCED ESSAYS AT UNDERGRADUATE LEVEL

The skills required for extended and advanced essays

When you are on the second and third year of your law degree you will be required to write longer and more advanced pieces of coursework. Not only will the word limits of such coursework be increased (from perhaps 1,500 words to 2,000–3,000 words or more), but also the marker will have greater expectations of both your essay writing skills and your substantive and theoretical knowledge.

This will be reflected in the type of work you will be set and the research and other skills needed to complete the task. You must, therefore, adjust to these new demands if you are going to succeed at these stages of the course.

Writing longer essays

Writing longer pieces of work is not in itself more difficult than tackling the shorter pieces you were given in year one. Students often have problems keeping within, for example, a 1,500-word limit, and might welcome a 2,500-word limit. However, students cannot simply use the extended word limit to pad out their answers with yet more substantive and descriptive material. You will be expected to use the word limit to display both the writing skills, which should have improved since the beginning of your studies, and your enhanced substantive and theoretical knowledge.

Thus, essays at this level, and of longer word limits, at the very least test your ability to sustain your legal skills and arguments over a longer period. They also test other skills, such as deeper and more careful research, enhanced powers of analysis and critical reasoning, and skilful use and referencing of legal sources.

Tackling more theoretical and demanding questions

The work set on years two and three of your programme will inevitably be more demanding. You will notice a shift away from largely descriptive and basic essay questions, to questions which test the student's ability to critically analyse the law, its application and, in some cases, its social, economic or political impact.

Theoretical and conceptual questions

In year one, when studying constitutional law, you may be asked, *'What are the principal grounds of judicial review* and *what is the constitutional purpose of such review?'* You will be given approximately 1,750 words in which to answer the question. The first part of the question requires a fairly descriptive answer and the whole question could be answered by looking at the main text, the central cases and perhaps an article or two.

On years two or three, if you were studying a specialist administrative law course, any question in this area would be more complex and challenging.

EXAMPLE QUESTION

'The grounds of judicial review ensure the maintenance of the rule of law and government accountability, and the observance by the courts of their proper democratic mandate.'

Examine this statement in the light of the modern law of judicial review. (2,500 words)

This question requires a strong theoretical appreciation of judicial review and a deep awareness of its constitutional significance, as well as a sound knowledge of the legal principles and case law.

There will be little room for purely descriptive material and the student will be expected to research and present a variety of academic theories in this area, some of which may be politico-legal.

This in turn will impact on the amount and type of research students must undertake – more articles and specialist texts and the need to look at some cases in great detail, using relevant extracts from the judgment.

Much of these differences are reflected in the word limit, the question allowing the student to undertake and include more research and to incorporate more complex arguments.

Critical legal questions

In addition, you may get more questions which require your opinion on the acceptability of the current law, possibly with a request to suggest possible reforms.

EXAMPLE QUESTION

'The current distinction in English law between murder and manslaughter is both incoherent and unsatisfactory.'

Consider possible reforms in this area in order to meet the above criticism.

As you can see, the examiner's expectations of you as an academic lawyer has changed since the first year, and they now require you to show an in-depth knowledge and appreciation of the law and of its application and impact.

However, this type of question is not as daunting as it seems. You will not be expected to lead academic opinion and to come up with startling new proposals; but ensure you display an appreciation of leading academic and other opinion.

This sort of task will require you to rely on sources other than your trusty textbook (see the section entitled 'Undertaking greater research'), but in turn those sources will provide you with the leading opinion in this field, which you can then incorporate and discuss in your essay.

The case analysis or case note

The case analysis or case note is a popular method of assessment on the later stages of your undergraduate programme and on postgraduate courses. You may be asked to critically analyse a central case in a particular legal area and assess its impact on that area of law. The case note assessment tests your ability to understand cases, what was actually decided and why, and their impact in a given legal area. It also tests your ability to analyse the decision in the context of academic opinion and any fundamental legal principles (such as the rule of law, justice and international law).

The rewards for getting it right in this assessment are, therefore high; and your marks will suffer if you do not display the necessary skills.

EXAMPLE QUESTION

Explain the significance of the House of Lords' decision in Attorney-General's Reference (2004) with respect to the compatibility of the reverse burden of proof in English law. (2,000 words for undergraduates, 5,000 words for postgraduates)

To tackle this assessment you will need to display a number of enhanced research and writing skills.

- Consult the case notes section of a number of academic journals for guidance on format and style. If the word limit is 5,000 words (postgraduate level), you need to consult those journals that include extensive case notes of about that length; the *Modern Law Review* is perhaps the best example, but other examples are *Public Law*, *International and Comparative Law Quarterly* and *Industrial Law Journal*. Other journals (*Cambridge Law Journal* and *Law Quarterly Review*) contain shorter case notes but can be cited as sound legal authority. The academic and critical style used in those journals will also be consistent with the level of your assignment, particularly where you will need to display sound postgraduate skills.

- Avoid adopting the style used for case notes in trade journals. Although these notes can often be useful, and can be expertly written, they tend to lack the appropriate detail and analysis of the previously mentioned journals; and they often employ bullet points etc.

- If the case has already been noted in an academic journal (or a number of journals), be careful not to copy that note or its style. You may, however, use the existing note as a secondary source and as an indication of modern academic opinion on the subject area and the case: in which case be careful to credit and reference this source.

- You can employ headings to break down your case note – for example, Introduction, Facts and Decision, Analysis, Conclusions or the like. Any case note should have an introductory section (explaining the legal issues raised by the case and the specific dilemma faced by the court in the case), a clear account of the facts, an analytical account of the decision, and a critical analysis of the decision and its impact (including your conclusions).

- Do not spend too much time on the facts of the case; one paragraph will generally be adequate, more than one paragraph when it is necessary to provide the full background. Your account of the facts should be clear and contain enough information to allow the reader to appreciate the context in which the legal dispute arose and to appreciate the court's reasoning and decision.

- Your analysis of the decision should not be too descriptive. Whilst detailing the exact decision of the judge(s), the account should take the opportunity to evaluate why the judge came to that decision, what authority they applied/distinguished/overruled, and whether that decision was flawed in any respect. At this stage you can add references (in footnotes) to inform the reader of your knowledge of existing principles and case law, and to draw attention to any possible errors that you feel the judge has made in coming to the decision.

- A substantial part of the case note should be dedicated to the commentary on and critical analysis of the case. You do not, of course, have to disagree with the decision, but you should at this point highlight the approach taken by the judge, consider whether the approach and decision is consistent with previous authority or sound legal principle, and explain the impact this approach and the decision might have in this legal area.

- A case note in assessment provides you with an opportunity to explain how a decision impacts on your study of a legal area. The style is, therefore, slightly different from the one adopted in case notes in journals because, unlike the author of a case note, you are addressing a set question.

Study the case note below (written within a word limit of 1,500–2,000 words) and note how the author has presented the case and divided it up into sections. Please note that this case does not represent the most current law and is presented as an example of how to set out a case note in an appropriate and critical fashion.

The right to demonstrate and the concept of *contra bones mores*: the decision in *Hashman and Harrap* v *United Kingdom*

Introduction

The last year or so has witnessed a number of successes for the right of demonstrators to exercise their right of peaceful protest. In October 1998 the European Court of Human Rights held that two peaceful protestors had had their rights of liberty of the person and freedom of expression unjustifiably interfered with when they had been arrested for handing out leaflets outside a conference centre (*Steel* v *United Kingdom* (1999) 28 EHRR 603; see Steve Foster and Rona Epstein, 'Binding over and the right to protest' (1998) *New Law Journal*, 1688). Further, in the domestic courts, the House of Lords held that people have the (limited) right to assemble on the highway for the purpose of peaceful and non-obstructive protest (*DPP* v *Jones* [1999] 2 All ER 257). Also, Sedley LJ recently held that the police had no power to arrest a peaceful demonstrator for obstruction of an officer where the threat to a breach of the peace came from another source (*DPP* v *Redmond Bate, The Times,* 28 July 1999).

Now, in *Hashman and Harrap* v *United Kingdom* ((1999) 30 EHRR 241) the European Court of Human Rights has held that the use of the ancient binding over power to control behaviour which is *contra bones mores* was contrary to the applicants' right of freedom of expression under Article 10 of the European Convention on Human Rights. In doing so the European Court has struck another blow for the right of peaceful demonstration, although as we shall see there remains a good deal of uncertainty surrounding the police's power of arrest for, and the court's power to regulate, such behaviour.

The facts and decision in Hashman and Harrap

The facts of *Hashman and Harrap* were as follows. Both applicants had attended a fox hunt – the Portman Hunt – with a view of disrupting it. During the hunt the applicants had blown a hunting horn and had engaged in shouting. The police had been called to the scene to investigate the death of one of the hounds which had run into the road, but it was accepted that the applicants were not responsible.

A complaint was made regarding the applicants' conduct and Gillingham Magistrates ordered them to keep the peace and be of good behaviour. On appeal it was held that their behaviour did not amount to a breach of the peace and neither was it likely to occasion one. However, the court was of the opinion that they had been guilty of conduct which was unlawful and which had exposed the hounds to danger, and which therefore amounted to conduct *contra bones mores* – conduct which was wrong rather than right in the judgment of the majority of contemporary fellow citizens. Accordingly the applicants were bound over.

The applicants lodged an application with the European Commission of Human Rights (Application No 25594/94) claiming a violation of Articles 5, 10 and 11 of the European Convention, and the Commission accordingly found that there had been a violation of Article 10 and referred the case to the European Court (decision of the European Commission on Human Rights, 6 July 1998).

In giving judgment, the European Court held that the proceedings taken against the applicants constituted an interference with their right of freedom of expression under Article 10, despite the fact that their expression took the form of impeding others' activities. The Court then considered whether the concept of *contra bones mores* was sufficiently certain so as to satisfy the requirement that a restriction be 'prescribed by law' within Article 10(2) of the Convention, which permits necessary restrictions on that freedom. On behalf of the Government it was argued that the concept provided an invaluable tool for controlling antisocial behaviour and that it was sufficiently certain to allow people to regulate their conduct. In particular, they argued that given the applicants' behaviour at the hunt they would, in this case, have been left in no doubt as to the nature of behaviour that the order covered.

The Court, referring to its previous case law on the meaning of the phrase 'prescribed by law' (*Sunday Times v United Kingdom* (1979) 2 EHRR 245) – that the law should be formulated with sufficient precision so as to allow a person to regulate his conduct, and that any prior restraint on freedom of expression calls for the Court's most careful scrutiny – came to the conclusion that the concept of *contra bones mores,* and its application in this case, was not prescribed by law. In coming to that conclusion it conceded that in the case of

→

Steel v *United Kingdom* (above) the European Court had accepted that the law relating to binding over orders requiring persons to be of good behaviour, although very imprecise, afforded the majority of the applicants in that case with sufficient protection under the Convention. However, in the present case the Court pointed out that in *Steel* the relevant applicants had been charged with causing a breach of the peace and that the proceedings brought against them were in respect of breaches of the peace which were later found to have been committed under laws which the Court in *Steel* felt were sufficiently precise in their definition so as to comply with the Convention.

Turning to the concept of *contra bones mores*, the Court distinguished the formulation of that concept with other provisions such as breach of the peace, which the Court noted only included conduct the natural consequence of which would be to provoke others to violence and which thus describes conduct by reference to its effects. For this reason the Court was prepared to accept the legitimacy of the general law relating to breach of the peace, including a law which makes it an offence to engage in conduct which is likely to cause annoyance, which was upheld by the European Court in the case of *Chorherr* v *Austria* (1993) 17 EHRR 358. With specific reference to the facts of the present case, the Court could not accept that it must have been evident to the applicants what they were being ordered not to do for the period of their binding over. Unlike the case of *Steel*, in the present case the applicants had not committed a breach of the peace and it could not therefore be assumed that the order applied only to similar behaviour. Thus the order by which the applicants were bound to keep the peace and not to behave *contra bones mores* did not comply with Article 10(2). This was, however, the decision of the majority, and in his dissenting opinion Judge Baka felt that given the concrete circumstances of the case the particular applicants would have known what type of behaviour was *contra bones mores*.

Analysis

Having decided the issue on the question of legality, the Court found that it was not necessary to consider whether the restrictions were 'necessary in a democratic society' for the purpose of achieving a legitimate aim under Article 10(2). In addition, the Court also held that it was not essential to examine the applicants' complaints under Article 11 of the Convention, guaranteeing the right of peaceful assembly. As a consequence the Court was not allowed the opportunity to comment on the necessity and proportionality of binding over orders with the Convention, assuming that any such order is sufficiently certain; neither did the Court rule on the compatibility, or otherwise, of the various legal provisions existing in domestic law, which are often used to control the behaviour (immediate and potential) of protestors (such as ss. 4 and 5 of the Public Order Act 1986).

In particular there is still a good deal of confusion, in both domestic law and under the Convention itself, as to whether behaviour which is not violent in itself, but which does or may provoke violence in others, can justify the use of the law against the protestors. The decision of the European Court in *Steel* v *United Kingdom* (above) seems to establish that *entirely* peaceful protest should not be restricted, but that the use of breach of the peace laws to control a potentially violent situation caused by the lawful actions of protestors would be justified within the Convention. In domestic law, leaving aside the use of *contra bones mores*, the courts appear to be resolving the dilemma by considering whether the protestors' behaviour is an unreasonable interference of another's rights. Thus in *DPP* v *Nicol and Selvanayagam* ([1996] 160 Justice of the Peace Reports, 155) it was held that the conduct of the protestors in throwing sticks into the water where anglers were holding a competition was an unreasonable interference with the anglers' rights and thus justified their arrests for breach of the peace.

In any case there must be evidence that the protestors' behaviour caused a breach of the peace. For example, in *Percy* v *DPP* ([1995] 1 WLR 1382) it was held that as the protestor's action of climbing a fence surrounding a military air base did not result in any breach of the peace – they had merely been escorted from the premises – the applicants' binding over orders should be quashed. Thus, in cases such as *Percy*, and cases such as *Steel* and *Hashman and Harrap*, there would be a violation of the Convention if protestors were in any way restricted in their activities, or where they are subsequently penalised for such conduct. Where, on the other hand, it is reasonable to assume that their behaviour is likely to

→

cause a breach of the peace then, provided such action is unreasonable and, thus, the reaction of the other parties' not unreasonable, protestors will have to take their crowd as they find them. In this respect, although the recent decision in *Redmond-Bate* may well protect speech and actions which are no more than annoying, it is still likely that the actions of hunt saboteurs and other protestors which has in effect caused or threatened a disturbance will, in the police officers' and the courts' view, amount to unreasonable conduct.

Conclusions

The decision of the European Court in *Hashman and Harrap* is an important one in that it calls into question the legal control of peaceful demonstrations via convenient and vague concepts which have in the past regulated conduct which poses little or no threat to public order. In addition, the decision will in all probability signal the demise of the use of *contra bones mores* in the area of demonstrations. In fact, the Law Commission recommended the abolition of the power to bind over to keep the peace and be of good behaviour (Law Commission Report on Binding Over, no. 224 at page 81). Nevertheless, the decision does not address many of the issues surrounding the necessity and proportionality of many public order laws, or whether such laws strike a fair balance between the protestor's right to demonstrate on the one hand, and the duty of the police and the courts to preserve the peace and allow others to enjoy their rights on the other. This problem will continue to occupy the courts, particularly in the post-Human Rights Act era.

Coursework on unstudied areas of law

Many questions on years two and three will test your ability to research and write in an area not covered in lectures and seminars. This will test your advanced research skills (**see below and covered in Chapter 6**) but, importantly, the student will not have the comfort of testing their appreciation of the legal areas in formal classes.

In other words, it is testing your ability to *study* the law. Again, this sort of task should not prove too difficult in practice, provided you display the research and other skills identified subsequently (**and those identified generally in Chapter 6**), and you engage with your course from the outset.

You will also notice the difference in the difficulty of problem questions. In year one the scenario will raise fairly familiar issues and problems, and the student should readily recognise them from their previous study and from established cases. However, in years two and three the scenario will raise more and varied issues, including some points which have not been judicially settled – the examiner is setting the question to address one or more 'moot' points.

This will require the student to display enhanced skills in advising the parties, because the answer will not be settled and the student will need to skilfully evaluate and distinguish previous authority.

Demonstrating enhanced writing and legal skills

Chapters 1, 2 and 6 of this book stress the need to display sound writing and legal skills – good grammar and spelling, a clear, crisp writing style, sound referencing and citation skills and so on.

You must continue employing these skills throughout the course, and markers will now be less tolerant of any lapses in these areas, deducting marks for poor practice: **this may jeopardise your marks and thus your final classification.**

In addition, they will expect you to have **refined** those basic skills by showing **enhanced** writing skills:

There should be no lapses in your citation and referencing skills. Full and proper citations will be expected; for example, *Carlill* v *Carbolic Smoke Ball* (1893) might be overlooked in year one, but in year two the marker will expect the full citation and reference.

By this stage you will be expected to use footnotes effectively and professionally, including the use of Latin abbreviations such as *ibid.*, *op. cit.* and so on (consult your course booklet to see if these abbreviations are to be employed).

Your writing style should now be mirroring the legalistic and professional style adopted in respectable texts and journals. Some casual phrases and colloquialisms might not be penalised too harshly in year one, but in years two and three they will be, which will be reflected in the marks you receive.

Bibliographies should be constructed appropriately and expertly – to cite the lecture notes in your bibliography in the first year might be forgiven, but to do so in year two (or worse, in year three) displays an ignorance of legal skills and/or an unwillingness to learn.

The shorter coursework

In addition to the longer essay, you may be given a smaller piece of work to submit, of approximately 1,000–1500 words, and sometimes used as a formative exercise – to test your knowledge and writing skills and to give the markers an indication of your ability – before the submission of the major piece(s) of work.

Indeed, in recent years sometimes these shorter pieces have replaced longer pieces as the coursework element.

These smaller pieces usually test your understanding of some of the basic principles of the legal area that you are studying and may not be that demanding. However, they will test various skills such as your ability to understand and explain central concepts and rules in a concise but academically appropriate style.

In addition, they provide you with an opportunity to employ your general research and writing skills and in particular become familiar with the sort of materials that you will be using throughout the course.

Although the pieces are relatively short, you should not expect descriptive questions. The questions will invariably require you to come to grips with quite wide and complex concepts and principles, and answering such questions within a short word limit is not without its difficulties.

EXAMPLE QUESTION

What are the fundamental characteristics and principles of public international law? (1,500 words)

The question does not require a detailed knowledge of the subject area, and such a question could be tackled quite comfortably by most undergraduate students. However, you will be expected to display a sound knowledge of these basic principles and to provide a competent answer to the question. In particular you would be expected to:

- Explain the principles in a particularly structured, logical and confident manner.
- Consult a reasonably wide range of primary and secondary sources, despite the word limit. Students will not be able to get the answer from a basic textbook, but instead must show that they have consulted a number of expert views on this topic.

- Digest and utilise complex and specialist secondary sources within this word limit. The skill here is to refer, briefly, to a variety of sources and to illustrate that you have read and understood these sources despite not having space to include them in any detail in the coursework. The student should use footnotes expertly in this respect, referring to various sources and alluding to the detailed arguments contained in them.

EXAMPLE

'Foster claims that the universality of international law is a myth created for the purpose of legitimising international treaties that were drafted by powerful Western states.'*

*See also the views of Simon Foster-Harrison, in 'The Myth of Public International Law' [2004] ICLQ 200, at 228. But contrast the opinion of Stuart Foster-Jones in 'Finding Conformity in International Law' (2005) OJLS 100, at 129, where the author claims that there is sufficient international consensus to warrant the use of the label 'public *international* law' (author's italics).

- Display a sound appreciation of those sources and arguments and an ability to contribute logical and informed opinion in that area and the issues raised by the question.

IN-DEPTH RESEARCH

The key to writing more advanced coursework is the ability to undertake in-depth research and to use such research in the presentation of the piece. Coursework in the second and third year will test your ability to cover either a specific aspect of, or a substantial amount of, the subject area, and this will test your ability to find and explain relevant and varied sources and to convey that material in an appropriate, analytical and critical style.

In particular, advanced essays will require you to:

- undertake advanced, careful and selective research;
- research and understand new and developed areas of law;
- research and then condense bulky legal information;
- research and discover recent legal developments in the form of new cases, statutory developments and proposals, and academic opinion.

Undertaking greater research

The essays that you will be set in years two and three cannot be answered simply by relying on your notes and the standard textbook. These sources will still remain essential to your basic understanding of the relevant subject area, but you will need to go beyond them to get the sort of information required to tackle advanced coursework.

In particular, you will need to make use of certain advanced sources that may not be used extensively on earlier parts of the programme.

- **Specialist texts:** Do not rely too heavily on basic or set texts which provide the student with a grounding in the subject area, for example a general text on domestic human rights. Specialist texts (for example on freedom of speech or police powers) allow you to acquire detailed information and analysis on specialised areas.

- **Quality journals:** At this level you will be expected to research, and engage with and the most respected and in-depth academic views.

- **Government reports and official documentation:** A this level, you need to be aware of any White or Green Papers, consultation documents, commissioned reports and so on, and to be able to access, use and cite them appropriately.

- **Comparative materials:** In some subjects you may be expected to use foreign cases and statutory provisions, international treaties and overseas academic journals in your work. Ensure you know how to access these materials – law websites sometimes have an international or European section – and cite and use them appropriately in your work.

TIPS FOR UNDERTAKING MORE DETAILED RESEARCH

- Unless your set text or notes do not cover the areas tested in the coursework, always begin your research with these basic sources.

- You must ensure that you are competent and confident in the area and these sources will provide you with at least a basic knowledge of the essential principles and primary cases and so on.

- In addition, a good textbook will have explored many of the most controversial and interesting issues surrounding the relevant legal areas. This will allow you to appreciate the legal rules and their impact and will begin to equip you in tackling the question.

- Lecture handouts are useful if the subject area of the work has been, or will be, covered in lectures. They will provide you with a basic structure, an indication of what the lecturer feels are the most interesting and controversial points and, often, a useful essential and additional reading list.

- Good textbooks (and in particular cases and materials texts) will provide you with references to further reading, which you can then explore as part of your research.

- Look at the references used by the author in footnotes and further reading lists at the end of the chapter or the text. This should not be used as an alternative to full research, but if an expert has compiled a list of useful sources, make use of their research.

- You should now be in a position to move on to advanced sources – articles, specialist texts, additional cases and so on.

- Do *not* 'jump in at the deep end' by starting your research here. You should build up your knowledge and appreciation of the subject and the relevant issues, but if you begin with specialist material and advanced arguments you and your answer will become confused and unconvincing.

- There is no golden rule about how many texts, articles and primary sources you should use in advanced essays. Your research and bibliography should be thorough and reasonably extensive, but remember you are not writing a dissertation or PhD thesis.

- You should show research beyond the basic texts, but avoid researching and using an inordinate amount of materials.

EXAMPLE QUESTION

Critically assess the impact of the Human Rights Act 1998 on the power of the police to detain and question suspected criminals. (3,000 words)

This question, to be found on a criminal justice or human rights course, requires a reasonably detailed analysis of the legal area and thus will require fairly detailed research.

Begin with the relevant chapter in your set text (either your human rights or criminal justice text). Then read similar chapters in one or two other main texts to see what views and ideas those authors have on the topic. This will identify the central issues and the main statutory provisions and cases.

You can now consult chapters in more specialist texts in areas such as police powers, human rights and criminal justice and the European Convention on Human Rights. More specifically, you will need to find and use a number of articles (say four) dealing with this specific topic and which will allow you to address the question in a critical fashion.

In this case, therefore, the student has used approximately ten secondary sources, which should, generally, be more than adequate to provide a suitably detailed and analytical answer (along, of course, with a proper analysis of any relevant statutes, cases and so on).

Keeping up to date with recent developments

One of the skills expected of students presenting advanced essays is the incorporation of recent legal developments. The set text will be at least six months out of date, and thus reliance on textbooks will lead to the omission of recent cases, statutory developments and new secondary sources.

Failure to keep up to date may result in students making legal errors in their work, or, at the least, providing an incomplete answer. Not only will students be penalised for omitting this information, but markers will also be impressed by the inclusion of it, particularly if it appears that students have taken the initiative in this respect. It is vital, therefore, to have a regime for keeping up to date.

- Get into the habit of checking daily and weekly updates on law websites. These will provide you with references to new cases, statutory law, proposals for reform, articles (including newspaper articles) and, sometimes, books.

- The sites may also allow you to access the specific source and to print it off. Also, access legal blog sites, especially those operated by lawyers.

- Get into the habit of looking at the most recent journal issues and law reports housed in your library and online. The websites mentioned in the preceding point may not refer to all journals and cases, particularly overseas journals, so this is a good way of ensuring that you don't miss any relevant developments.

- Always listen in lectures and seminars for information on new cases. Very often the lecturer will notify the students of a new case or development, covering it in the lecture and alerting the student to academic opinion on it.

- The lecturer will also place such reading on their online sites. Understandably, the lecturer will be disappointed if the student shows ignorance of it in their assessed work.

- Make use of websites that accompany textbooks. These very often provide updates on the law as they affect the content of the textbook.

Finding and using appropriately advanced sources

By employing your basic research skills (learned in year one and covered in Chapter 6 of the text and the preceding section with respect to undertaking greater research and finding recent developments), you will be able to locate the type of sources required to write advance essays.

You need to know how to make the most of these advanced sources in order to show off your research skills and to enhance the quality of your work.

TIPS FOR FINDING AND USING ADVANCED SOURCES

- Use your research skills and your knowledge of the subject area to find *appropriate* journals and texts. In addition to researching mainstream journals, such as the *Modern Law Review* and *Law Quarterly Review,* which contain articles and case notes on all manner of legal subjects, you will need to identify and consult the leading journals in specific subject areas. These journals can be used by students studying particular subjects – human rights (*European Human Rights Law Review, Human Rights Law Review*), commercial law (*Business Law Review, Journal of Business* Law), criminal law and justice (*Criminal Law Review, Howard Journal of Criminal Justice*) and European Union law (*Common Market Law Review, European Law Review*).

- You may also need to consult overseas journals, whether their content is general (*Harvard Law Review, Yale Law Review*), or subject specific (*Netherlands Human Rights Quarterly*). Many of these journals contain articles on English law, especially Commonwealth journals, and many overseas journals contain articles on European and international law.

- Search your library catalogue, and the library catalogues of other libraries, for books in a specialised field. These texts are also often referred to in more general textbooks in footnotes and bibliographies.

- Show a wide reading in the area by using a variety of texts and journals – basic and specialised, domestic and overseas, academic and 'trade' journals.

- In particular, ensure that you refer to appropriately detailed and respected journals and avoid the overuse of 'trade' journals. For example, do not just use articles from the *New Law Journal* and *Law Society Gazette* when tackling an advanced essay. These journals provide an invaluable source of information on recent developments and include some excellent, yet brief, analyses of legal issues. However, some of them are written by, and for, practitioners and might not be suitable for essay purposes. Students should use them alongside more respected and weightier journals if they are going to tackle the issues raised by advanced essays fully and effectively.

- Use your skills to refer to and cite these journals and texts properly.

- Do not cite or refer to journals or texts that you have not read. It is not a competition to put as many books and articles in your bibliography as you can, and you should not try to mislead the marker in this respect.

- Do not try to use academic opinion unless you understand the author's views and try to avoid overcomplicated and esoteric sources.

- Ensure that you understand the source so that you can explain the meaning and significance of views expressed in them and add your own views (see the section entitled 'Adopting a critical and analytical approach').

- Ensure that the sources are fully credited, and cited and referenced properly; and that your analysis and views are separated from those of the authors.

WRITING IN A PROFESSIONAL AND ACADEMIC, CRITICAL AND ANALYTICAL STYLE

At this stage, students should be able to write in a reasonably professional and academic style, imitating the style (as opposed to the exact words) of academic writers. Importantly, students must be able to incorporate all their research and a variety of legal materials into their work in an expert fashion.

Remember, it is not permissible simply to copy and paste academic opinion into your answer without credit *and* analysis: you will be guilty of plagiarism, or, at least, poor academic practice.

Examine the style adopted in the following passage (an introduction on a commercial law question relating to sales by a non-owner) and notice how the piece is constructed and how it uses a mixture of secondary sources and personal reflection.

EXAMPLE

When a non-owner sells goods to an unsuspecting purchaser, two strong claims are in conflict – the right of the true owner to assert his title if another person lays claim to those goods, and the right of the innocent third party who has paid for the goods in good faith to keep those goods as his own.[1] Somehow the law has to reconcile these rights and determine 'Who is the owner?'[2] The answer is vital because, although the person who is held not to be the owner will, in theory, have a remedy against the unauthorised seller,[3] that seller will probably be a 'rogue' who has disappeared, and, if he can be found, may be penniless and any unsuccessful (and innocent) party will lose out financially. The starting point in law is that the true owner's rights are paramount, although many exceptions have been created to this rule by both common law and statute.[4] This has created an unsatisfactory situation, with the law being developed in a piecemeal fashion and being interpreted restrictively, and often inconsistently, by the courts.[5]

---

[1]See Ivan Davis, 'Transferability and sale of goods' (1987) LS 1, where the author explores the property rights of the true owner and the claims of bona fide purchasers.
[2]In many cases a number of innocent parties may be involved, as where a rogue sells the true owner's goods to X, who then sells them to Y. See Paul Dobson, *Sale of Goods and Consumer Credit* (Sweet & Maxwell, 2000), at pages 72–73.
[3]By virtue of s. 12 of the Sale of Goods Act 1979.
[4]Under ss. 21–27 of the Sale of Goods Act 1979.
[5]See Michael Bridge, *The Sale of Goods* (OUP, 1977), at page 410.

Adopting a critical and analytical approach

Advanced coursework will require you to do more than provide descriptive material. The marker will expect you to analyse the area and the cases, to criticise, and to draw your own rational and supported conclusions. The skill here is to merge established academic opinion with your own understanding and arguments. In other words, draw on academic opinion in this area as the basis of your critical examination of the question and then show that you critically understand those views.

Look at the following section, where the student begins to examine the possible reform of the rule relating to sales by non-owners. Note how she uses her research of primary and secondary sources and adds her own reflections and views.

EXAMPLE

Given the complexity of the legal rules, their potential for unfairness and the continual problem of non-owners selling and pledging goods to innocent purchasers, it is surprising that this area has resulted in little proposal for reform and even less actual law reform. In 1966 the Law Reform Committee looked into the area,[6] and in 1994 the Department of Trade and Industry published a Consultation Paper, proposing reforms to the *nemo dat* principles, which resulted only in the removal of the 'market overt' rule.[7] Whatever proposals, if any, are introduced, the present general rule combined with its exceptions cannot be described as satisfactory. The cases discussed in the earlier part of this essay show that the rules are technical and that the rights of the innocent parties are often determined by complex and often inconsistent application of commercial legal rules. For example, Thornely refers to a system of complicated and duplicated provisions that require a thorough overhaul.[8] It is essential therefore, that other possibilities of reform are addressed.

---

[6]Law Reform Committee: 'Twelfth Report on the Transfer of Title to Chattels' (Cmnd. 2958, April 1966). For a discussion on the Committee's findings, see Diamond (1966) MLR 413.
[7]Transfer of Title: Sections 21 to 26 of the Sale of Goods Act 1979 (20 January 1994).
[8]JWA Thornely, 'Thieves, Rogues, Innocent Purchasers and Legislative Tangles' [1988] CLJ 15, at page 18.

UNDERGRADUATE PROJECTS

Introductory points

Whilst on your law course, you may be given an opportunity to submit a project (or dissertation as they are commonly known) as part of your programme. Indeed, on some law courses it is compulsory to undertake a dissertation.

This normally occurs in the final year of your course and will generally take the form of a 12,000- to 15,000-word piece on a legal topic of your choice, which you will need to get approval for from the dissertations tutor; if you are taught in semesters, it is common for the project to be between 6,000 and 10,000 words, but the guidance below still applies.

Undertaking a project will provide several benefits. It will allow you to research and study a legal area of your choice and interest in detail. This will enhance your research and writing skills and will equip you for further academic study on postgraduate courses and research degrees. In addition, it is often useful to include details of individual research in letters of application for both academic and professional courses and for employment.

Choosing to do a project

If the dissertation is optional, you must think very carefully before choosing to embark on a dissertation instead of studying another taught subject.

- *Be guided by interest, not just by the desire to avoid exams.* Many students think that the dissertation will be a 'soft option' because there is no examination and it is only a 'large coursework'. As we will show, nothing could be further from the truth, but the cardinal rule is this: Do not undertake a project unless you have the interest to start and finish it. Unless you are interested in the topic area, and can maintain that interest throughout the whole academic session, you will not succeed in the dissertation (**the results in this module often determine the classification of your degree**).

- *Ensure that you have got the necessary skills to embark on a dissertation.* Some students think they are better at coursework than examinations, but the evidence does not always bear that out. To finish a dissertation you need patience, good intellectual and academic ability, and very good writing and academic skills.

- If you are receiving regular negative comments in coursework about your writing style and your coursework skills, the dissertation is probably not for you. If the dissertation is compulsory, then you need to work on acquiring those skills by the time you reach your final year.

- *Expect the dissertation to be demanding and be prepared to research thoroughly.* The dissertation will involve a tremendous amount of in-depth research, discovery, comprehension and collation of legal materials, writing and rewriting and extensive proofreading. Unless your heart is in it, it is best to choose a taught subject. However, if your interest in the subject and the project is maintained, you will find the dissertation an enjoyable and stimulating experience. It gives you an opportunity to acquire a specialist knowledge and appreciation of the law, but it does come at a price.

- *Be prepared to meet deadlines and to practise self-discipline.* This is often the most difficult aspect of a dissertation. You must settle on your area and title at an early stage, present the supervisor with a viable plan well in advance of starting the dissertation (usually in the early summer preceding the final academic year), meet with your supervisor at regular intervals and take into account any advice and recommendations, present individual chapters throughout the academic year for checking and amendment, and leave ample time to write, rewrite and proofread your work.

An effective way of meeting deadlines (for the completion of chapters and the final project) is to make proper use of your supervisor and to follow the instructions on seeking their advice. Always attend the meetings with supervisors and ensure that you have the necessary work for them to check. If you submit drafts in good time, supervisors will generally look at that work and make recommendations. However, you cannot expect them to do this if you have not kept your appointments through the year and then suddenly hand them a 12,000-word project to look over in the three days remaining before the submission date. Always incorporate the changes recommended by the supervisor and ensure that you understand what the recommendations are and how to execute them.

In short, you need the following skills to undertake a project:

- ability to write extended assessments and to sustain research and other skills over a long period of time;
- ability to learn new areas of law and to grasp a variety of complex legal theories and arguments;
- ability to undertake in-depth, selective and specialised research;
- ability to cover a substantive amount of a chosen subject area and to condense bulky legal and other information;
- ability to practise advanced writing skills and to convey the information in an appropriate style;
- ability to time manage the dissertation with the remainder of your law studies.

Choosing a legal area and title

You will be given a fairly wide choice and remit with respect to choosing your area and title; although you will need to get this ratified by the supervisor, who may reject it because the title and plan is too vague or not viable – because it covers too specialised an area or because there is insufficient legal content.

Although students might welcome choosing their own title, after years of being forced to answer other people's questions, choosing an area and an appropriate title has its difficulties. Your supervisor will help you out in this respect, but you should follow this guidance.

Ensure that the area of law is interesting, suits your skills and is reasonably familiar

As you are going to be working on this project for a number of months, it is essential that you choose an area that is of interest to you and that will sustain your interest over that time.

You should choose an area that you will look forward to researching and studying. This might not necessarily be a topical or generally controversial social or other issue. In fact, there is often a danger of choosing something simply because it has received wide media coverage (see the next section). However, it should be an area in which there are plenty of unresolved and academically interesting issues. You will not be allowed to write a project describing entirely established substantive law; there will need to be some 'edge' to the project.

Also, ensure that the subject area suits your knowledge and skills. It is usually a good idea to choose an area that will allow you to display your existing skills. For example, you may be better at legal theory rather than 'black letter' law, or better in the commercial law subjects rather than subjects such as human rights or criminal justice. Although you will need to research new aspects of the law and a variety of new sources, you should choose an area that is reasonably familiar to you.

For example, a student who chooses to look at the legal and social implications of domestic immigration law without the benefit of any previous study in this area might run into subsequent difficulties with respect to researching and understanding this complex area of law. In contrast, if that student has studied (or will be studying) administrative law and/or human rights, it would be feasible to undertake a project on the impact of judicial review/human rights law in that area. At least the student is aware of the underlying principles of judicial review/human rights and can now undertake research on immigration law in the context of that understanding.

Similarly, students should not attempt projects on, say, the US law on copyright unless they have studied intellectual property and even then intend to examine the US law as a comparator with the domestic law.

Ensure that the topic and title have sufficient legal substance

Some topic areas appear very interesting and controversial yet do not raise sufficient (current) legal issues. For example, basing a project idea on a recent event such as the proposed ban of smoking in cars, or the resignation of a government Minister over a national scandal, may appear to be an interesting basis for study, but if there are insufficient *legal* issues to examine, the project will end up as a general discussion on a matter of social interest.

Similarly, a project on, for example, the interference with literary speech by domestic obscenity laws was a very topical area in the 1960s and 1970s but is now largely academic. In this case the student needs to change the focus of the project to study a live legal issue relating to obscenity, such as the control of child pornography or obscenity laws and the social media.

Equally, where the area does raise a number of legal issues, the student's title and aims and objectives must focus on those issues. For example, the controversy surrounding the publication of blasphemous cartoons in Paris, causing offence to Muslims and leading to violence against journalists, is a suitable topic for a project, but only if the student is made aware of the relevant domestic and international rules on blasphemy laws, freedom of speech and the protection of religious observance (and is aware that the offence has recently been abolished in domestic law).

Study the following project plan, proposing to look at the controversial area of terrorism and public safety.

EXAMPLE

Terrorism and the protection of the state

The aim of this project is to study the evils of terrorism and how the state may take steps to control it. It will be argued that in the light of the atrocious events in New York and London, and later events, that Parliament and the courts require additional powers to control terrorism and that the normal safeguard of due process and civil liberties should not be available to terrorists.

The proposal has several flaws. First, the title is too wide and vague – it does not suggest that the student is going to research the *legal* issues involved in the law against terrorism. Second, the aims are vague and there is little indication what the focus of the project will be, including which laws are going to be studied. Third, the language used in the aims is too subjective and passionate, indicating that the project will simply include the views of the author on 'what we should do with terrorists'!

In this case, the student needs some assistance in focusing on the legal issues – the relevant legislation, its compatibility with domestic and international law, and the compatibility of recent laws with human rights norms.

Ensure that you can access sufficient information on the subject quickly and easily

You will be expected to choose something novel and interesting, but you must ensure that you will be able to find and access the sources necessary to complete your project. There is no point choosing an area that, although exciting and controversial, will pose too many problems in accessing the necessary information. For example, if you choose to study the law of another jurisdiction, you may run into difficulties when you attempt to access relevant texts, articles and cases.

Many projects will require you to go beyond sources available in your own library (or available on legal websites), but, at least initially, check whether the information is available at these points. If it is not, then you can identify that early on and explore other possibilities.

If your project is going to involve empirical research or questionnaires, check whether you are likely to be allowed access to this information; **and ensure you comply with rules regarding ethics**. Always have a back-up just in case these sources or information do not materialise. For example, if you intend to do a project on prisoners' rights, and intend to interview prisoners and prison officers, always have a library-based project to fall back on if your interviewees let you down. The key is to start your research early, just in case it does not go as expected.

As with any coursework, get to the library early and never underestimate the benefit of early research. Although photocopying is not the same as research, it is often a good idea to get paper copies of relevant articles as soon as possible. That way, at least you know that you have your copy and you will not be competing with others for that source at a more vital time.

Devise an appropriate and interesting title

Students often find it difficult to devise an appropriate title for their project, but it is an essential part of the whole exercise.

Your title should clearly reflect the focus of your project and provide the reader with a clear idea as to its content. For example, *'The protection of the right to celebrity privacy in English law'* identifies the legal area and the focus of the study, implying that the central thrust of the project is the inquiry into whether the law provides adequate protection of this right. Although there will be much discussion on press freedom and the public right to know, if there is too much emphasis on this aspect, then the content of the piece will not reflect the title, and vice versa.

Do not choose a title that looks like an essay question. Students are used to essay questions and often use similar questions for their projects.

EXAMPLE

It would not be appropriate to title your project 'The existing laws on privacy protection are inadequate and incoherent. Discuss.'

Make your title snappy and informative. You can always add a subtitle for fuller description.

EXAMPLE

'Protecting celebrity privacy: An examination of domestic privacy laws on the protection of the private lives of public figures.'

You can choose an eye-catching title, provided it is not too sensational or frivolous.

EXAMPLE

'An insult to humanity or plain free speech? The acceptability of criminal laws for denying the Holocaust' is acceptable.

Not: 'Political correctness and denying the Holocaust: Is Austria the new fascist state?'

Ensure you have a thesis

A dissertation must have a thesis – a central argument – upon which you can research the law and construct your dissertation. Do not simply construct a dissertation from existing law and theories without first thinking about *your* central argument and what you hope to prove at the end of the dissertation.

For example, if you are undertaking a dissertation on privacy versus press freedom, decide whether your main argument is that there should be less interference with press freedom in this area, or that press freedom should be further restricted to allow fuller protection of privacy interests

Your dissertation, and its aims and objectives, should follow this thesis, and this will allow you to construct convincing arguments in the various chapters, constructive proposals for reform, and clear and cogent conclusions; although you will obviously need to be aware of laws, cases and arguments that run contrary to your thesis.

Set yourself a realistic and clear remit

Make sure you choose a realistic area of study and set yourself a realistic and attainable remit. Whilst you want to choose something sufficiently novel and controversial, you should not choose something that is going to be too technical or complex to research, digest and explain. 'A study of blasphemy laws in Central and South Eastern Asia' would require an inordinate amount of research and is more suited to a doctoral thesis than an undergraduate project. It would also require you to undertake very comprehensive and difficult research and to digest quite complex individual laws and theories.

Equally, ensure your aims are clear, both to you and your supervisor. Plan the aims and content of the project so that you can get a picture of the end product and how it is to be divided, and avoid submitting vague and unfocussed proposals.

EXAMPLE

Freedom of expression

The aim of this project is to explore the juristic and philosophical basis of the fundamental right to free speech. The project will begin with a theoretical exploration of the notion of free speech and its values. I will then identify the possible justifications for its control, detailing the case law of both domestic and international courts in the specific areas of press freedom, censorship and obscenity and indecency laws. Finally the project will make a study of Article 10 of the European Convention to examine the extent to which the Convention and the European Court of Human Rights upholds freedom of speech.

This proposal is far too extensive, and it would not be realistic for the author to cover that much ground, unless he did so very superficially and mechanically. The proposal contains about five separate project areas, and the author has simply copied the contents of a book on freedom of speech and used it as his proposal.

Preparation and research for your dissertation

Settle on your area and its scope at an early stage

You should start thinking about whether you wish to do a project and the topic area in the middle or at the end of your second year. By that time, you should be aware of your best skills and your favourite legal areas and will have encountered enough substantive law and legal issues to make an informed decision about what sort of area you would like to research.

You will then (late in the third term/second semester) be able to approach your tutor or dissertations supervisor with a coherent and viable idea, and get his or her advice on the scope and direction of the piece.

Although the direction of the project may change slightly during the next few months, you should have a general idea of:

- what you are going to cover;
- how it might be broken into chapters (a difficult task that needs a good deal of thought);
- what angle the piece is going to take;
- whether it is going to be largely substantive law or legal theory;
- whether it will require solely library-based research or empirical study.

Get to know the area involved

It is essential that before you launch into full research of the topic that you acquaint yourself with the basics of the legal area. You may have acquired this foundation knowledge as part of your previous or concurrent law study, but it is vital that you are comfortable with the basic principles and conversant with any relevant institutions or theories. For example, if you are embarking on a project with a comparative element (e.g. USA) you must acquaint yourself with the basic framework of their legal and/or constitutional system. Similarly, if your project will require a study of international law and institutions, you will need to get some grounding in those areas and principles before you start looking at detailed areas of your project topic.

Before you make a final decision on your topic, spend a couple of weeks reading around the subject and seeing if it is interesting and understandable. Then, conduct some basic research and learn the general principles, the statutory framework and the essential case law. You are now in better position to make a final choice of title and this preliminary reading and the knowledge you acquire from it will aid your subsequent research and understanding.

Researching for your project

As you will be looking at a specialist area and will be writing a 12,000- to 15,000-word project, you will need to undertake quite extensive research. Principally you will have to find all sources – primary and secondary – that are relevant to your project, and you should not leave any substantial gaps in this respect.

Your preliminary reading (as mentioned previously) should have uncovered a good number of sources and in turn these sources will identify further reading, cases and so on.

You must conduct a thorough search in your, and other, law library catalogues to find both basic and specialist texts in the area, and if your project involves the study of another jurisdiction, you must conduct a proper research on relevant academic and general websites. Conduct this search early, because you may have to order these texts or visit other libraries.

You need to do similarly thorough research for articles, statutory law and cases on law websites, and these searches should be conducted on a regular basis throughout the academic term to ensure that you remain up to date.

You must become familiar with specialist journals in the relevant legal area and conduct a regular search of their content to see if any relevant articles have been published. You will also need to research overseas journals to see if anything relevant has been written in them, especially if you are making a comparative study.

You will need to consult a number of websites that have relevance to your legal area. The websites of specialist bodies, such as human rights groups, commercial organisations and governmental agencies, will provide you with invaluable information on their work, recent developments and proposals and access to reports. In addition, they will have helpful links to other legal and non-legal websites.

You need to check whether the items you have found are actually relevant to your project. In this respect, if your aims and objectives are vague, you will find it difficult to distinguish the relevant from the irrelevant. If you have a clear idea of what you are looking for, you will be able to identify relevant sources by simply looking at the abstract provided by the website.

You need to check daily and weekly updates on a regular basis. You will be expected to be completely up to date, and new cases or academic opinion must be incorporated into your project. Also, you should check quality newspapers every day for relevant and useful articles and points of discussion.

Presentation

The presentation of your dissertation is of great importance. You have been working on this piece for the whole academic session, and the supervisors and markers will expect a high standard of presentation; **the quality of presentation will reflect greatly in the mark you receive.**

Your university will have guidelines and instructions about font size, spacing and layout, and you must make yourself aware of these rules and follow them. You may have to get at least one copy of the dissertation bound within the university, with the university markings on it.

The abstract

Your abstract, anything between 200 and 800 words, should provide a brief explanation of the topic area, its topicality, why you have chosen the area, how you researched it and a general indication of the project's content and conclusions.

One of the purposes of the abstract is to provide the reader with a clear explanation of the area, and to demystify what might be a complex or specialist area. Thus, it can be written in a reasonably informal manner, and generally it does not need to be supported by legal citations and references.

The content of the abstract can differ depending on the nature of the project and the individual university, but below is a typical abstract, in this case relating to a project on the changing status of non-executive directors in English companies.

EXAMPLE

The subject of this dissertation was chosen due to its topicality and relevance to modern company law. The concept of corporate governance has become a byword for corporate responsibility and accountability. Criticisms of 'fat cat' directors and other unconscionable

---

corporate practices have fuelled both public and legal debate and have led to a number of reports and reviews to consider these aspects. In particular, there have been many recommendations in respect to the traditional role of company directors and suggestions regarding the increased role of non-executive directors in company regulation.

This dissertation looks at the role of the non-executive director in corporate governance and details the various committees and their recommendations with respect to these officers. The research for the dissertation did not follow a traditional academic pattern, the information not being contained in the weightier academic journals. This led me to research in practical and trade journals that concentrated on the practical aspects of the law and its possible reform, as well as, of course, considering in-depth the Higgs Report. The dissertation was also informed by high-profile corporate activities.

Great thought was given to the approach and layout of the dissertation, in particular whether to consider the material on an issue basis or, in the alternative, in a chronological manner, the latter approach being adopted. This was primarily because the material lends itself to some repetition and considering each report in turn was a mechanism to avoid undue repetition and to provide the reader with a clear understanding of the historical treatment of these issues.

I would like to thank [my supervisor] for all her assistance during the supervision of this dissertation.

The introduction

After your abstract, you will need to provide an introduction.

This can be a separate chapter before your main chapters or can be included as part of your first main chapter.

The purpose of the introduction is to provide the reader with essential background information to the legal issue that you are going to cover in the project.

Thus, the introduction should provide an explanation of any legal dilemmas that the project area might cover, some explanation of the basic legal principles or a historical account of the legal area, and some indication of how the remainder of the project will deal with the relevant issues.

Examine the following introduction (or at least extracts from the introduction) and see how it introduces the reader to the nature of the legal concept to be discussed in the project (the non-executive director), how that concept has been the subject of proposals for reform and how each part of the project will cover those issues.

EXAMPLE

During the 1990s new life was breathed into the role of non-executive directors and as a consequence their role on the board has gone through a dramatic change. The increase in profile is due to the valuable part most commentators feel they can play in corporate governance and, particularly since the Cadbury[9] and Higgs[10] reviews, non-executive directors are now seen as the mainstay of good corporate governance, the governance debate emphasising the distinctive contribution of outsiders in helping to ensure that managers act in the interests of shareholders.[11] The Cadbury Report emphasised the contribution that independent non-executive directors could make, opining that the calibre of the non-executive members of the board is of special importance in setting and maintaining standards of corporate governance.[12] Similarly, the Higgs Review stated that a board is strengthened significantly by having a strong group of non-executive directors with no other connection with the company as these individuals bring a dispassionate objectivity that directors with a closer relationship to the company cannot provide.[13] We shall see during this dissertation how the role of the non-executive director is becoming critical not only for the transparency and accountability of companies, but also for their capability and business credibility. This in turn has raised questions concerning how non-executive directors are selected, how their independence is assured, what their functions are and how their effectiveness may be assessed . . .

---

[9]Report of the Committee on the Financial Aspects of Corporate Governance (Cadbury Report, 1992), hereafter called the Cadbury Report.
[10]The Higgs Review of the Role and Effectiveness of Non-Executive Directors (January, 2003), hereafter called the Higgs Review.
[11]W. Beekes, P. Pope and S. Young, 'The link between earnings timeliness, earnings conservatism and board composition: Evidence from the UK' (2004) Corp Gov. 12(1), 47–59, at page 47.
[12]The Cadbury Report, paragraph 4.10.
[13]The Higgs Review, paragraph 9.5.

To fully appreciate how the role of the non-executive director has changed it is necessary to spend a little time detailing their role prior to examination of the Higgs review. Therefore, Chapter 1 will consider the role of the 'old-style' non-executive director and the reports commissioned prior to the Higgs Review. This is necessary, as although the Higgs Review was the most specific report concerning the role of the non-executive director it cannot be considered in isolation, otherwise an incomplete picture of how the report came about and the ideas behind its recommendations would be produced. Chapter 2 is devoted to the Higgs Review, its recommendations and its shortcomings. Chapter 3 will deal with the post-Higgs situation, in particular the new revised combined code, recent legislative proposals and the 'new-style' non-executive director. Finally conclusions will be drawn in Chapter 4.

Laying out chapters

It is essential that you have some idea of how you are to split the project up into chapters, even before your meeting with the supervisor, although the supervisor will help you refine or redraft those initial ideas. If you have no idea how to split and label your chapters, then you are probably not ready to research and proceed.

The chapters should cover the issues that you have identified in the title, your aims and objectives and the abstract. Thus if your title is 'Protecting celebrity privacy', and your aims were to critically examine the legal protection of the private life of public figures against press intrusion (in the context of your central thesis in your dissertation, above), your chapter headings might be as follows:

EXAMPLE

Chapter 1 – The protection of privacy interests in domestic law (Provide a general overview of how statute and the common law protect a variety of privacy interests, both before and after the passing of the Human Rights Act 1998.)

Chapter 2 – Privacy protection and self-regulation (Explain the rules relating to press regulation by the Press Complaints Commission including recent calls for reform in that area, together with a critical analysis of the effectiveness and shortcomings of such.)

$\rightarrow$

Chapter 3 – Privacy protection and the European Convention on Human Rights (Provide a clear and detailed account of the relevant principles of the Convention and specifically the case law of the European Court of Human Rights in this area. This will allow you, in the next chapter, to measure the domestic law and its effectiveness against those principles. It will also allow you to make informed proposals for reform and conclusions.)

Chapter 4 – Privacy v Freedom of the press: getting the right balance (Examine the present position, in particular the recent case law, to assess whether the current law is consistent with the principles and case law of the Convention and the thesis on this area: that a legal system should provide a robust protection of privacy against press intrusion.)

Chapter 5 – Recommendations for Reform and conclusions (Consider proposals for reform in the light of the above observations and arguments, leading to final conclusions. Draw on any ongoing reforms which are consistent or otherwise with the thesis.)

Note, if the dissertation relates to one specific aspect of the above – privacy and free speech and the European Court of Human Rights – then you need to think of chapter headings that will cover different aspects of that study: developing privacy and the European Court; balancing free speech with privacy; the public interest defence; remedies and the European Court; conclusions.

Quality word-processed work

The quality of the presentation of your dissertation is vital. The work should be professionally presented, and the quality of your word-processing and style are very important. If you are not very proficient at word-processing, then get someone to type it up for you; it will be worth it in the end because you are likely to lose marks for a poorly presented dissertation.

Clear, coherent and professional writing style

As with advanced essays, you should employ an academically professional style when writing your dissertation.

This style must be maintained throughout the whole work, so you must take great care in how you present your research and with your style of writing.

Always write clearly and maintain a critical and analytical style.

Examine the following extract and notice how the style is clear, and shows a confidence with the subject matter and the various sources.

EXAMPLE

The Higgs Review recognised and addressed this concern, providing what may be regarded as a 'comply or explain' approach with respect to independence. Thus the definition, above, allows boards to regard a director as independent, even if he or she would not be so regarded by following the strict wording of the definition; there remains, therefore, scope for interpretation.[14] Interestingly, research conducted for the Review suggests that among board members independence can simply have the meaning of being able, as an outsider, to see things differently. If interpreted in this way, the characteristic of independence essentially amounts to a non-executive director's ability to retain an 'independence of mind' that allows him or her to test and challenge the thinking of executive directors on the basis of the non-executive director's experience elsewhere. In short, among directors, 'independence of mind' was felt to be the key characteristic of non-executive directors.[15] Therefore a weakness of the Review is that it allows companies to say who is independent or not without any additional, external scrutiny.[16]

---

[14]Indeed, it would seem that the essential issue is to ensure that the directors, who decide whether a director is to be regarded as independent, are accountable to shareholders and take decisions in their interests.

[15]Hans-Christoph Hirt, *supra*, note 6.

[16]John Lowry and Alan Dignam, *op. cit.*, note 5, at pages 383–385.

Advanced citation and referencing skills

Your university will provide specific guidance on citation and referencing of sources, and it is essential that your skills are very strong in this respect. You will be expected to display expertise in this area, and it is advisable to consult (good) previous projects before submitting your project.

Check whether the university prefers the Harvard or Oxford style of referencing, and follow that style rigorously. (**See Chapter 7 of the text for details and examples.**)

Ensure that you are conversant with the appropriate citations and abbreviations of specialist journals, statutory provisions and cases (particularly if those sources are overseas).

Ensure you are conversant with the appropriate use of Latin phrases, such as *op. cit., supra, ibid.* and so on. (**See Chapter 7 of the text for details and examples.**)

Appropriate, true and properly cited bibliography

Your bibliography, appearing at the end of the project on separate pages, is a reflection of the research that you have conducted for the project. It must be expertly constructed but must also provide the reader with a favourable impression regarding your research and understanding of the subject area.

Follow the rules about construction of bibliographies (**see Chapter 7 of the text**) and in particular any advice provided by the university in this respect.

Again, it is important that you know which style of referencing and citation is expected (Harvard or Oxford).

Ensure that your bibliography reflects a thorough research of the subject, including appropriately specialist secondary sources, and does not include inappropriate sources (e.g. too many basic texts, too many trade journal articles). The inclusion of a nutshell text or other basic material could be fatal at this level.

Your bibliography should contain everything that you have *read* in preparation of writing your project. The source does not have to be referred to in your project; you may, for example, have read a (good) basic text(s) to gain a background or foundation knowledge, and these can be included in your bibliography even though they do not appear in the main body of the project or footnotes.

Do not include sources that you have not read or sources you do not know the content and gist of. Although you do not have to refer to every source in your project, you must have at least read that source for it to be included in your project. If your bibliography has 100 entries, and only 20 of them have been referred to, the marker will get the impression that your bibliography is not a true one and that you have not read the majority of those sources.

Try to find room in the project for the majority of your sources, even if they are merely cited in footnotes. In such a case, prove that you have read the source by making some reference to the content of the source.

EXAMPLE

'For further commentary on the impact of the Act on prisoners' rights, see Steve Foster . . . ' Alternatively, 'See Steve Foster, "Prisoners' Rights and the Human Rights Act 1998" [2005] PL 333, where he argues that such rights have been extended since the passing of the Act (at page 346).'

You should split your bibliography into primary and secondary sources. If you wish you can create sub-headings; for example, under 'Secondary sources' you can have sub-headings of texts, journal articles, newspaper articles and websites.

Reading over your work before submission

The quality of your presentation is a vital factor in gaining a high mark for your project. In particular, ensure that you:

- Take great care with the proofreading of your project and ensure that it is as free as possible of typographical and spelling mistakes, poor grammar, and vague or inappropriate phrases.

- Leave ample time (at least one week) before the submission date to check these fine details. It will be worth it in the end, as a project with countless errors will create an impression of hurried work and a lack of care and pride in the work.

- Get someone else to check for style and grammar and to proofread for you after you have looked at it several times. Unnoticed mistakes can often be spotted by carrying out this exercise.

- Before you take it for binding, make sure the page numbers are in order and that the piece looks cohesive; for example, ensure that headings are not placed at the bottom of the page with the text on the next page.

Further reading

The advice given in this book on preparing and writing law assessments is intended to complement your law studies and your study of legal skills. In addition to reading this text, it is necessary that you consult a number of other texts that provide assistance in acquiring and practising general and specific legal skills. The texts listed here should help in this respect.

There are a number of very good texts on how to study law and how to acquire the skills necessary to survive on a law course. These texts will include some advice on how to research and write essays, but contain more general information on matters such as reading cases, interpreting statutes and employing critical and analytical skills.

Bradney, A. et al. *How to Study Law* 6th edn (Sweet & Maxwell, 2010)

Finch, E. and Fafinski, S. *Legal Skills* 5th edn (Oxford, 2017)

Hanson, S. *Legal Method and Reasoning* 4th edn (Routledge, 2015)

Holland, J. and Webb, J. *Learning Legal Rules: A Student's Guide to Legal Method and Reasoning* 9th edn (Oxford, 2016)

McBride, N. *Letters to a Law Student: A Guide to Studying Law at University* 4th edn (Longman, 2017)

Rivlin, G. *Understanding the Law* 7th edn (Oxford, 2015)

Stychin, C. and Mulachy, L. *Legal Method: Text and Materials* 3rd edn. (Sweet & Maxwell, 2007)

Wilson, S. and Kenny, P. *The Law Student's Handbook* 2nd edn (Oxford, 2010)

In addition, there are more specialist texts on matters such as how to conduct advanced research, how to use a law library, how to use legal language and how to cite and reference legal authorities.

Clinch, P. *Using a Law Library: A Student's Guide to Legal Research Skills* (Oxford, 2001)

Haigh, R. *Legal English* 4th edn (Cavendish, 2015)

Knowles, J. and Thomas, P. *Effective Legal Research* 3rd edn (Sweet & Maxwell, 2012)

Lammasniemi, L. *Law Dissertations: A Step-by-Step Guide* (Routledge 2018)

Manchester, C. and Salter, D. *Exploring the Law* 4th edn (Sweet & Maxwell, 2011)

Murray, R. *How to Write a Thesis* 4th edn. (Open University Press, 2017)

Nolan, D. and Meredith, S. *Oscola – The Oxford University Standard for Citation of Legal Authorities* 4th edn (Hart 2012)

Salter, P. and Mason, J. *Researching and Writing Legal Dissertations* (Longman, 2007)

Stein, S. *Law on the Web: A Guide for Students and Practitioners* (Pearson/Prentice Hall, 2003)

Index